THE LANGUAGE OF BREXIT

THE LANGUAGE OF BREXIT

*How Britain talked its way
out of the European Union*

STEVE BUCKLEDEE

Bloomsbury Academic

An imprint of Bloomsbury Publishing Plc

B L O O M S B U R Y
LONDON · OXFORD · NEW YORK · NEW DELHI · SYDNEY

Bloomsbury Academic

An imprint of Bloomsbury Publishing Plc

50 Bedford Square
London
WC1B 3DP
UK

1385 Broadway
New York
NY 10018
USA

www.bloomsbury.com

BLOOMSBURY and the Diana logo are trademarks of Bloomsbury Publishing Plc

First published 2018

British Library Cataloguing-in-Publication Data
A catalogue record for this book is available from the British Library.

ISBN: HB: 978-1-3500-4797-6
PB: 978-1-3500-4796-9
ePDF: 978-1-3500-4799-0
eBook: 978-1-3500-4798-3

Library of Congress Cataloging-in-Publication Data
A catalog record for this book is available from the Library of Congress.

Cover design by Olivia D'Cruz
Cover image © Getty Images/Gary Waters

Typeset by Newgen KnowledgeWorks Pvt. Ltd., Chennai, India
Printed and bound in Great Britain

To find out more about our authors and books visit www.bloomsbury.com.
Here you will find extracts, author interviews, details of forthcoming events
and the option to sign up for our newsletters.

CONTENTS

Introduction 1

1 'The EU isn't much cop but . . .'. Remain supporters' use of coordinative constructions 7

2 Hedging and modality versus strident claims and apparent absence of doubt 19

3 More to imperatives than meets the eye 45

4 Inclusive *we*, the former City broker as champion of the common man, and good old Bojo: How the pro-Brexit press created the illusion of a classless alliance 53

5 Democracy myths and facts: A double defeat for David Cameron 69

6 'Free': A little word that did a big job for Brexit 79

7 Nominalization, presupposition and naturalization 85

8 The language of racism lite, and not so lite 95

9 Comparison with the Scottish independence referendum of 2014: How Project Fear worked in 2014 but not in 2016 109

10 Leave's appointment with history and Remain's another day at the office 119

11 Little Englanders or reaching out to the world beyond Europe? Comparison with the 1975 referendum on remaining a member of the European Economic Community 129

12 From 'Up Yours Delors' (1990) to 'Stick it up your Juncker' (2016). Was it *The Sun* wot won it once again? 139

13 Dirty tricks: Lies, personal attacks and the Queen supports UKIP 151

14 The Day After: How could this happen? 163

15 The issue that would not go away: The general election of 2017 181

The Epilogue So Far 201
References 211
Index 229

Introduction

Language can invigorate or dismay, inspire people to commit heroic deeds or justify their most despicable acts, illuminate our successes or expose our self-inflicted wounds.

This book is about the power that language possesses. It investigates how the Brexit campaigners used language much more persuasively than their counterparts in the Remain camp in the build-up to the referendum of 23 June 2016, which was to decide whether the United Kingdom should continue to be a member of the European Union. It is, of course, difficult to sound impassioned and to employ coruscating rhetoric when your message is that, on balance, it is better to stick with the status quo and just leave things as they are. It is harder still if leaving things as they are means persevering with a historically uneasy relationship with an unloved and sometimes overbearing partner. If, in contrast, your message is an appeal to a love of liberty, a traditional sense of justice and national pride, then it naturally follows that urging people to have the courage to make a bid for freedom will involve more grandiloquent language, powerful metaphors and a rousing tone.

In a democracy, however, it is not automatically the case that whoever campaigns more vigorously will win, for in the privacy – and loneliness – of the voting booth, electors may lose their nerve and go for the boring but safe option rather than take the bold step towards an uncertain future. In the 2014 referendum on Scottish independence, a majority of Scots decided it was better the devil they knew despite the fact that the Scottish National Party had campaigned energetically and effectively.

Two years later many of us chose not to stay up till dawn on 24 June to follow the referendum results as they came in because we expected something similar to the outcome in Scotland, that is, that a lot of people who had toyed with the idea of voting to leave the EU would nevertheless cast an unenthusiastic vote to stay in once they had the ballot paper in front of them. The news on breakfast TV soon informed us that the Remain camp's complacency had been misplaced.

Inquests into the cause of the unexpected result have offered a number of hypotheses: it was an anti-establishment protest vote that proved to be more successful than the protesters themselves really intended; an underestimation of public concern over immigration from EU member states; too many pro-Remain young people were so confident of the outcome that they did not bother to vote; it was a genuine protest by those who perceived themselves as economic losers ignored by the decision makers; heavy rain on voting day deterred lackadaisical Remain supporters while their more committed adversaries splashed through puddles to get to the polling station.

The first half of this book concentrates primarily on the question of language, the highly effective linguistic strategies employed by the Brexit campaigners compared with the dispassionate, at times spiritless language used by pro-Remain supporters. It would be a gross exaggeration to claim that the language issue swung the vote in favour of Leave, but a case can be made that it was at least a contributing factor in what was, after all, a narrow 52–48 per cent victory for the side that expressed its message with greater force and conviction.

Chapters 9 to 15 relate language use to the wider sociopolitical and historical context since 1945, including Britain's accession to the original European Economic Community (which was enthusiastically greeted by the same newspapers that were ferociously anti-EU in 2016), the souring of relations with

Brussels during Margaret Thatcher's long premiership, and the deep divisions in British society that were painfully exposed by Leave's victory.

I began collecting data in January 2016 and continued to do so up to and including voting day on 23 June. The main sources of material were the official and unofficial websites devoted to the Remain and Leave campaigns, speeches and interviews involving mostly politicians but also economists and bankers, and editorials and articles from online newspapers.

The websites of the following political parties, pressure groups and individuals were regularly monitored:

REMAIN

- The Britain Stronger in Europe movement
- The pro-Remain Labour site
- Will Straw's blog

LEAVE

- UK Independence Party (UKIP)
- The Vote Leave Movement
- Labour Leave
- Better Off Out
- Grassroots Out (GO)
- Leave EU
- Dominic Cummings's blog
- Left Leave

Will Straw and Dominic Cummings were directors of the Britain Stronger in Europe and Vote Leave campaigns respectively.

While the lexical blend Brexit was quickly adopted by the media throughout Europe, Lexit (the fusion of Left and exit) did not acquire anything like as wide a currency. Because of the prominent roles of high-profile Conservatives like Boris Johnson, Iain Duncan Smith and Michael Gove during the referendum campaign, in the eyes of many the pressure to leave the EU came primarily from the political right. In reality, the existence of the Labour Leave and Left Leave movements, and the strength of the Leave vote in areas in which the Labour Party is strong, attest to the fact that there was also a left-of-centre argument for leaving the EU, although the Lexit campaign did not enjoy the kind of funding that fuelled Brexit, and its leaders were mostly not as well known to the general public. In terms of language use, Brexit and Lexit were very different phenomena, and although the former will receive more attention in this work, the latter will not be entirely neglected.

The problem with websites and blogs is that posts may be taken down, and in this work I have endeavoured to cite materials that can still be accessed. Online newspapers, in contrast, have archives from which content is rarely if ever cancelled, and from a linguistic point of view, a rich source of material was the articles written by journalists with decades of experience in using words to influence public opinion. The various papers were divided almost 50-50 during the referendum campaign: predictably, the right-wing *Daily Express*, *The Telegraph* and *Daily Star* campaigned for Leave, and *The Sun* maintained its long tradition of insulting Europe in general and France in particular, and it was equally predictable that *The Guardian*, *The Observer*, *The Independent* and *Daily Mirror* would take up the Remain cause. There were also surprises, however: *The Times* campaigned to stay in the EU while its sister newspaper, the *Sunday Times*, encouraged its readers to vote to leave, and the *Daily Mail* campaigned aggressively for Leave but the *Mail on Sunday* opted for Remain. The UK's newest national daily, *The i*, adopts a centrist stance on many issues, although it did appear to be mildly in favour of staying in the EU. The low-circulation *Morning Star* was the only paper that featured Lexit editorials, although journalists promoting the Lexit case were given space in some of the pro-Remain newspapers, particularly *The Guardian* and the *Daily Mirror*.

Some of the issues discussed in this work really merit an entire volume rather than a chapter. That is certainly the case for the theme of immigration and border controls that featured so prominently in the EU debate, and the detection of explicit or implicit racism in linguistic strategies. At the time of writing, however; we do not yet know how the media will react to whatever sort of agreement London and Brussels reach on the question of borders and residence rights, so a lot of data still need to be collected.

Although this book concentrates on language, I hope that non-linguists, including people whose first language is not English, would also wish to read it. I have endeavoured to strike the right balance between accessibility and appropriate linguistic analysis, but if I fail at times, if colleagues feel that I sometimes do not quite get it right, I apologize.

Finally, readers are bound to wonder where I personally stand on an issue that divided the country of my birth, so I may as well come clean about it from the beginning. I am British but I have lived most of my adult life outside the UK. Because I am not resident in Britain, I could not vote in the referendum, but had I been able to do so, I would certainly have looked after my own interests, which would have meant voting to maintain my pension rights and access to medical care in the country in which I live. I have no great love for the European Union, however; my view of the EU is similar to that of the first two journalists quoted in Chapter 1.

1

'The EU isn't much cop but . . .'. Remain supporters' use of coordinative constructions

On 24 June 2016, shortly after the full results of the referendum were known, the online edition of the *Financial Times* quoted the senior Labour MP, Margaret Hodge, attacking the leader of her own party, Jeremy Corbyn, over his allegedly inadequate campaign for Remain: 'The EU referendum was a test of leadership and I think Jeremy failed that test. He came out too slowly. He was very halfhearted about his attempts to campaign and Labour voters simply didn't get the message' (Pickard et al. 2016). In the same article, Lord Mandelson, a key figure in Tony Blair's government, is quoted as saying of Corbyn's campaign, 'At best his voice was curiously muted but when he did say anything, there were mixed messages.' Over the next five days twenty-one members of Corbyn's shadow cabinet resigned, all citing dissatisfaction with their leader's lacklustre performance in the build-up to the referendum as a major reason for doing so, while the shadow foreign secretary, Hilary Benn, displayed such disloyalty that he left Corbyn with little option but to sack him.

It is true that less than two weeks before voting day Jeremy Corbyn announced on Channel 4's comedy show *The Last Leg* that his enthusiasm for remaining in the EU could be rated at 'seven, or seven and a half out of ten' (*Jeremy Corbyn on the Last Leg* 2016), but, as I hope to demonstrate in the following chapters, he was hardly alone in damning the EU with faint praise. Although the Leave campaign had been expected to do well in certain parts of the country, Labour MPs were genuinely shocked when it emerged that the pro-Brexit vote had also been strong in Labour's traditional heartlands in the north and midlands, but instead of asking themselves why their own constituents had ignored advice to vote to stay in, they made a somewhat disingenuous attempt to lay the entire blame at the party leader's door. In reality, no individual could have swayed the result one way or the other, while Remain supporters of the right, left and centre have a certain collective responsibility for not employing language more convincingly.

This section begins by looking at a syntactic structure that recurred with remarkable frequency in written and spoken texts supporting the case for Remain, a construction that actually concedes that the Leave camp also have a credible argument themselves. Further investigations of grammatical and lexical features, conscious linguistic strategies and the sometimes fuzzy distinction between rhetoric and spin aim to show that on a series of fronts the Brexiteers won the language war. What is highly persuasive may not be highly truthful, however, and it could be argued that Remain campaigners were more honest in using language that acknowledged the complexity of the issue at stake. A referendum requires a binary choice while the European Union, an institution that encompasses twenty-eight nations (still, at the time of writing) and well over 500 million permanent residents, is such a complicated amalgam of the good, the bad and the perplexing that it is practically impossible to either love it or hate it unconditionally. If Leave won the language war they did so partly by simplifying matters in keeping with the essential in-or-out question on the ballot paper, while Remain paid the price of openly admitting that the EU was far from perfect.

There is no simple answer to the question of when (or whether) it may be justifiable to practise a certain judicious selection of truths in order to achieve greater exhortative efficacy, and it is probably fair to say that we demand different levels of sincerity from different writers or speakers: we want historians to favour impartiality and truth over ideological issues, hope but do not really expect journalists to do the same, and in the case of politicians, fully expect them to put a spin on what they are pleased to call facts. David Runciman (2010: 9) argues that since politicians have a series of conflicting loyalties – to their heterogeneous electorate, to their party and factions within it, to their principles but also to their assessment of what is feasible – they cannot possibly be 100 per cent truthful with all interlocutors at all times. However, the same author makes a provocative distinction between lying and hypocrisy:

> A lie creates the immediate impression that one believes something that happens to be false, but that does not mean that one is not what one seems (indeed, people who have a well-deserved reputation for lying may by telling a lie be confirming exactly who they are). Hypocrisy turns on questions of character rather than simply coincidence with the truth.

If politicians who sincerely believed that leaving the EU would be an enormous mistake had 'sexed up' their message for the good of the cause, they would, by Runciman's distinction, have been true to themselves, and therefore anything but hypocritical, even as they uttered half-truths and total lies. Indeed, the president of the European Commission, Jean-Claude Juncker, has made no attempt to sue or even contradict journalists who have reported on his propensity to lie to achieve his political objectives (*Jean-Claude Juncker's most outrageous political quotations* 2014). The primary aim of this work, however, is not to evaluate the honesty of those actively involved in the Brexit debate, but to consider the linguistic features that distinguished the Remain and Leave campaigners in order to gauge the relative efficacy of each side's message.

The following three sentences provide the same information but with different syntactic constructions:

(i)　I had done a first-class job but the boss did not thank me.

(ii)　Although I had done a first-class job, the boss did not thank me.

(iii)　Although the boss did not thank me, I had done a first-class job.

Sentence (i) is an example of coordination (sometimes referred to as *parataxis*) while sentences (ii) and (iii) are examples of subordination (or *hypotaxis*). Huddlestone (1984: 382) explains the difference with admiral conciseness: 'In coordination the terms in the relationship are of equal syntactic status, in subordination they are not – one is subordinate, the other superordinate.' Coordination creates syntactic parallelism: in (i) the two clauses on either side of the coordinating conjunction *but* have equal weight and each could stand alone as a short sentence in itself. Subordination creates syntactic hierarchy: in (ii) and (iii) the clauses containing the subordinating conjunction *although* could not be stand-alone sentences because they are clearly incomplete and need to be linked to a main or superordinate clause.

In sentence (ii) the fact that I had done a first-class job is expressed in a subordinate clause and is therefore assigned reduced importance, while the stressed information, the fact that the boss did not thank me, is placed in a main clause. The focus of the sentence is on the boss's ingratitude. In sentence (iii) the situation is reversed: the boss's refusal to thank me is less important and the main focus switches to the high quality of my work.

Assigning a piece of information greater importance by expressing it in a superordinate clause can be a double-edged sword, however. As Lesley Jeffries notes (2010: 86): 'Putting something at a higher syntactic level may mean that it is more important, but it is also likely to make it more susceptible to questioning, so that text producers who wish their ideas not to be questioned too closely may well make something quite uncontentious the main proposition of their sentences.' Sentence (iii) would probably not be uttered by someone who harboured doubts as to whether his/her claim to have produced top-quality work could really stand up to close scrutiny.

In written and spoken texts produced by Remain supporters during the referendum campaign, the following structure was used with extraordinary frequency:

> Finite clause critical of EU + BUT + Finite clause presenting Remain as preferred option

In the language of anti-Brexit politicians, journalists and bloggers this coordinative construction was ubiquitous and even occurred in the headlines or leads of articles. In the following examples, the first two are the headline and the lead respectively of two articles written by George Monbiot (2016) for *The Guardian*. The third quotes both the headline and the lead of a piece written by Adam Ramsay (2016) for the website of openDemocracyUK.

(iv)   I'm starting to hate the EU. But I will vote to stay in

(v)   The EU is a festering cesspool. But it's a crystal spring compared with what the outers want to do – surrender Britain's sovereignty to the United States

(vi)   I hate the EU. But I'll vote to stay in it
      The European Union is an undemocratic corporate stitch-up. But leaving would be worse

Although most of us can remember a teacher of English telling us that you cannot start a sentence with *but*, here we have four cases in which a journalistic convention prevails over the grammatical rule that a conjunction should not be placed in initial position. By making the clause that precedes the word *but* a sentence in itself, these two writers stress the fact that the two clauses on either side of the conjunction are of equal syntactic status. Had they opted for subordination, the subordinating conjunction *although* in initial position would have immediately signalled to the reader that the proposition of the first clause would be overridden by that of the main or superordinate clause (in as much as language as strong as 'festering cesspool' and 'undemocratic corporate stitch-up' can be overridden).

In their less-than-ringing endorsement of the European Union, Monbiot and Ramsay appear to be practically in agreement with the central argument of the Lexit campaign, that is, the EU is fundamentally undemocratic and has come to represent the interests of multinational corporations rather than those of the public at large. Their unenthusiastic vote to maintain membership is based on nothing more than the fear that stepping out of the frying pan will lead to somewhere even hotter, so it is hardly surprising if they do not present their case with a great deal of fervour. One would expect a little more vim from professional politicians known for their pro-EU stance or from an online newspaper that supported the case for remaining a member from the moment the referendum date was announced, but in the following examples the same coordinative construction is evident: (vii) is the concluding sentence of an open letter written by five senior figures in the Labour Party, including Jack Straw, a minister in Tony Blair's government and father of Will Straw, executive director of the Britain Stronger in Europe movement (Nelson 2016); (viii) comes from an article written by Labour MP Yvette Cooper (2016); (ix) is from an unsigned editorial in *The Independent* entitled *The right choice is to remain* (2016).

(vii)   The EU is not perfect and improvement is always worth making, but the benefits far outweigh the costs.

(viii)   Europe's not perfect and there's plenty we should keep campaigning to change. But we still get a better deal if we work together than if we walk away.

(ix)   The institution is not without its flaws of course – there is bureaucratic inefficiency and the maintenance of Strasbourg as the official seat of the European Parliament is wastefully expensive. But membership of the EU benefits our economy, boosts global security and aids our connectivity with the rest of Europe.

The 'five Labour heavyweights' (*The Mirror*'s description) – Neil Kinnock, David Blunkett, Margaret Beckett, Jack Straw and the rather more middle-weight Hilary Benn – might argue that in ending their twelve-sentence open letter as they did, their intention was to show that they had reached their pro-EU position after an honest appraisal of the merits of both sides of the issue, and had elected to eschew the simplistic and exaggerated approach of the Brexiteers. That they were capable of understanding the Leave supporters' point of view is clear from their admission at the start of the letter that in the 1975 referendum (see Chapter 11) all five had voted against Britain's continued membership of what was then the European Economic Community. Given their political history, it is remarkable that so little of the zeal of the convert entered their prose that in their concluding sentence they did not even down-grade the reference to the EU's imperfections to a subordinate clause.

In content as well as in structure, Yvette Cooper's words in (viii) are similar to those of the five heavyweights: in both cases the first clause acknowledges the EU's imperfection and the need for improvement while the second features a comparative (*outweigh* and *better deal* respectively) to illustrate the advan-tage of staying in. There is no sexing up of the message to make it more persua-sive, which once again can be seen as either admirable honesty or ineffectual campaigning by an experienced politician.

In (ix) it could be argued that the first sentence actually has more impact than the second in that it contains a highly specific example of one of the EU's flaws – the cost of maintaining Strasbourg as the seat of the European Parliament – while the second mentions general benefits without saying any-thing concrete. Indeed, it is not even clear what is meant by 'our connectivity with the rest of Europe'.

David Cameron's great gamble was that he could emulate Harold Wilson in 1975 and convince a majority of voters that he had renegotiated Britain's conditions of membership to such an extent that Eurosceptics' worries had already been addressed. On 19 February 2016, in an official statement to the media just one hour after the conclusion of talks with the European Council, he began by reassuring TV viewers in the UK that 'Britain will be permanently out of ever closer union – never part of a European superstate', then made his case for voting to stay in the EU. Given that he had failed to make any headway on the one issue that might have persuaded some Brexit supporters to change their voting intentions – the thorny question of the free movement of citizens within the Union – he could hardly assume a gung-ho attitude. Instead he emphasized his 'hard-headed assessment of what is in our national interest', but in doing so he also found himself admitting that he could understand public discontent with the EU:

> (x)   Like many, I have had my doubts about the European Union as
> an organisation. I still do. But just because an organisation is
> frustrating it does not mean that you should necessarily walk out
> of it, and certainly not without thinking very carefully through the
> consequences. (Cameron 2016)

One has the impression that Cameron would not even give the EU a mark of seven and a half out of ten. He conceded that the doubters were not an insignificant minority and that his own misgivings had not been completely assuaged. After the coordinating conjunction *but*, a subordinate clause provides more negativity concerning the EU, then the advice not to walk away is hedged (see Chapter 2) by the adverb *necessarily*. The concluding nonfinite clause creates an interesting implicature: perhaps it is all right to walk away from the European Union if you have carefully thought through the consequences.

Ross Clarke (2016) in the *Daily Express* reports that two days later, Cameron's defence secretary, Michael Fallon, sounded even less enthusiastic when speaking on BBC radio's *Today* programme:

(xi)   No one likes commissioners, harmonisation or directives. It has its faults but if you were outside the European Union it would still be there.

The subject of the first sentence makes dislike of three aspects of the EU universal, while the clause after *but* in the second sentence presents the existence of the European Union as just a disagreeable fact of life that we must learn to live with because it will not go away.

Posters designed by the German fine arts photographer Wolfgang Tillmans were among the most effective propaganda materials used by the Remain campaign. Tillmans focused on themes to which the Brexit camp had no real answer, such as the emergence of a de facto European identity as greatly increased mobility, particularly among the so-called Erasmus generation, has led to a situation in which huge numbers of Europeans live and work in nations other than that of their birth and the continent is now home to more mixed-nationality couples (with their bi- or trilingual children) than ever before. One poster from his *Between Bridges* pro-EU collection (Tillmans 2016) follows the same structure of acknowledging the EU's defects before saying something positive (the graphical layout has been modified):

Flawed? Yes   Slow? Yes   Attractive? Uhh
So, why?
The EU has brought peace to 28 member states.
In Poland and Hungary the EU is seen as the last defence against their authoritarian governments.
Don't leave them alone.

Tillmans presents the view that the 1957 Treaty of Rome set in motion a process that has brought nearly sixty years of peace to countries that were twice ruined by war in the first half of the twentieth century. Like the politicians and journalists discussed earlier, Tillmans also acknowledges the EU's faults before making the case for voting Remain. The difference, however, is that the second part of his message is a great deal more powerful than the less-than-inspiring appeals to opt for the lesser evil in the quotations considered previously. In texts (iv) to (xi), the second part of the coordinative construction presents staying in the EU as being in Britain's interest. In Tillmans's poster, the issue is not Britain's interests; it is Europe's interests and the multinational project that has guaranteed peace and democracy in the greater part of the continent, which takes the debate to a higher level than calculations of benefits outweighing costs or securing a better deal. It is actually a claim that can easily be challenged – some would argue that peace in Europe has had more to do with NATO and the mutually assured destruction of the nuclear arms race than with developments following the signing of the Treaty of Rome – but it is a theme that can raise passions in a way that appeals to maintain access to the single market cannot.

By repeated use of coordinative constructions, anti-Brexit politicians and journalists showed that they had sufficient confidence in their pro-EU arguments to allow them to be 'susceptible to questioning' (to repeat Jeffries's words) in a main clause, but the question remains as to why they decided to give equal prominence to the Brexiteers' views, not even relegating them to the lower syntactic level of a subordinate clause. It is difficult to believe that career politicians were so committed to telling the unvarnished truth that they elected to forego even mild subterfuge and spin to downgrade the validity of the case for leaving the EU and render more persuasive the counterargument. In the short texts quoted here, very little editing would be required to make the case for staying in the club a little more convincing; in (vii) and (viii), for instance, it would be sufficient to insert a factive verb, that is, a verb such as *know*, *learn*, *realize* or *regret* that presupposes the truth of its clausal complement:

(xii)   The EU is not perfect and improvement is always worth making, but *we have realized that* the benefits far outweigh the costs.

(xiii) Europe's not perfect and there's plenty we should keep campaigning to change. But *we know that* we still get a better deal if we work together than if we walk away.

The next chapter looks at further syntactic and most of all lexical characteristics of the language used by the Remain campaigners, linguistic features that give the impression that they were not wholly convinced by their own arguments. In contrast, the Leave campaigners opted for bold claims and seemed untroubled by doubts or the need to exercise caution.

2

Hedging and modality versus strident claims and apparent absence of doubt

In everyday speech we talk about 'hedging your bets' when you reduce your risk of serious loss by placing money on at least two possible results, the principle being that the gain made on one bet will at least partially compensate for the loss made on another. The expression is then extended beyond the domain of gambling to all transactions or dealings in which one tries to be prepared for two or more outcomes. We also say that people hedge when they do not make a firm commitment or do not give a direct response, and in this case the word has mildly negative connotations as it implies that our interlocutor is not being entirely straight with us.

When linguists talk of hedging, the word is stripped of its negative connotations and assumes the status of a technical term. For Bloor and Bloor (2013: 103), 'Hedging is a linguistic avoidance of full commitment or precision. It is a vague but useful term covering a range of phenomena.' This brief definition provides no information as to why people resort to hedging, and for this we can turn to Machin and Mayr (2012: 192): 'Hedging can be used to distance ourselves from what we say and to attempt to dilute the force of our statements and therefore reduce chances of unwelcome responses.'

A 'bald on-record strategy' (Brown and Levinson 1978) – that is a direct, clear, concise and unambiguous assertion – can lead to a range of unwelcome responses: direct contradiction in an equally bald on-record way, a challenge to provide proof or at least evidence, and, in some cases, an accusation of slander or libel. Tabloid newspapers dedicate considerable space to gossip about celebrities and the objects of such treatment can hardly complain about invasion of their privacy when it is in their interest to be in the public eye as frequently as possible. If a newspaper oversteps the mark, however, those same celebrities do not hesitate to sue. In the following text about the model Kate Moss, the expressions in italics show how an unnamed reporter for the *Daily Mail* employed hedging strategies to avoid the risk of legal action in an article with the clumsy headline *What's that party girl Kate Moss has popped out for?* (2008).

> (i) Kate Moss popped out for a spot of shopping last night – and returned home with two bottles of what *could have been* amyl nitrite.
>
> The substance, also known as 'poppers', is not illegal but *is popular among clubbers* who sniff its vapours to achieve a head rush. *It is also often combined* with other drugs.
>
> . . .
>
> *Speculation has been mounting* in recent weeks that Moss *could be pregnant*, although *health experts have warned* against the use of amyl nitrite during pregnancy. *Moss has also been spotted* drinking alcohol in recent weeks.

The reporter uses the modal verb *could* and a past conditional construction rather than the unequivocal affirmation that Kate Moss bought amyl nitrite; it is merely a hypothesis and s/he does not exclude the possibility that the bottles actually contained mineral water. We learn that the substance is popular among 'clubbers' but it is not explicitly stated that Kate Moss leads that kind of hedonistic lifestyle, while the passive voice is used to avoid stating directly that Moss herself would ever do something as reprehensible as to combine amyl nitrite with other (illegal?) drugs. The passive voice is again used to hide the identity of those responsible for fomenting 'mounting speculation' and the question of whether the famous model is indeed pregnant is again no more than a hypothesis signalled by a second use of the modal *could*. We have no information about the identities and medical credentials of the 'health experts' and a third use of the passive voice avoids any suggestion that it was paparazzi employed by the *Daily Mail* who spotted Kate Moss drinking alcohol. Any reader of normal intelligence would interpret the article as an accusation that the selfish and irresponsible Kate Moss is guilty of the despicable act of endangering the health of the baby she is carrying by indulging her own appetites and desires, but the judicious use of hedging techniques means that the text is almost certainly not actionable (note *almost*, a hedge used by someone who is not qualified to make authoritative pronouncements on legal matters).

Text (i) feature two of the most frequently employed hedging strategies: the use of modal auxiliary verbs that indicate 'speakers' attitudes towards the factual content of an utterance' (Crystal 1994: 257) and passive constructions without an explicit agent. Other techniques to avoid appearing excessively assertive or dogmatic include:

- Non-factive verbs such as *seem*, *appear* and *suggest* that allow the possibility that superficial appearances do not correspond to reality.

- Lexical verbs that indicate that what is stated is an opinion, not an objective fact: *I think, it is believed to be, we suppose* etc.

- Adverbs of frequency like *sometimes, often* or *usually*.

- Modal nouns: *likelihood, assumption, possibility* etc.

- Modal adjectives and adverbs: *(un)likely, conceivable/conceivably, probable/probably* etc.

- The use of approximators: *sort of, more or less, roughly* etc.

- Attributing responsibility to an anonymous third party: *they say*, *a lot of people think* etc.

- Metalingual glosses that diminish the speaker's or writer's authoritativeness: *as far as I know*, *to the best of my knowledge* etc.

A theory of communicative behaviour that has stood the test of time is Grice's Co-operative Principle (1975), which is concerned with the extent to which we comply with four maxims of collaborative interaction. We normally tell the truth or what we believe to be the truth (the Quality Maxim), we endeavour to give enough but not too much information (the Quantity Maxim), we try to make our contribution pertinent (the Maxim of Relation) and we try to express ourselves clearly without obscurity or ambiguity (the Maxim of Manner). Grundy (2008: 299) defines a hedge in relation to the Co-operative Principle as 'a means of indicating weak adherence to a conversational maxim'.

If the relevant maxim is that of quality, weak adherence implies questionable sincerity, or at the very least a certain evasiveness: 'Hedging is the use of language features that allow a speaker or writer to avoid coming cleanly and quickly to the point, to avoid being specific and therefore providing 'padding' to the consequences of what they say.' (Bloor and Bloor 2013: 13).

Hedging is inextricably linked to the broader issue of modality, which can be defined as the grammaticalized expression of a speaker's or writer's attitudes towards matters of possibility, likelihood, permissibility, ability, necessity, obligation and desirability with regard to what s/he says or writes. It is most commonly indicated by modal auxiliary verbs (*can*, *might*, *should* etc.) but can also be expressed by semi-modals such as *have to* or *need* (which are semantically similar to modals but are grammatically different in their negative and interrogative conjugations), and, as we have seen above, lexical verbs plus modal nouns, adjective and adverbs.

A distinction is made between epistemic modality, which is concerned with possibility and likelihood, and deontic modality, which involves necessity and obligation. The verbs most commonly associated with the former are *may*, *might* and *could*, while for the latter we use the modals *must* and *should* and the semi-modal *have to*. A third type of modality, boulomaic or volitive modality, is concerned with (un)desirability and is expressed through the modal auxiliary *would* (especially *would like*) and non-modals such as *wish* and *hope*.

Norman Fairclough (2001: 105) distinguishes between relational modality – 'a matter of the authority of one participant in relation to others' – and expressive modality, which is 'a matter of the speaker or writer's authority with respect to the truth or probability of a representation of reality'. The former often involves verbs of deontic modality such as *must* and *should*: *you must do as I say* implies that the speaker has the authority to impose an obligation upon the interlocutor, while *you should do as I say* reduces the exhortation to the level of advice that the interlocutor can choose to ignore. The expressive type involves *will*, *could* and other verbs associated with epistemic modality: *the consequences will be disastrous* indicates that the speaker is sure of the accuracy of his/her prediction, whereas *the consequences could be disastrous* does not convey certainty but merely presents a hypothesis that will be much easier to disown if current fears prove to be unfounded. The verb *may* is sometimes used for relational deontic modality – *you may go home now* means that the speaker has sufficient authority over the interlocutor to grant him/her permission to go home – and sometimes for expressive epistemic modality – *you may well be right* is a judgement upon the likelihood that the interlocutor is right.

This chapter is primarily concerned with expressive and epistemic modality as it focuses on how speakers and writers evaluate the truth of what they themselves say or write. However, relational modality is also relevant, particularly with regard to what Fairclough, in a different work, calls the 'texturing of identities'. How people signal the degree of certainty and truth to be assigned to their utterances tells us something about them as individuals and in relation to others.

> Modality is important in the texturing of identities, both personal ('person-
> alities') and social, in the sense that what you commit yourself to is a signifi-
> cant part of what you are – so modality choices in texts can be seen as part
> of the process of texturing self-identity. (Fairclough 2003: 16)

The texts analysed below demonstrate how the use of epistemic modality
and hedging by Remain supporters – including some whose political futures
depended upon a vote in favour of staying in the EU – tended to give the
impression that they were not 100 per cent convinced by their own arguments. In contrast, Leave campaigners expressed rock-hard certainties and
were remarkably untroubled by self-doubt. The closer we got to 23 June, the
more I thought that Remain campaigners ought to read W. B. Yeats's poem
The Second Coming, which contains the lines: 'The best lack all conviction,
while the worst / Are full of passionate intensity.' Yeats ends his poem with
a desperate question: 'And what rough beast, its hour come round at last, /
Slouches towards Bethlehem to be born?' As demonstrated in Chapter 13,
some Remain supporters used epithets far worse than 'rough beast' to
describe Nigel Farage and Boris Johnson; this chapter is concerned with the
issue of 'passionate intensity', which was conspicuously absent in the speech
and writing of prominent figures urging the public to vote for continued
membership of the EU.

The following text, a warning about the economic consequences of leaving
the EU, comes from a piece entitled *Facts: Jobs* (2016) on the Labour Party's
labourinforbritain site:

> (ii) Over three million jobs which are linked with our trade with the EU
> could be put at risk. British companies could face tariffs to export to Europe.
> For example, it is likely that UK-based car manufacturers [. . .] would sud-
> denly face the same 10% tariffs on exports to Europe as the United States
> and Japan.

In the first two sentences the verb of epistemic modality, *could*, indicates that the loss of three million jobs and the imposition of tariffs are possibilities rather than certainties. Similarly, in the third sentence the modal adjective *likely* refers to a negative economic scenario that is probable but not certain. We are told that UK-based car manufacturers *would* face, not *will* face, 10 per cent tariffs, which makes the warning a hypothesis rather than the inevitable consequence of leaving the EU.

As noted in the previous chapter, it could be argued that such linguistic choices represent an honest admission that the issue was complex. In reality, no one could predict with any great confidence what would happen after a vote to quit the EU. After the referendum it was immediately obvious that few people, least of all certain leaders of the Leave campaign, had given much thought to the practicalities of negotiating a divorce. Before the vote there was some talk of the 'Norway solution', and later of 'soft Brexit', a compromise that would permit the UK to leave the EU but continue to have access to the EU's single market, thus ensuring that there would be no imposition of tariffs and no loss of jobs. Alternatively, the consequence of 'hard Brexit', a clean break with all EU institutions, would most definitely be the imposition of tariffs (though not necessarily the loss of such a huge number of jobs). If the author(s) of text (ii) had assumed that Brexit would be of the hard variety, it would have been possible to use the modal verb *will* and the modal adjective *certain* in describing economic consequences that were not hypothetical at all, but the inescapable price to pay for a reckless decision.

A consistent feature of the Brexit (but not Lexit) campaign was concern that freedom of movement within the EU had resulted in the arrival of unsustainable numbers of migrant workers from such countries as Poland, Romania and Bulgaria. Texts (iii) and (iv), both from *The Guardian*, present entirely different scenarios of what a victory for Brexit would mean with regard to immigration. The first quotes an article in the May 2016 edition of the *National*

Institute Economic Review by the economist Jonathan Portes, who maintains that Brexit would probably not lead to a substantial fall in the number of EU migrants (Travis 2016). The second cites a report published by the Social Market Foundation think tank that estimates that if Britain left the EU the majority of the 1.6 million EU citizens resident in the UK would not meet the requirements to obtain a work visa, and that a mass exodus of migrant workers would be disastrous for the economy (Mason 2016).

> (iii) Brexit 'unlikely to mean deep migration cuts and could lead to 2p tax increase'
>
> Economist Jonathan Portes says Brexit is likely to cut net migration to UK by only 100,000 but reduction will cause financial harm
>
> (iv) Leaving the EU could cause catastrophic staff shortages in some sectors, as 88% of EU workers in Britain would not qualify for a visa under current rules, remain campaigners have warned.
>
> . . .
>
> There could be a severe impact on the UK labour market if freedom of movement were to end and workers of all countries were treated according to the current rules, the study found.
>
> . . .
>
> Filling this gap may pose a real challenge for UK employers.

Text (iii) gives the headline and lead of an article by Alan Travis, *The Guardian*'s home affairs editor. Again we see the modal verb *could* and the adjectives *likely* and *unlikely* to indicate that the article that follows is not an assertion of facts but a description of a possible outcome. Given that the prospect of Britain's regaining control of immigration policy was fundamental to the UK Independence Party's (UKIP) programme (and is explored in more detail in Chapter 8), a convincing explanation of why Brexit would not lead to great cuts in the number of EU migrant workers could have done considerable damage to the Leave camp's case. It is curious, therefore, that the home affairs editor of a newspaper that supported Remain did not vigorously declare that leaving the EU *will not* mean deep migration cuts, or *will* reduce the number of migrants by no more than 100,000. Since a number of UK employers made it clear that they would continue to require imported labour regardless of the outcome of the referendum, unequivocal affirmations about the negligible effect of Brexit on immigration would have been easy enough to justify. The modal verb *will* is used in the lead but with reference to unspecified financial harm rather than the potentially vote-swinging issue of immigration.

That economics is not an exact science is evident from the fact that text (iv) presents the opposite scenario of Brexit leading to an enormous cut in the number of EU migrants and 'catastrophic staff shortages' as an immediate consequence. In the first sentence the modal verbs *could* and *would* are used although the situation described is not really a hypothetical one. Visa requirements for non-EU citizens exist, as do data concerning the qualifications and family status of those EU workers currently resident in Britain. Similarly, the second and third sentences could be rewritten as statements of fact based upon the reality of existing visa requirements and the low percentage of migrant workers who meet those requirements: there *will* be a severe impact on the UK labour market and this *will* pose a real challenge for employers. This too is an argument that could have greatly damaged the Leave campaign if expressed through the first conditional form and a modal verb indicating the certain consequence of taking back control of immigration policy: for example, 'be careful what you wish for because if you get rid of the Poles earning the national minimum wage, care homes *will* close and all you *will* take back is Auntie Mabel with her advanced state of dementia'.

Text (v), by the Australian journalist Andrew Dewson (2016) for *The Independent* deals with the danger (or hope, depending on one's point of view) of renewed calls for Scottish independence following a victory for Leave, while text (vi) features *The Mirror's* heavily hedged report of Prime Minister

Cameron's warning that Brexit would signal the end of low-cost flights (Hughes and Wheeler 2016).

(v) But there's one very real possibility that Brits are ignoring: that a vote in favor of a Brexit could conceivably lead to the breakup of Britain and then of the Commonwealth.

. . .

Every business that might consider leaving England for mainland Europe following a Brexit might instead consider moving to Scotland.

. . .

Plenty of Brexit supporters want Britain to remain whole: they argue that Scotland wouldn't become an automatic member of the EU and may not achieve favorable membership terms. But alternatively and just as likely – the EU desperately, wanting to stick it to England, might fasttrack Scottish membership, granting the country very favorable terms indeed.

. . .

What about the Commonwealth? The British monarch is still the official head of state in Commonwealth nations, but for how much longer? It's possible that an independent Scotland could decline membership of the Commonwealth. Support for republicanism isn't at the levels reported a decade ago, but if Britain no longer existed then sentiments may change.

(vi) Cheap flights between European destinations could be put at risk by the UK leaving the EU, David Cameron has suggested.

The Prime Minister sought to cast doubt on the ability of low-cost airlines such as Easyjet and Ryanair to freely operate routes between EU member states after a Brexit.

. . .

The Prime Minister made the claims as he sought to rejuvenate his campaign for a Remain vote at June's referendum after an Easter holiday in Lanzarote.

The first sentence quoted in text (v) features a noun (*possibility*), a verb (*could*) and an adverb (*conceivably*) that serve the epistemic function of presenting the prospect of the breakup of the UK as a potential development but not a certainty. The one thing that is asserted without hedging – the claim that the Brits are ignoring the risk of dismantlement of the UK – is open to challenge since Nicola Sturgeon, leader of the Scottish National Party (SNP), ensured that in the run-up to 23 June the entire nation understood that a second referendum on Scottish independence was on the SNP's post-Brexit agenda.

The modal verb *might* is then used twice, first for the possibility of businesses relocating from England to mainland Europe, then for the prospect of their choosing Scotland as an alternative destination.

As regards the third part of text (v), epistemic modality is expressed through *wouldn't* and *may not* in the presentation of the Leave argument that an independent Scotland would find itself outside the EU with no guarantee of an easy return, then through *likely* and *might* in the alternative scenario of Brussels deciding to give Scotland favourable treatment in order to punish England. Twenty-five days after the publication of Dewson's article and two days after the referendum, the European Commission made it abundantly clear that Brexit involved all of Britain and that Scotland would first of all have to achieve independence from the UK before applying for EU membership in the normal way.

The final part of text (v) features an informal register with aspects usually associated with spoken communication, such as direct questions and contracted verb forms. The second direct question may be seen as a hedging device since Dewson avoids a bald on-record statement that the British monarch will not be head of state in Commonwealth nations for much longer but leaves it to the reader to interpret the implicature created by his flouts of the maxims of quantity and manner. He also appears to be unaware of the fact that thirty-two of the fifty-two members of the Commonwealth are republics that already have their own president as head of state rather than Queen Elizabeth II. The

British monarch has no constitutional role in independent republics like India, South Africa and Nigeria, where her status as head of the Commonwealth is purely symbolic.

Modality is expressed through the use of *possible* and *could* with reference to the prospect of an independent Scotland electing to leave the Commonwealth, and no explanation is given as to why the government in Edinburgh might choose to abandon a voluntary association of sovereign states in which Britain has no political control whatsoever over the other members. In the final sentence the reference to a rise in republican sentiments is hedged by the use of the modal verb *may*, but the suggestion is in any case irrelevant given that fifteen Commonwealth nations chose to adopt a republican system of government on gaining independence and seventeen others became presidential republics some years after becoming independent. It was noted earlier that the use of modality tells us something about speakers' or writers' attitudes towards the factual content of what they say or write, and in the case of text (v) it appears that indicators of uncertainty do not only signal an honest recognition of the complexities of the issues at stake, but also reflect the personal uncertainty of a writer who has not researched his subject sufficiently.

One immediate consequence of the vote for Brexit was the widely predicted devaluation of sterling. This led to the phenomenon of 'staycation' – a lexical blend of *stay* and va*cation* – as British families realized that they would get fewer euros for their pounds in Spain or Portugal and opted to rediscover the attractions of Blackpool and Brighton. The same devaluation obviously made Britain a more appetizing destination for holidaymakers from eurozone countries, Asia and the United States, and by 23 August 2016, *The Independent* could cite a number of sources with figures to demonstrate a significant increase in tourist spending in the UK during the month of July (Rodionova 2016). For low-cost airlines staycation meant that a drop in the number of British passengers was, and still is, offset by a rise in the number of non-British passengers flying to and from the UK.

Text (vi) reports on David Cameron's warning that Brexit could mean that budget airlines might not be able to operate in the EU. The claim is not difficult to challenge given that companies based outside the European Union such as Norwegian Air Shuttle, Pegasus (Turkey) and UP (Israel) currently fly to EU destinations, and *The Mirror*, the one daily tabloid that supported Remain, employed a series of hedging techniques to establish a certain distance between the prime minister's views and the journalists reporting them.

In the first of the quoted sentences the modal verb *could* is used and we read that the possible risk to budget flights is something that Cameron 'has suggested' rather than stated or affirmed or simply said. The next sentence does not tell us that the prime minister cast doubts on the ability of Ryanair and Easyjet to continue to operate freely but 'sought to cast doubt', which implies that he did not necessarily succeed in his intention. Then in the third of the quoted sentences we learn that Cameron's warning are 'claims' as opposed to declarations or statements, and that he made them 'as he sought to rejuvenate his campaign for a Remain vote', which again establishes the distinction between seeking to do something and actually doing it. In terms of relational modality and Fairclough's notion of texturing identities, the intensive use of hedging in this article can be seen as indicative of the journalists' wish to ensure that, on this specific question of budget airlines, their own self-identities are not too closely associated with the prime minister's views.

Switching our attention to the Leave campaign, we find considerably less use of hedging and an entirely different approach to modality. Text (vii) comes from a post entitled *Why Vote Leave* on the official Vote Leave Take Control website of the Leave campaign.

(vii) If we vote to leave the EU

   We will be able to save £350 million a week

   We can spend our money on our priorities, like the NHS, schools, and housing.

We'll be in charge of our borders

In a world with so many new threats, it's safer to control our own borders and decide for ourselves who can come into this country, not be overruled by EU judges.

We can control immigration and have a fairer system which welcomes people to the UK based on the skills they have, not the passport they hold

We'll be free to trade with the whole world

The EU stops us signing our own trade deals with key allies like Australia or New Zealand, and growing economies like India, China or Brazil. We'll be free to seize new opportunities which means more jobs.

We can make our own laws

Our laws should be made by people we can elect and kick out – that's more democratic.

If we vote to stay in the EU

The EU is expanding

Turkey is one of *five* new countries joining the EU

. . .

The EU will cost us more and more

The EU already costs us £350 million a week – enough to build a new NHS hospital every week. We get less than half of this back, and have no say over how it's spent.

Immigration will continue to be out of control

Nearly 2 million people came to the UK from the EU over the last ten years. Imagine what it will be like in future decades when new, poorer countries join.

We'll have to keep bailing out the €

The countries that use the Euro already have a built-in majority, meaning they can always outvote us. You will be paying the bill for the Euro's failure.

The European Court will still be in charge of our laws
It already overrules us on everything from how much tax we pay, to who we can let in and out of the country, and on what terms.

This work is primarily concerned with the use of language rather than the semiotic significance of graphical and layout choices or the use of photos and cartoons. To reproduce the full content of the relevant part of the site in question would occupy several pages of the traditional book format. However, in this case some mention should be made of certain aspects of visual communication, particularly in the light of Machin and Mayr's observation that, just as words can denote one thing and connote another, so images can depict physical reality – people, places or things – and at the same time evoke abstract concepts, ideas and values (2012: 49).

The text is neatly divided into two parts: following the condition 'If we vote to leave the EU' there are five positive consequences beginning with the pronoun *We*; in the second part we have the condition 'If we vote to stay in the EU' followed by five negative consequences. Much of the text in the first part is of a soft shade of blue while the second part uses red, the colour traditionally associated with danger.

Some of the images are neither original nor particularly persuasive (the white cliffs of Dover, a blindfolded Lady Justice with her balance and sword etc.), but two merit some discussion. Beside the positive consequence 'We can make our own laws' there is an image of a large Union Jack in the background and in the foreground twenty-three hands raised, presumably in support of the national flag. What is significant is the fact that eleven of those hands are black or brown, evidently a choice made to counter the accusation of scarcely concealed racism frequently aimed at Leave supporters.

The second powerful image accompanies the warning that 'The EU is expanding'. A map shows Europe plus Turkey, with Britain coloured blue and Turkey red. Additional text informs us that the population of Turkey is seventy-six million and a broad red arrow indicates the direct route from that country to the heart of England. That Turkey has a large population is underlined by a circle at the base of the arrow containing a number of the man and woman icons found on the doors of public toilets, but there are more male than female icons. There are no words to tell us that expansion of the EU will result in Britain having to absorb great numbers of Turkish migrants, but the image used depicts precisely that scenario while also invoking concerns about trying to assimilate men coming from a society where attitudes towards gender issues are very different from those in the UK.

To return to language use, the most striking feature is the recurrent choice of the modal verb *will* to indicate the certain outcome of a vote for or against leaving the EU, a stark contrast with the hypotheses and uncertainty signalled by Remain supporters' repeated use of *may, might* or *could*. When, as in text (vii), the modal verb *can* refers to ability of some kind, it does not fall neatly into one of the categories of epistemic or deontic modality, and in such cases it is sometimes described as representing *dynamic modality*. However, it suggests a definite ability comparable with that indicated by the expression *will be able to*, and therefore conveys a sense of self-confidence.

The outcomes of either a yes or a no vote described in text (vii) are not in themselves any more likely to come about than those offered in the Leave camp's predictions and hypotheses described above. Indeed, all of them can be and were hotly contested, especially the claim that leaving the EU would save Britain £350 million a week. While it is true that the UK was, and at the time of writing, still is one of the major contributors to the EU budget, the figure of £350 million is quite simply a lie. Member states are normally required to pay 1 per cent of their GDP but Britain has been contributing less than that since 1984 when Mrs Thatcher negotiated a rebate. When that rebate is taken into account, the weekly sum drops to £248 million, but that is a gross figure that does not consider the money that returns to the UK in the form of aid to economically deprived areas like South Wales and Cornwall, agricultural subsidies and the funding of research programmes such as Horizon 2020. Once all the receipts from Brussels are included in the calculation, the UK's net contribution to the EU budget is found to be £136 million a week, which is 'still a lot of money but is less than 40 per cent of the figure claimed by the Leave campaign throughout the referendum campaign (Henley 2016). Later in text (vii) there is in fact a rather oblique reference to finance received from the EU but it is described as 'less than half' of the £350 million allegedly sent to Brussels each week when an accurate calculation would show it to be 61 per cent.

In text (vii), and indeed in practically all Leave propaganda during the referendum campaign, the issues of immigration and border controls were discussed in terms of certainties or confident predictions, usually with the modal verbs *can* and *will*, and without hedging strategies. The question of whether Brexit would be hard or soft did not fully emerge until after the vote, although some Leave campaigners were effectively touting the soft variety by reassuring their supporters that leaving the EU would not damage the British economy because the government could opt for the Norway-solution of negotiating a deal to retain access to the single market. This conveniently overlooked the fact that Brussels had made it abundantly clear that maintaining free movement of labour was a non-negotiable condition of tariff-free trade with the single market. It was not made sufficiently clear that taking back control of immigration policy, and also of breaking free from the European Court, could only be achieved through hard Brexit, a prospect that might well have deterred some voters.

Other confident claims in text (vii) that were challenged during the campaign are the conviction that an independent UK would be able to negotiate favourable trade deals with rapidly growing economic powers like China and Brazil, and the fear that Britain would have to keep 'bailing out' a failing euro.

It is not at all clear why China would cut a deal with Britain when it has not done so with the much larger market of the EU, while in today's interconnected world it is difficult to see how any trading nation or bloc could be unaffected by a crisis in the eurozone. The only point made in text (vii) that cannot be contested is the typically Lexit argument concerning the desirability of laws made by people 'we can elect and kick out'; it is undeniable that the European Commission is unelected and that throughout the period of the referendum campaign was involved in the Transatlantic Trade and Investment Partnership (TTIP) negotiations with the United States that citizens of the member states were not allowed to know anything about.

Texts (viii) and (ix) do not require detailed comment; both are further examples of the use of *will* and other expressions of epistemic modality to present certainties rather than possibilities or hypotheses.

(viii) BREXIT FACTOR 10 reasons why choosing Brexit on June 23 is a vote for a stronger, better Britain.

Leaving the EU will save our sovereignty, rein in migration and boost our economy

(Lord Green et al. 2016)

(ix) [*omissis*] The eurozone crisis isn't just economic – devastating as it is. It's also going to be political and will spread beyond the eurozone, convulsing the EU in ways we have not yet even come close to seeing. As EU members we would be part of this, even outside the eurozone.

. . .

We have already seen low-level rioting in Greece – it will surely get much worse as voters' impotence becomes ever more intolerable. But if voters cannot change direction through the ballot box the lure of extremists is bound to increase as it has already with the rise of Golden Dawn in Greece and other fascist parties elsewhere.

. . .

So the issue we have to address before June 23 is whether we want to remain tied to the EU and the chaos that is bound to engulf it. Inside the EU, as the eurozone collapses and the politicians attempt to rescue it and their precious European project, there will be no escape. We will suffer the consequences of a currency we never joined and a political union we never wanted. Or we can get out now and leave them to it.

It's not really much of a dilemma, is it?

(Pollard 2016)

Text (viii) shows the headline and lead of an article from *The Sun* online on the eve of voting day. The article itself – which is surprisingly long for *The Sun* – contains the modal verb *will* thirty-four times, while the combined total for *can, would, should, could* and *must* is twenty-eight. *Would* appears thirteen times, usually in second conditional constructions concerning the hypothesis of a victory for Remain.

Stephen Pollard's article in *The Express* online (text ix) is closely based on the book *The End of Alchemy: Money, Banking and the Future of the Global Economy* by Baron King of Lothbury who, when he was plain Mervyn King, was governor of the Bank of England from 2003 to 2013. The book's contents are wide-ranging but Pollard homes in on those parts that predict tough times ahead for the eurozone. The journalist writes of the collapse of the eurozone as a certain outcome: apart from the modal verb *will* that is used four times in the sentences cited above, there is also an instance of the *going to* future form, which is an even stronger indicator of certainty. In addition, epistemic modality is also expressed through the adverb *surely* and two instances of the form *is bound to*, which conveys a sense of inevitability. At no point do we find even the slightest concession to the notion that the euro might not be doomed after all.

Both the Brexit and the Lexit campaigns drew attention to the lack of democratic accountability in the EU but there were also significant differences

in their programmes that convinced most Lexit supporters that it was pru-
dent not to be seen alongside high-profile Brexit figures. Conservative MPs
like Boris Johnson and Michael Gove had no problem with the EU's neoliberal
agenda, including the privatization of public services and the prohibition of
state aid to industry, while Lexit supporters argued that European laws made
it impossible for a future Labour government to implement its election manifesto, notably the promise to renationalize the railways, a proposal that had,
and still has, considerable support in the country. Similarly, a key element of
the Brexit platform, the need to reintroduce border controls and reduce the
numbers of EU migrants coming into the UK, was largely ignored by Lexit
proponents, who feared accusations of barely disguised racism if they were
seen as sharing UKIP's highlighting of public concern about migration levels
(although a notable exception was the MP Gisella Stuart, herself an immigrant
from West Germany, who served as chair of the Vote Leave campaign and on
her blog – *Gisela Stuart and Team Gisela* – and in interviews made it clear
that she thought Labour was committing a tactical error in not addressing
the legitimate concerns expressed particularly by second and third generation
British Asians).

Texts (x), (xi) and (xii) give the Lexit point of view. They are respectively
the final part of an unsigned editorial entitled 'Why the *Morning Star* supports
a Leave vote' (2016) in the radical left-wing newspaper the *Morning Star*, the
headline, lead and opening paragraphs of an article by Brendan Chilton (2016),
the chair of Labour Leave, published, rather surprisingly, in the right-wing
Daily Express (a common enemy creates strange bedfellows), and the headline
and conclusion to an article by Suzanne Moore (2016) in *The Guardian* that
turned out to be prophetic.

(x) Falling wages, mass unemployment and battered public services are
feeding the resentment that gives birth to fascism. And the EU's commitment to endless austerity contributes to that.

Nor is the EU's record on racism good. A deal with Turkey widely condemned as illegal has allowed it to wash its hands of desperate refugees. In Ukraine it supported a fascist-backed coup against an elected government. When France decided to deport tens of thousands of Roma in 2009–10, the EU looked the other way.

There is no evidence that a Remain vote would help defeat the far right. The struggle against racism and intolerance is one we will have to wage anyway.

Since the beginning of the neoliberal era in the 1980s, we have seen corporate power strengthened at the expense of democracy again and again.

The 'big bang' deregulated the banks, putting big finance beyond our control. Independence for the Bank of England removed our ability to set interest rates. Global trade treaties are giving private companies the right to enter new markets whatever the people think about that, and increasingly the right to sue governments if they don't like their policies.

The EU is part and parcel of all this. A vote to Leave today will not bring about socialism. But it would be a step towards restoring democratic control of our economy, and would remove an obstacle to progress.

The Morning Star advise you to take that step.

(xi) EU does NOTHING for working people, says Labour Leave's BRENDAN CHILTON

MAKE no bones about it: the EU is anti-democratic

It is fundamentally against the interests of working people here in the UK and across Europe. The EU referendum is a once-in-a-lifetime opportunity for working people to take back control of our country from the unelected and unaccountable institutions of Brussels.

Millions of Labour supporters should vote to leave the EU on June 23 because it is the only progressive option in this referendum campaign. We are told by the international elite that we must remain a member of the

European Union because it has brought democracy, peace and progress to the member states. What utter nonsense!

The EU is not a benevolent institution that protects people and guides social progress. Instead it is an institution that ruthlessly crushes all who oppose it and has caused many of the social inequalities which are rife in Europe today.

(xii) Voters will stick two fingers up to those lecturing about Brexit's dangers

Every discussion of the referendum assumes that a Labour government is an impossibilty, so the left case for Brexit is a nonstarter. Instead, hope must be invested in 'young people', who it is assumed all think the same thing and go to Glastonbury.

So, we are told that this is a hugely important vote and that one must vote with head not heart, as though we have already lost. Somehow the EU will be reformed. We just don't know how.

But surely once the leave camp feels its strength, it will keep pushing? This matter won't be settled. The complete lack of credibility among the main players (Cameron, Corbyn and Johnson may all be arguing the opposite case to the ones closest to their hearts and histories) is ridiculous. The public senses this but, again, we keep being told that what this is really all about is immigration, the democratic deficit or sovereignty. Or 'I'd like to teach the world to sing' Eurovision. Maybe it's about all those things. Meanwhile, the complete loss of nerve by the left means that the low paid, the bottom 10%, are deemed worthy of sacrifice for some greater good.

I share this loss of nerve because of the company I would be in: the apocalypse of Borisconi. But I sense that, for many, a strange game is being played out whereby voting leave is not seen as such an enormous gamble. Much of England is ready to roll that dice; this part of England, so often despised, demonised and disrespected by those who claim to represent it, does need to be spoken for. This England will not do as it is told. This England may not be London and may not be subsumed into the fantasy of Great Britain, whichever side is selling it. When government, opposition and businesses are speaking with one voice, many feel there is not much of an actual choice here.

In the first two paragraphs of text (x) the indicative mood is employed to describe the nefariousness of the EU in a series of factual assertions that are not softened by any hedging devices at all. Epistemic modality is avoided and value-loaded lexis – facism, racism, facist-backed coup, desperate refugees, deport – underscores the strength of the accusations.

The modal verbs *will* and *would* both appear in the third paragraph, the former with reference to a certainty – the war against racism that socialists will have to wage irrespective of the referendum result – and the latter to refer to the consequences of a victory for Remain, an inexpedient outcome for the anonymous author who, in texturing his/her self-identity, chooses a verb that renders a vote to stay in the EU a mere hypothesis.

The third and fourth paragraphs return to direct, hard-hitting attacks on the EU's past and present policies, before the modals *will* and *would* reappear in the sixth. The article was posted on 22 June when most opinion polls were predicting a narrow victory for Remain, so the author uses a conditional construction with *would* to refer to two highly desirable gains resulting from an unexpected vote to quit the EU, but *will* for the rather obvious observation that there is no causal link between a victory for Leave and the creation of a socialist society.

In the paragraphs quoted in text (x), and indeed in the entire article, bold assertions are made and nothing is mitigated by hedges. Epistemic modality is primarily used in assessments of the likelihood of a victory for one side or the other, while the sustained attack on EU policies that the *Morning Star* considers detrimental to the interests of European citizens conveys the clear message that a vote for Leave is not the less bad option but a positive step forward.

When the article was written most people agreed that the radical left had very little chance of gaining political power in the UK any time soon, so the *Morning Star* had nothing to lose in electoral terms by eschewing circumspection and shooting from the hip. Labour, in contrast, has been a party of government on numerous occasions and hopes to become so again at a future general election, yet text (xi), from an article by Brendan Chilton, general secretary of the Labour Leave campaign, displays a similarly direct approach with no hedging devices to reduce the risk of hostile responses. It covers similar ground to the piece in the *Morning Star*: the EU's lack of democracy and accountability, austerity as a political choice rather than as an economic necessity, and neoliberal policies that benefit multinational corporations but not ordinary citizens. In the part quoted above we may presume that the headline and lead, emphatic capitals included, are the work of a *Daily Express* editor, while the first three paragraphs of the article are faithful to Chilton's words.

In text (xi) we find the opposite of hedging; the idiom *make no bones about it*, the adverb *fundamentally* and the exclamation *what utter nonsense* all serve to inform us that Chilton's assertions are not up for debate. The same tone of certitude is maintained throughout the article.

Instead of epistemic modality, in the second paragraph we have the deontic modals *should* and *must*. As noted earlier, *should* tends to indicate advice rather than a definite obligation that the addressee cannot feasibly refuse to obey, and here Chilton uses it in urging his readers to vote for leaving the EU. *Must*, in contrast, implies that the speaker or writer has the authority to impose an obligation on the addressee, and in text (xi) it is the 'international elite' that instructs Britain to remain part of the European Union. Modality is not used with regard to the factual content of the author's words – not a hint of doubt appears anywhere in the article – but to draw attention to the high-handed way in which the international elite tell EU nation states what to do.

If *The Express* is an unlikely place to find an article by a member of the Labour Party, *The Guardian* is not where one would expect to read a series of pieces expressing understanding of and sympathy with people intending to vote for Brexit, yet Suzanne Moore (2016) did precisely that between February and June. The headline of text (xii) – 'Voters will stick two fingers up to those lecturing about Brexit's dangers' – correctly predicted the outcome of the referendum two weeks before voting day. In an earlier piece, Moore (2016) admitted that her stance had shocked many of her university-educated friends: 'My instinct now is pretty Brexitty, much to the horror of many of my left/liberal friends who equate being anti-EU with being anti-Europe.' The extract quoted here is typical of her approach in that it makes a net distinction between Farage, Johnson and other Brexit leaders – men for whom she clearly has no respect – and the ordinary men and women planning to vote Leave more to defy the establishment than because of the specific issue of EU membership.

Text (xii) consists of the concluding paragraphs of the article. The deontic modal verb *must* is used twice in the first two short paragraphs, first in a passive construction ('. . .hope must be invested. . .'), then with the impersonal pronoun *one* ('. . .one must vote with head. . .'). Although the agent of the obligation signalled by *must* is not explicit, it is not difficult to work out who is imposing the obligation, and it is the same establishment that Chilton attacks in text (xi). In her final sentence Moore identifies that establishment as 'government, opposition and businesses . . . speaking with one voice'.

In addition to the modal verb *must*, a series of other expressions reinforce the idea of a powerful elite ordering people about, from the 'lecturing' of the headline to 'we are told', 'we keep being told' and the England that 'will not do as it is told'. That Suzanne Moore has little time for the leaders of the Brexit campaign is abundantly clear from her use of the lexical blend *Borisconi* (*Boris* [Johnson] + Berlus*coni*), which equates the most prominent figure in the final weeks of the Leave campaign with Italy's gaffe-prone and often clownish former prime minister. However, her view of those 'so often despised, demonised and disrespected by those who claim to represent it' is entirely different, and it is significant that she does nor write that this part of England *may* or *might* not do as it is told, but 'will not'.

From this and the previous chapter it is clear that Brexit/Lexit supporters couched their arguments in ways that were not necessarily full of W.B. Yeats's 'passionate intensity', but usually exhibited far greater certitude than Remain campaigners' hedged and cautious warnings. In the next chapter we see that Leave used language to good effect even in an apparently straightforward, optionless matter like the use of the imperative.

3

More to imperatives than meets the eye

The simplicity of certain features of English grammar sometimes reduces our communicative options. Modern English only has one second-person pronoun, so we can neither distinguish between singular and plural (although the plural *youse* and variations upon the archaic singular *thou/thee* occur in a number of dialects), nor employ a pronominal honorific as a politeness strategy, to acknowledge our addressee's age or status, or to establish a certain distance between ourselves and our interlocutor.

The same simplicity is then carried over to imperative sentences, in which the pronoun is usually not stated explicitly but is understood to be *you*. There is just one way, the use of the base form of the verb, to express a positive imperative, so 'Listen!' is the only option available to us whether we are addressing one person, two or more, a naughty child or a dowager duchess. For a negative imperative we are restricted to *don't* + base form, as in 'Don't tell anyone'. Unlike negative declarative and interrogative sentences, negative imperatives take the auxiliary *don't* even when the main verb is *be*, as in 'Don't be late'.

Occasionally the subject *you* is overtly present, either for contrastive purposes in a sentence such as 'You wash and I'll dry', or 'when there is a somewhat bullying or aggressive tone' (Huddlestone 1984: 360) as in 'You just show a bit of respect'. There is a certain ambivalence when there is an overt third-person subject, as in 'Somebody call an ambulance!', although a pragmatic interpretation of that subject would extend its meaning to 'somebody among you', and the addition of a tag question would require *you*: 'Somebody call an ambulance, will you?'.

Another type of imperative entails the use of *let*[gr], or grammaticalized *let*, as opposed to *let*[lex], or lexical *let* (ibid.: 361). *Let*[lex] can be used in all clause types, including imperatives that are no different from those considered above in that the unstated subject is *you*: 'Let me/us see your tattoo' directly commands, or more realistically in this case, implores a person to do something. *Let*[gr] is only used in imperatives, and when it is followed by the *'s* contraction of *us* the subject is first-person plural, as immediately becomes apparent if we add a tag question: 'Let's eat out this evening, shall we?' As will be investigated further in the next chapter, the pronoun *we* can be interpreted either inclusively or exclusively; inclusive *we* includes the interlocutor(s), as in 'your aims are not so different from ours, so I'm sure we can reach an agreement acceptable to all', while exclusive *we* excludes the addressee(s), as in 'you go your way and we'll go ours'. The *let*[gr] imperative obliges an inclusive interpretation, and some grammarians prefer to call it the *cohortative* mood (from the Latin *hortatorius*, meaning encouraging or cheering) since it tends to be used to urge a course of shared action rather than to issue a command in a peremptory fashion.

Returning to the unequivocal imperative with the implicit subject *you*, many languages have a far more elaborate system because they also have a more complex pronominal system that distinguishes between singular and plural second-personal addressees as well as between familiar and formal relationships. 'Tell me!', for instance, can be translated into Italian in four ways:

- Dimmi

- Ditemi

- Mi dica

- Mi dicano

The first two options are unequivocal imperatives with implicit second-person subjects, the first being the singular *tu* and the second the plural *voi*. Neither would normally be used with an adult stranger or strangers, or with a person or people whose age or status the speaker wishes to acknowledge. In such situations, it would be normal to use the third and fourth options, whose implicit subjects are the third-person *lei* (singular) and *loro* (plural) respectively, the pronouns required to express courtesy or respect for one's addressee(s). Technically speaking, the third and fourth options are not imperatives at all, but *congiuntivi esortativi*, or exhortative subjunctives (Trifone and Palermo 2007: 138), but they are listed here because they are two of the four most direct translations of 'Tell me!'. The crucial difference, however, is that saying 'Mi dica' to an Italian is unlikely to cause offence (in service encounters it is used as a broad equivalent of 'How can I help you?'), while a blunt 'Tell me' will not always be appreciated by an anglophone interlocutor.

Because of the lack of alternative forms in English, there is often the risk of sounding bossy or aggressive if we use the imperative. We can take some of the sting out of the command by adding *please* or the tag questions *will you?* or *would you?*, but we often prefer to use an indirect speech act, typically an interrogative clause to transform the order into a polite request, such as 'Could you bring me Ms Baker's file?'. The request formula is generally chosen even when the speaker clearly has the authority to issue an order; most managers have enough sense to understand that barking orders at staff does not produce the best response, and most staff do not confuse a polite boss with a weak boss.

Imperatives are freely used when the unstated *you* does not refer to anyone in particular, such as in written instructions on how to use a device or machine, or in a recipe. When using a series of imperatives to give street directions, the speaker may be addressing the hapless tourist directly but the information provided would be equally pertinent to anyone standing on that particular spot, so there is again an impersonal element. During elections the most basic campaign slogan of all involves the imperative form of the verb *to vote.* In the slogans *Vote Remain* or *Vote Leave*, the implicit subject is a non-specific *you*, and those publishing or uttering what is superficially an order know perfectly well that millions of people will disobey. In terms of Speech Act Theory (Austin 1962, Searle 1969), the illocutionary force is one of proffering advice rather than issuing a command, and the speaker or writer knows that in many cases the perlocutionary effect will be the opposite of that which is intended. In a one-to-one situation, however, *Vote UKIP* might be interpreted as a genuine command, and one quite likely to be resisted.

Given the potential dangers involved in using grammatical imperatives, it is helpful to think in terms of *jussives*. A jussive may be defined as a clause or verb form that indicates an order or command but is not necessarily an imperative in purely syntactic terms; indeed, imperatives should rightly be considered a subclass of the wider class of jussive clauses (Huddlestone 1988: 133). 'You will sort this out immediately' is a declarative sentence but the uncontracted and emphatically pronounced *will* makes it abundantly clear that the illocutionary force is an order rather than a mere statement of fact. A number of fixed expressions involving the subjunctive mood are non-imperative jussives: *So be it, Long live the King* and so on. An important jussive when the intention is to depersonalize an order is the employment of an introductory subordinate clause like 'It is vital that . . .' or 'It is essential that . . .'. In this way responsibility for imposing a directive is shifted away from the bossy speaker or writer and towards unspecified external circumstances.

A feature of the Leave camp's referendum campaign was that one type of imperative sometimes masqueraded as another. The most frequently published slogan was the double imperative *Vote Leave Take Control* (also the URL of the main pro-Brexit website) or the slight variation *Vote Leave, take back control*.

Vote Leave, take back control

FIGURE 1 *Downloadable campaign resource from the website of the Vote Leave movement.*
Source: http://www.voteleavetakecontrol.org/campaign_resources.html.

This slogan appeared on billboards, posters, vehicles and, somewhat con-troversially, was also superimposed upon a photograph of one of Britain's best-known works of contemporary art, the 20-metre tall Angel of the North sculpture near Gateshead in the north-east of England (prior permission from the artist, Antony Gormley, was neither obtained nor even requested).

Although the slogan appears to involve two standard imperatives with an implicit second-person subject, during the referendum campaign it was often linked to texts or public speeches that suggested that its true illocutionary force was that of a cohortative with an inclusive first-person plural subject. Indeed, when space permitted (e.g. on the side of a truck) the imperative with *let*[gr] was preferred: *Let's take back control*.

Ambiguous imperatives did not begin with the 2016 referendum campaign. On the eve of voting day, Alice Foster for the *Daily Express* reminded us that her news-paper had started working for Brexit long before the referendum had even been announced by showing us again the cover of a special edition published in January 2011 (Foster 2016). After the conventional second-person imperative *Get Britain out of the EU*, St George atop the white cliffs of Dover uses the first-person plural pronouns *we* and *our* in an underlined demand that the country be reclaimed, thus suggesting that the preceding imperative should be interpreted as having a cohortative illocutionary force with the initial *Let's* unstated but understood.

The words *yes* and *no* can function as jussives, as we see in the following 'Britty Brexit' downloadable poster from the website of the Better Off Out cam-paign. Indeed, the slogan *No to the European Union, Yes to the Wider World* could be converted into two conventional imperative clauses by the simple insertion of the verb *say* before *no* and *yes* respectively. This poster counters one of the main accusations launched at Leave supporters, that is, that they were Little Englanders, nostalgic for past glories and turning their back on internationalism and openness. The implication is that it is the EU that is beset by provincial attitudes and that by saying no to this limited institution we – the pronoun is apposite – would be opening up to genuine internationalism of a

FIGURE 2 *Special edition of the* Daily Express, *8 January 2011, republished 22 June 2016.*

global scale. Given the nature of the choice presented, a cohortative interpretation is appropriate since the 'wider world', with its connotations of adventure and enormous potential, is obviously the option most of us would prefer. The EU is not explicitly described as *narrow* or *limited*, but the very absence of a premodifier to counterbalance *wider* is a flout of the Gricean maxim of quantity, and this creates the implicature that the European Union lacks the broad range and limitless possibilities offered by the alternative choice.

FIGURE 3 *Downloadable campaign resource from the website of Better Off Out.*
Source: http://www.betteroffout.net/campaigning/campaigning-materials/.

The same idea that it is the EU that has limited horizons is presented in
a poster on the cross-party Twitter account *Stop the EU*. The main slogan is
Think outside the EU box (2015), followed by 'There's a world of trade out there'

and 'Vote no to end this madness'. The confines of the EU box are contrasted with the limitless opportunities offered by the world of trade out there in such a way that the first imperative clause is not so much a command as an inducement to collective action by addressers and addressees together. The images reinforce the contrast as a globe inside a cardboard box and a ballot box symbolize entrapment and the route to liberation respectively. The cohortative illocutionary force of the second imperative clause is once again established by rendering the alternative course of action unthinkable; who among us would vote yes to retain madness?

The implicit *Let*[gr] of the imperative clauses investigated here leads naturally to further examination of the inclusive *we* successfully employed by Leave campaigners. In the next chapter we see how the marginalized and the unemployed learnt that they were in the same boat as Old Etonians.

4

Inclusive *we*, the former City broker as champion of the common man, and good old Bojo: How the pro-Brexit press created the illusion of a classless alliance

The Remain and Leave campaigns were well funded and both received substantial private and corporate donations. According to the Electoral Commission, the independent watchdog set up by the UK Parliament to oversee party and election finances, in the ten weeks to 21 April 2016, registered Remain campaigners raised £7.5 million, which included donations amounting to £2.3 million from the supermarket magnate Lord Sainsbury, as well as other substantial donations from the hedge fund manager David Harding, the Tower Limited Partnership and Lloyd Dorfman, the founder of Travelex. In the same period registered Leave groups amassed £8.2 million, including

£3.2 million from the stockbroker Peter Hargreaves and nearly £2 million from companies owned by the businessman Aaron Banks (*Leave and Remain EU donations and loans revealed* 2016). Both sides also raised funds by appealing to the general public but neither could claim to have organized a Bernie Sanders-style campaign financed by millions of small donations from ordinary men and women.

At 4:00 a.m. on 24 June, when the definitive result of the referendum was not yet known but Leave's victory was practically certain, Nigel Farage announced to cheering supporters: 'This will be a victory for real people, a victory for ordinary people, a victory for decent people. We have fought against the multinationals, we fought against the merchant banks, we fought against big politics' (Peck 2016). Throughout the referendum campaign the leader of UKIP presented the central issue as one of honest, hardworking people wresting back control from a self-serving elite in the worlds of finance and business whose path to ever greater wealth and privilege was favoured by the political establishment in Brussels. To cultivate his personal image as an ordinary bloke he frequently had himself photographed in a pub, holding a pint of real ale (never Eurofizz lager) and chatting amicably with fellow customers. Farage's CV, however, is hardly that of a typical *Occupy Wall Street* protester. The son of a stockbroker, he chose not to go to university but went directly from his independent school, Dulwich College, to the City of London, where he had a modestly successful career as a commodities broker until he became a full-time politician. Over the years he has flirted with economic ideas hardly designed to benefit low-wage earners, such as the proposal to introduce a flat-rate tax for all regardless of a person's income.

Other prominent leaders of the Leave campaign are even less likely candidates as champions of the common man. The Conservative MP and former mayor of London, Boris Johnson, comes from a wealthy, upper-middle-class background, was educated at Eton and Balliol College, Oxford, and had a successful career as a journalist at *The Times*, the *Daily Telegraph* and then as editor of *The Spectator*. Although he takes a liberal stance on many social issues, in economic matters he is an orthodox free-market Conservative.

Another product of Eton and Oxford is Jacob Rees-Mogg, pro-Brexit Conservative MP and son of the late William Rees-Mogg, who was editor of *The Times*. He combines his work as an MP with professional activity as a fund manager in the City and running his company, Somerset Capital Management, which he set up in 2007. He supports the controversial zero-hours work contracts currently being used in the UK and opposes same-sex marriage.

Michael Gove is not from a privileged background and to earn a place at an independent school in Aberdeen had to win a scholarship. He then followed a path not dissimilar to that of Boris Johnson: Oxford, followed by journalism, a post at *The Times* and selection as a candidate in a safe Conservative seat. In 2005 he co-authored with other Conservative MPs *Direct Democracy: An Agenda for a New Model Party*, which advocates, among other things, the dismantlement of the National Health Service (*Michael Gove* 2017). During a controversial spell as Secretary of State for Education in David Cameron's government he managed in a single year (2013) to collect motions of no confidence at the conferences of the Association of Teachers and Lecturers, the National Union of Teachers (a unanimous vote) and, crucially, the National Association of Head Teachers. In 2009 the *New Statesman* estimated his personal wealth at about £1 million, which makes him rather hard up by the standards of Johnson and Rees-Mogg but very rich indeed compared with the overwhelming majority of people who voted Leave in the referendum. The same article revealed that though an MP (but not yet a minister), Gove continued to receive £5,000 per month from *The Times* for writing a weekly column, a task that he claimed to complete in an hour (*The new ruling class* 2009).

This is not to say that all Brexit-supporting Conservatives MPs are wealthy, Oxbridge-educated white men (Priti Patel, for instance, is the daughter of Ugandan Asians expelled by President Idi Amin in the 1960s), but it is nevertheless extraordinary that certain newpapers managed to present such obvious establishment figures as those described above as tough little Davids with the spunk to take on the Goliaths of the banks, the multinationals and the Brussels bureaucracy. This was achieved in various ways, but the most basic linguistic technique employed was clever use of the word *we*.

Some languages have two first-person plural subject pronouns, one that includes the addressee and one that does not. For example, Tok Pisin (which derives from 'Talk Pidgin'), a creole used as a first or second language by more than five million people in Papua New Guinea, has the inclusive pronoun *yumi* ('you + me') and the exclusive *mipela* ('me + fellow', but not you), a neat division that removes any risk of ambivalence (Crystal 1994: 183). English only has *we* and the addressee has to infer from context whether the pronoun is being used inclusively or exclusively, something that rarely creates difficulties. Margaret Thatcher (1988), in her address to the College of Europe on 20 September 1988, which immediately entered the political lexicon in the UK as the *Bruges Speech*, switched repeatedly between the two types of *we*:

- 'We have not successfully rolled back the frontiers of the state in Britain, only to see them re-imposed at a European level with a European super-state exercising a new dominance from Brussels.' (Clearly an exclusive *we* that refers only to the speaker and her government);

- 'We must ensure that our approach to world trade is consistent with the liberalism we preach at home. We have a responsibility to give a lead on this, a responsibility which is particularly directed towards the less developed countries.' (Inclusive *we* urging the member states of what was then the European Community to work together to encourage global free trade).

A feature of the way Brexit-supporting newspapers reported on the key issues was the repeated use of inclusive *we*. To a certain extent this is understandable since a great many people only read newspapers that reflect their own beliefs, opinions and prejudices, but for the significant minority who also like to read opinions contrary to their own, the *we* that implies all of us pulling together for the good of the cause is bound to grate.

In a speech delivered at Landudno in North Wales (Burrows 2016), Nigel Farage emulated Mrs Thatcher in switching between inclusive and exclusive *we*. The latter is used to claim that the very fact that a referendum was going to be held was a concession forced upon the government by Farage himself and UKIP activists: 'We have forced our political class into giving us this referendum that they never wanted us to have.' In reality a government with a comfortable majority in Parliament was not pressurized by UKIP or anyone else into allowing the referendum; it was a monumental political error by David Cameron who, following the disastrous advice of the American strategist Jim Messina, chose to use a referendum he was confident of winning as a tactic to take the wind out of UKIP's sails.

Inclusive *we* is evident in the UKIP leader's claim that the mismatch between official immigration statistics and the number of National Insurance numbers issued to migrants suggested that the entire population of the UK was being lied to by the British government and, because of EU membership, was powerless to avert a demographic calamity.

I do not believe that we are being told the truth about the number of people coming to this country. I believe that the true figures would shock us. It is not good for our quality of life, it is not good for our social cohesion in our society, and our population headed inexorably towards 70 or 75 million will not make this a better, richer or happier place to be. But as EU members there is nothing we can do about it.

In the same speech, the sense of inclusivity is reinforced by Farage's assertion that 23 June could become the UK's 'Independence Day', an expression that

implies self-determination, a universally desired outcome achieved by a population all pulling in the same direction.

Interference, or perceived interference, by outsiders is always likely to unite
people in a short-lived manifestation of national identity, and in April 2016
President Obama's rather cack-handed attempt to support David Cameron
probably did the Remain cause more harm than good. His warning that
Britain outside the EU would go to the back of the queue for trade deals provoked indignation, not least because his use of the word *queue* rather than
the American equivalent *line* made it rather obvious that his statement had
been prepared for him by Downing Street. Carole Malone (2016), an outspoken political commentator and TV personality, expressed her outrage at
this unwelcome interference in the pro-Remain *Daily Mirror*. The following
extract quotes the opening sentences of her piece and her splenetic reaction
to Obama's intervention, and the concluding sentences in which she reminds
the president of what happened when Piers Morgan, a British journalist and
former editor of the *Daily Mirror*, expressed his opinion of America's gun laws.

> How dare Barack Obama tell the British people we must stay in the EU and
> threaten that if we don't he'll make sure we're shoved 'to the back of the
> queue' for any new trade deals?
>
> Is this the act of an ally or is it a bully telling a country he clearly thinks
> he has under his thumb to do what he says – or else?
>
> How dare this outgoing president, who very soon will be politically
> defunct, ask us to do something he'd never in a million years ask his own
> people to do permanently relinquish their sovereignty? (*sic*)
>
> . . .
>
> Remember what happened when our own Piers Morgan dared to tell
> America to change its gun laws?
>
> There was a petition to deport him because the people's attitude
> was: 'How dare an Englishman interfere in our constitution?'

The Yanks don't take kindly to being told what to do in their own country. Neither do we!

Carole Malone makes repeated use of inclusive *we* – and most emphatically in her concluding sentence – as if she speaks for the entire nation in giving voice to a collective fit of pique afflicting men and women the length and breadth of the land. A similar tone of indignation marked reports of Obama's comments in the pro-Leave *Sun, Daily Mail, Daily Express* and *Daily Telegraph*, and the fact that such responses were published on St George's Day (23 April), the day on which England's patron saint is remembered, was not lost on some observers. In all likelihood the US president's intervention in the Brexit debate was not the main topic of conversation in British homes, workplaces, cafés and pubs on 23 April 2016, but his warning of the consequences of leaving the EU was grist to the mill for Brexit supporters wishing to present themselves as plucky little battlers taking on the mighty forces of the political and economic establishment led by the most powerful man on the planet.

The idea of we the people against the elite was taken up by *The Sun* in two pieces published in June 2016. In the first – an unsigned editorial entitled *SUN SAYS We urge our readers to beLEAVE in Britain and vote to quit the EU on June 23* (2016) – the exclusive *we* of the headline is immediately replaced by inclusive *we* in the opening sentences, the components of the elite are clearly identified, and the concluding sentences are a Trump-like appeal to restore greatness.

SUN SAYS We urge our readers to beLEAVE in Britain and vote to quit the EU on June 23

This is our last chance to remove ourselves from the undemocratic Brussels machine . . . and it's time to take it

We are about to make the biggest political decision of our lives. *The Sun* urges everyone to vote LEAVE.

We must set ourselves free from dictatorial Brussels.

Throughout our 43-year membership of the European Union it has proved increasingly greedy, wasteful, bullying and breathtakingly incompetent in a crisis.

Next Thursday, at the ballot box, we can correct this huge and historic mistake.

It is our last chance. Because, be in no doubt, our future looks far bleaker if we stay in.

. . .

The Remain campaign, made up of the corporate establishment, arrogant europhiles and foreign banks, have set out to terrify us all about life outside the EU.

Their 'Project Fear' strategy predicts mass unemployment, soaring interest rates and inflation, plummeting house prices, even war.

The Treasury, the Bank of England, the IMF and world leaders have all been wheeled out by Downing Street to add their grim warnings.

Nonsense! Years ago the same politicians and economists issued apocalyptic predictions about our fate if we didn't join the euro.

Thank God we stopped that. The single currency's stranglehold has since ruined the EU's poorer nations and cast millions on the dole.

. . .

Our country has a glorious history.

This is our chance to make Britain even greater, to recapture our democracy, to preserve the values and culture we are rightly proud of.

A VOTE FOR LEAVE IS A VOTE FOR A BETTER BRITAIN.

The *we* of the headline refers to the owner and editorial board of *The Sun*, but thereafter the pronoun is used inclusively. With imagery that borders on the militaristic, *we* are depicted as freedom fighters taking on a sinister coalition of powerful interests mobilized by Downing Street to 'terrify us all' into toeing the establishment's line. It is not difficult to challenge the accuracy and/or credibility of certain assertions: 'our 43-year membership of the European Union' over-looks the fact that the EU was not established until 1993 following the Maastricht Treaty, and while David Cameron obviously exercised a considerable degree of control over the treasury, he could not dictate policy to the Bank of England and it beggars belief to think that the International Monetary Fund (IMF) would do his bidding. The use of the comparative adjective in 'our chance to make Britain even greater' implies that the UK is still a great power, which conflicts with most people's perception of a nation that has been steadily losing influence on the world stage for at least a century. It is likely that many British citizens would pre-fer not to be included in a *we* associated with patriotic references to 'a glorious history' given that the glory was underpinned by imperial expansion.

On the eve of voting day *The Sun* invited three experts (Lord Green et al. 2016) to explain the case for leaving the EU, including the Conservative Member of the European Parliament (MEP), Daniel Hannan, who focused on wresting power from the elites and restoring sovereignty.

British history is the story of how we gradually took power away from the elites.

As power spreads, the people in charge find it harder to rig the rules. The country as a whole becomes freer, fairer and richer.

Countries around the world have flourished by copying the British model. But we are losing it at home.

Power is shifting to Brussels, from people we can sack to people we can't.

. . .

It's a similar story when it comes to the economy. What's at stake isn't just which policies we follow, it's who gets to set them.

Plenty of groups have suffered from EU rules, including steelworkers. In each case, Britain is forced to apply laws which damage us.

Who does best out of the system? Those lobbies and vested interests that can get their way in Brussels without having to worry about the voters.

Look at who is funding Remain: Goldman Sachs, JP Morgan, Citibank and
Morgan Stanley.

The multinationals and megabanks have spent millions pushing through
EU rules that suit them.

No wonder they're terrified of leaving. So are the failed British politicians who turned to Europe after losing here.

Here the Conservative David Hannan is straying into Lexit territory in focusing on matters such as the fact that the most important figures in the EU
power structure are unelected and unaccountable, EU regulations that prevent
national governments from saving jobs by aiding companies in difficulty, and
the cosy relationship between Brussels and the giant corporations and banks.
The points he makes can be documented by referring either to the EU's internal
rules or to the legislation it has passed. The weakness in his power-to-the-people
appeal, however, is that very similar criticisms could be levelled at a succession of UK national governments, in particular those led by the Conservative
Party to which Hannan belongs. The process that has led to the UK ranking
fourth in the income-inequality league behind Singapore, the United States
and Portugal (Wilkinson and Pickett 2010: 17) began in 1979 with the election of the Eurosceptical Margaret Thatcher. The European Community of the
time did not have a great deal of control over the economies of member states.
Today the Conservative Party, which has MPs who have worked for the likes
of Goldman Sachs and JP Morgan, does not espouse policies aimed at saving
Britain's steel industry or making a serious attempt to prevent corporate tax
avoidance, so while David Hannan's criticisms of the EU have a certain ring of
truth about them, it is difficult to believe that a British government free from
EU interference and dominated by the Brexiteers of 2016 would be any better. Indeed, if we return to the articles by George Monbiot and Adam Ramsay
analysed in Chapter 1, we see that both are more scathing about the EU than
Hannan is, but both conclude that the alternative, a right-wing Conservative

government without the restraints of European regulations, would be worse. Paul Mason (2016), writing in *The Guardian*, takes the same view, first noting that 'The EU is not – and cannot become – a democracy' before warning that 'If Britain votes Brexit, then Johnson and Gove stand ready to seize control of the Tory party and turn Britain into a neoliberal fantasy island.'

As noted earlier in this chapter, the backgrounds and the policies of prominent Leave campaigners place them clearly within the establishment. As things turned out, *The Sun* and other newspapers were right to detect a groundswell of opinion against the elite, but many of those who led the protest were actually part of that elite, not representatives of a classless rebellion of the ignored and the marginalized.

The two pieces from *The Sun* cited above feature short sentences, direct questions and simple, non-technical lexis. Nick Cohen (2017), consciously or unconsciously, adopts a similar style of prose in pointing out that the very simplicity of such language should put us on our guard, while accusing one's political opponents of elitism is an easy, no-risk but often hypocritical strategy.

> Propaganda hides best behind simple words. The plainer the language, the more devious it can be. A speaker's apparent lack of pretence promises the audience that in front of them is a man of 'the people', who scorns political correctness, and 'tells it like it is.'
>
> Ah, 'the people.' What lies are told in your name. To be with 'the people' is to be a good neighbour and a good citizen. To be against 'the people' is to be against the sole source of legitimacy in a democracy. If you are not a traitor or an agent of a hostile foreign power, you are at the very least an 'enemy of the people'; an aloof member of 'the elite' that fixes the system for its own benefit. Who does not want to be on the people's side? Who will admit to standing with their enemies in the 'elite'?

One of the most distasteful attacks on an alleged elite figure appeared in the *Daily Mail* (Buckley et al. 2016). Both sides in the referendum campaign welcomed celebrity endorsements, with the scientist Sir Stephen Hawking, the author J. K. Rowling and the former footballer David Beckham supporting Remain and the Monty Python star John Cleese, the actress Elizabeth Hurley and the former cricketer Sir Ian Botham speaking up for Leave. When the actress Emma Thompson, interviewed while filming in Germany, made an impassioned appeal for Britain to stay in the EU, the *Daily Mail* responded with carefully crafted indignation and a personal attack in a piece entitled *Luvvie Emma sneers at Britain: I'm European, she claims in bizarre tirade against us quitting Brussels* (2016). In British slang *luvvies* are people in show business, especially actors, who take themselves too seriously and imagine that they are qualified to comment upon all manner of subjects. The use of luvvie in the headline implies that Ms Thompson's words need not be taken too ser-iously, a suggestion reinforced by describing her comments as a *bizarre tirade*. The choice of the reporting verb *claims* instead of *says* is perhaps an attempt to cast doubt upon what ought to be indisputable, that is, that a citizen of the UK, a country belonging to the continent of Europe, is European. The opening sentences continue in the same vein.

> She has never been afraid of spouting her London metropolitan elite views on matters of political importance.
>
> So it no surprise that she has waded into the referendum debate with a bizarre rant against the UK.
>
> The outspoken darling of the Left sparked outrage yesterday by deriding Britain as a 'tiny cake-filled misery-laden' island which must stay in the European Union.

Emma Thompson is not merely guilty of being a member of the 'London metropolitan elite'; she is additionally culpable because she has a history of supporting left-wing causes. Her greatest sin, however, is that she is a woman. The adjective *outspoken* often has positive connotations of frankness and hon-esty, and tends to be used in this sense in descriptions of Boris Johnson or

Nigel Farage. It becomes a derogatory term in 'The outspoken darling of the Left', as if Ms Thompson does not have the same right to express her views that a man has. But she is not known for *expressing* her views at all, but for 'spouting' them, while the content of her spoutings, a 'tirade' in the headline, are a 'rant' in the second paragraph of the article. She 'waded into' the referendum debate, a prepositional verb that suggests a clumsy intervention rather than a reasoned argument.

Readers of online articles often have the opportunity to comment upon them, their identities hidden behind a nickname. This particular article spawned a huge number of comments, many of them overtly sexist and extremely vulgar. The *Daily Mail* chose to highlight a comment sent by Godfrey Bloom, a former UKIP MEP who was forced to resign from the party in 2013 for, among other instances of intemperate behaviour, describing women in the audience at the party conference as 'sluts'. His response to Emma Thompson's opinions was expressed in the form of a polite request, or possibly of a generous offer: 'May I be the first to spank her silly bottom? Something her mother should have done years ago.'

As mentioned earlier, most people read newspapers that confirm rather than challenge what they already believe, so it is probable that the *Daily Mail*'s attack on Emma Thompson galvanized support among people who had no problems with comments like Godfrey Bloom's but did not win over new converts. Neither did it create apostates, however, for Remain supporters missed the opportunity to bring this article to a wider and different readership in order to expose the nasty strain of sexism exhibited by certain readers of *The Mail*.

People may be more willingly to identify themselves with an inclusive *we* if the pronoun is used in contexts that demonstrate, or claim, that *we* are smarter or more competent than a clearly identified *they* are. The Brexit camp chose the field of security and military might to show that we, the British, do a far better job than our European partners.

Although the idea of establishing a European Rapid Reaction Force has been discussed over the years, nothing concrete has yet emerged. In 2016 Brussels began to prepare the way for a military research and development programme, which put the prospect – or the threat – of an EU army very firmly on Leave's agenda. The former head of MI6, Richard Dearlove (2016), writing in a pro-Remain magazine, noted that Britain's active role in NATO and history of sharing intelligence with the United States meant that leaving the EU would not endanger the UK's security in the slightest. Charles Moore (2016) in *The Telegraph*, in an article bearing the splendidly disparaging head-line 'The EU is a huge version of Belgium – and it can't deal with the modern world' (written days after suicide bombings at Brussels airport and a metro station in the city had exposed the limitations of the Belgian security services), argued that Britain was already part of a far better intelligence-sharing alliance than anything the EU could ever construct.

> By far the highest level of intelligence trust in the world is the 'Five Eyes' alliance, between the US, Britain, Australia, Canada and New Zealand. They share an experience of cooperation in wars, a language, a Common Law tradition and, in four cases, the Crown.

Dearlove and Moore both refer to the UK in the third person in articles based on real data. Nick Gutteridge (2016) in the *Daily Express* adopts an altogether more emotive approach with quotes by army veterans, photographs of the Queen inspecting the troops and of British tommies in a trench during the First World War, references to past victories, a soundbite from UKIP's defence spokesman and, of course, the pronouns *we* and *us*.

> Britain has by far the biggest and best equipped army in Europe and is to plough some £2.2bn into developing new weapons this year alone.
> But under the new EU plans we could in future be blocked from research-ing new military technology which would benefit the British army, instead

being forced into ploughing money into projects for the wider benefit of the whole EU project.

. . .

But UKIP's defence spokesman Mike Hookem – himself a former serviceman in the RAF – warned an EU army would leave the UK unable to defend its own interests in the world, including the Falklands.

He said: 'When you sign up you pledge allegiance to her Majesty the Queen. Who are you going to swear allegiance to in the future, Jean-Claude Juncker?

'Are we going to be pulling the Union Jack off our uniforms and stitching on the EU flag. It's scandalous.

'During the Falklands war France was selling weapons to the Argentinians. If they try to take back the Falklands again will France let us use this EU army to defend them? I doubt it.

'There's only one people who can defend the British, and that's the British themselves.'

Many British citizens would not identify themselves in the inclusive *we* employed by Gutteridge and Hookem despite the alleged superiority of Britain's military capability with respect to other EU member states. Plenty of people believe that the UK's military budget should be cut and the money diverted to other purposes, while others see little point in retaining the Falklands and other anachronistic remnants of a lost empire. Few of them, however, would ever read the *Daily Express*. As with *The Mail*'s attack on Emma Thompson, *The Express* could use *we* secure in the knowledge that it really was an inclusive pronoun as far as its readers were concerned.

5

Democracy myths and facts: A double defeat for David Cameron

In a referendum offering a choice between change and maintenance of the status quo, it is incumbent upon those wishing for reform or innovation to be proactive in stating their case clearly and convincing the voters of the credibility of their position. For people aiming to leave things as they are, there is the risk of slipping into reactive mode, merely gainsaying whatever arguments their opponents propose and presenting their own position as the safe option. The Remain camp's attempt to be proactive, the so-called Project Fear, was ultimately ineffectual, as we will see in Chapter 9. Much of their time and energy, however, was spent reacting to Leave's claims; indeed, David Cameron's lengthy negotiations with Brussels in early 2016 to secure a special deal for the UK was essentially an attempt to defuse the Brexiteers' position by arguing that their concerns had already been met.

Leave campaigners (though generally not those of the Lexit persuasion) made immigration a key topic in the debate, and this is looked at in Chapter 8. An issue that saw UKIP, Conservative Leavers and Lexit supporters in total agreement, however, was the alleged lack of democracy and accountability in how the European Union is run and, more specifically, the European

Commission's disregard for the views expressed by the electorates of member states. Seldom do the right-wing *Daily Express* and the hard-left *Morning Star* find themselves on the same side but that is what happened when Nick Gutteridge (2016) in the former and an unsigned editorial entitled *It's Operation Desperation* (2016) in the latter reported on the EU's free trade treaty with Ukraine, a move widely seen as the first step in Ukraine's eventual accession to the Union, despite the fact that a referendum in the Netherlands had seen 61.1 per cent of Dutch voters reject the deal.

'Your vote means NOTHING' Brussels insists land grab plot WILL go ahead despite Dutch 'no'

EUROPEAN UNION leaders were tonight plotting to override the democratic wishes of the Dutch people and plough ahead with a rejected plan to tighten their grip on Ukraine.

Arrogant Brussels politicians insisted the plot to bring Kiev further into their sphere of influence will go ahead, even though last night it was overwhelmingly rejected by the Dutch people.

Germany's Angela Merkel told journalists the Dutch 'no' vote 'will be managed as we have managed other difficult issues before', whilst French president Francois Hollande said the EU 'will implement and apply' the rejected treaty.

And EU President Jean-Claude Juncker today expressly REFUSED to rule out steamrollering the Dutch people's democratic rights and enforcing the deal on them anyway.

No country was more pro-EU dream than the Netherlands. It was a model European country in every aspect.

But things have changed. Living conditions have deteriorated. Insecurity has increased. The 'social Europe' gains proclaimed in the 1980s have been whittled away.

The dream has turned sour for the Dutch, so they have rejected the EU free trade deal with Ukraine.

The EU elite is intent on constant expansion of the bloc's borders, disregarding its failure to harmonise relations in the wake of previous headlong enlargement.

Brussels turns a blind eye to rampant corruption in Kiev, the undemocratic banning of the Communist Party and the role of neonazi armed militias.

Why should the EU stance be surprising? It was up to its neck in the Maidan 2014 coup d'etat, rejecting Ukraine's right to have relations with both the EU and Russia and demanding all or nothing.

Given that Nick Gutteridge is unlikely to be unduly concerned about the fate of the Communist Party in Ukraine, it is not difficult to identify which extract comes from an article in the *Morning Star*. However, what strikes the reader is the fact that in two newspapers that have very different ideological stances, the eagerness to sign a deal with Ukraine is not seen in terms of trade but of territorial expansionism and both use highly emotive language. Gutteridge's headline contains the expression 'land grab', the lead refers to the EU's wish to 'tighten their grip on Ukraine' and his first sentence describes the 'plot to bring Kiev further into their sphere of influence', which reminds us of the kind of language used during the Cold War when the United States and the USSR competed to draw developing countries towards their respective visions of the world. Allusions to the Cold War are even more explicit in the *Morning Star*, particularly with the use of the word 'bloc', which recalls the days when the continent of Europe was divided between the Western Democracies and the Eastern Bloc. It is a word that evokes images of a bureaucratic monolith unable, or unwilling, to permit change or reform, and in 2016 the bloc is the European Union seeking 'constant expansion' of its borders and 'headlong enlargement'.

That the right-wing *Daily Express* and the left-wing *Morning Star* should both describe a free trade treaty in almost militaristic terms is remarkable enough, but their respective reasons for doing so might also share some common ground. The *Morning Star* has repeatedly warned that in prematurely admitting the Baltic states and Poland, the EU was recklessly provoking Russia, and in the lines quoted above, Brussels is accused of having a role in the overthrow of Ukraine's democratically elected but pro-Moscow president, Viktor Yanukovych. In June 2015 UKIP MEPs voted against a European Parliament resolution condemning Russia for human rights abuses, a year earlier Nigel Farage accused the EU of 'having blood on its hands' for encouraging the turmoil in Ukraine that eventually led to Russia's annexation of Crimea (Morris 2014), and a number of Brexit campaigners argued that the EU's imposition of sanctions against Moscow was harming Europe's economies more than Russia's. Gutteridge expresses outrage at the EU's disregard for a referendum result in the Netherlands, something he sees as symptomatic of Brussels' disdain for democracy, but his use of the language of territorial occupation and control suggests that he sees the proposed treaty with Ukraine as being about far more than free trade, and in this he is an unlikely bed fellow for the *Morning Star*.

Criticism of the EU's lack of democracy was expressed in powerful language and Remain's response was feeble by comparison. In the lead-up to the referendum much was made of the EU's five unelected presidents: Jean-Claude Juncker (European Commission), Mario Draghi (European Central Bank), Martin Schulz (European Parliament), Donald Tusk (European Council) and Jeroen Dijsselbloem (Eurogroup of economy ministers). Anti-EU commentators of various political shades portrayed the British public as being at the mercy of five bureaucrats they could not even name (with the possible exception of Juncker), much less vote out of office, while the elected European Parliament, if it was mentioned at all, tended to be described as weak and ineffectual.

Suzanne Moore (2016), in an article previously cited in Chapter 2, adopted the simple style and short sentences usually associated with the tabloids:

It doesn't look to me like a democracy. Nor does it appear accountable. This matters. Not a single one of my pro-EU friends could name their MEP when I asked them. Maybe this pales among issues like security, workers' rights and border control, but as a representative democracy it is sorely lacking.

In the right-wing *Sunday Express* the novelist Frederick Forsyth (2016) argued that the EU was never meant to be democratic because Jean Monnet and the other architects of the post-war European project, obsessed by the fact that Hitler had risen to power via the ballot box, concluded that 'the people, any people, were too obtuse, too gullible, too dim ever to be safely entrusted with the power to elect their government'.

Przemek Skwirczynski (2016), an activist for the little-known *Poles for Britain* campaign, also took the view that the development of the European Union had been planned from the beginning as a process leading towards an undemocratic superstate, and claimed that the last president of the USSR, Mikhael Gorbachev, had described the EU as 'the old Soviet Union dressed in Western clothes'.

Lexit supporters tended to avoid undocumented, arguably rather hysterical accusations that the post-war plan for Europe was designed from the beginning to deprive citizens of their democratic rights, and focused instead on how the best of original intentions had been betrayed over the years, resulting in the refusal in recent times to accept views expressed by the electorates of supposedly sovereign member states. Another unsigned editorial in the *Morning Star*, entitled *The Opposite of Democracy* (2016), recalled such incidences as the 2008 Irish referendum that rejected the Lisbon Treaty and the subsequent pressure on Dublin to hold a second vote, and, more recently, interference from Brussels that led to the replacement in Italy and Greece of governments that were democratically elected but deemed to be incapable of running the economy.

> For an organisation that parrots the word 'democracy' relentlessly, whether in criticising other world powers or preparing the way for another illegal invasion, the EU record on respecting democracy is shaky.
>
> When voters in countries like Ireland and France have erred by voting against EU treaties, they have been ordered to try again until they redeem their mistake by getting it right.
>
> Elected governments in Italy and Greece have been replaced by appointed 'technocrats' – effectively bankers and their nominees – to run the show and drive through economic 'reforms' that benefit the rich and powerful.
>
> The balance of income and wealth across the continent has swung from rich to poor as the inevitable consequence of wage freezes, unemployment and benefit cuts.
>
> Even now as the working class is over a barrel, our unelected and unaccountable EU bosses are negotiating the TTIP trade deal with Washington to further distance economic life from democratic accountability.

Remain campaigners made little attempt to counter such attacks, either avoiding the issue of democratic accountability, or, as we saw in Chapter 1, conceding the validity of the criticism before the adversative conjunction *but* followed by a counterbalancing clause stating something positive about the EU. In an article urging left-wing readers to vote Remain, Toby Moses (2016) has no qualms about describing the EU as 'that bloated, undemocratic bureaucracy' but asks the rhetorical question 'What self-respecting lefty wants to line up alongside Boris Johnson, Nigel Farage and Iain Duncan Smith?'. The choice is between a rock and a hard place.

Leave was allowed to set the agenda on the democracy question and forced Remain onto the defensive. What was lacking was a clear counter attack to explain how the EU actually worked, an approach that would have allowed Remainers to point out that in reality the European Union is nowhere near as undemocratic and unaccountable as is often claimed, and in some respects is more democratic than the national government of the UK. The very small number of attempts to do just that were well-researched and well-written, but their contribution turned out to be too little and, crucially, too late. An unsigned piece on the website *The Conversation* set out to answer the question *How democratic is the European Union?* (2016), and concluded: 'So all in all, the EU is, or is at least working to be, a democratic organisation. It has its failings but national governments have just as many – if not more.' Nine days before voting day Jennifer Rankin (2016) asked the similar question 'Is the EU undemocratic?' and pointed out that, contrary to popular misconception, the European Commission does not pass laws, but enforces and monitors laws and treaties decided by EU governments via the Council of Ministers and approved by the directly elected European Parliament. She also demonstrated that qualified-majority voting does not mean that the UK is frequently out-voted, citing research conducted by the London School of Economics showing that between 2009 and 2015 Britain was on the winning side 87 per cent of the time. Her verdict:

> The idea that laws are dictated by Brussels by unelected bureaucrats is simply wrong. In fact EU laws have to pass high hurdles before they get onto the British statute book. The British government has considerable clout in shaping those laws despite the growth of qualified-majority votes.
>
> When leave campaigners talk about laws made by Brussels, what they mean is 'laws made by the EU's directly elected governments and more often than not the European parliament through the co-decision procedure'. Not as snappy, but more accurate.

Another carefully researched piece was posted by Simon Hix (2016) on his blog on the website of the London School of Economics and Political Science, but on 21 June when it was rather late to have much impact. He notes that the allegedly unelected president of the European Commission and the individual commissioners, though not directly elected by the populace, are at least indirectly elected in that they are first of all proposed by the twenty-eight heads of government on the European Council, then confirmed by a majority vote in the European Parliament. He finds this no less democratic than the way in which the Queen effectively chooses the British prime minister – by convention the leader of the largest party – who then chooses members of the cabinet as s/he sees fit. Furthermore, he believes that EU procedures have become more democratic in the last decade.

Jennifer Rankin and Simon Hix were lone and late voices. Brexit and Lexit campaigners were allowed to promulgate the line that the EU was irredeemably undemocratic and that there was nothing Britain could do to get rid of unelected bureaucrats who proved to be inadequate or worse. Remainers tended to admit that there was a 'democratic deficit' that needed to be addressed and did not counter attack by pointing out that the European Parliament has the power to dismiss members of the European Commission. No one noted that the EU, like any governing body in a democracy, is subject to scrutiny by the fourth estate, or recalled that in 1999 the entire European Commission led by Jacques Santer was shamed into resigning following very public allegations of financial mismanagement which eventually resulted in one commissioner, Édith Cresson, being prosecuted in the European Court of Justice. Attention was not drawn to the fact that when a British government has a comfortable parliamentary majority, the House of Commons may become little more than a rubber-stamping service for decisions taken in the cabinet office.

Ironically, it can be argued that Remain lost the referendum because of faults in the democratic process not in Brussels, but in the UK. The precise margin of the Brexit victory reported by the Electoral Commission was 1,269,501 votes. David Cameron's first and second governments made two decisions that deprived a great many British citizens of the opportunity to vote in the referendum, and most of them were the sort of people who, given the chance, would have expressed a preference to stay in the EU.

In 2014 the Cameron government introduced individual voter registration. Previously, just one member of a household could register all the residents eligible to vote, while institutional landlords could complete the registration for tenants. Universities, with their halls of residence, are major institutional landlords and under the old rules they simply sent the relevant local authorities a complete list of students eligible to vote. Individual voter registration resulted in many of Britain's nearly two million students failing to register. The date of the referendum – 23 June – created further problems for those students who had finished their exams and had already moved away from their term-time address since they either had to re-register at the address they would be living at on referendum day (if they knew where they would be), or apply for a postal or proxy vote at their term-time address. Despite the efforts of individual universities and the National Union of Students to inform students of the registration requirements, a considerable percentage ended up being unable to vote on 23 June.

Post-referendum analyses of how the various sectors of British society voted revealed that those university students who did vote mostly voted for staying in the EU. That is hardly surprising: the so-called millennials had grown up taking freedom of movement for granted, had no memory of residence and work permits, and had most to lose from an outcome that jeopardized their right to study and work wherever they wished in the twenty-eight member states. As Megan Dunn (2016) put it:

We are instinctively internationalist, as lives lived online do not respect national frontiers. We travel, work, and study abroad to a greater degree than previous generations. Politically, we involve ourselves in global struggles, such as climate change, international development and global justice.

Of course, we will never know whether those students who failed to get on the electoral register would have voted in a similar way to those who did go to the polling station, and it is perfectly legitimate to say that young people who did not make the effort to register had no right to complain when the result was not the one they would have wished for. They were not so much disenfranchised as victims of their own apathy. However, as a particularly mobile population, they had registration hurdles to overcome that other sectors of society did not have, and it is reasonable to assume that David Cameron has wondered what would have happened if more of them had managed to put a cross on that ballot paper.

Other UK citizens really were disenfranchised: a significant percentage of the approximately 1.3 million Britons who, like me, live in another EU member state. British citizens who have lived abroad for more than fifteen years lose their right to vote in UK elections and referenda, so those of us who have put down roots in another EU member state could not make our opinions count. In the case of long-term expatriates, we are on fairly safe ground in saying that if they had been able to vote in the referendum, the overwhelming majority would have voted to protect their rights to health care, social services and possibly a state pension in their host country.

To sum up, the democracy question contributed to Remain's defeat in two ways. First, David Cameron, George Osborne and other high-profile figures made little or no attempt to confute Brexit and Lexit supporters' exaggerated, sometimes dishonest statements about the undemocratic EU, unaccountable bureaucrats, dictatorship from Brussels and the like. Leave campaigners were given a clear run on the democracy question, and some went so far as to write of a dastardly conspiracy to suppress democracy (inspired by a Frenchman) that began in the years immediately after the Second World War. Second, imperfections in the UK's democratic system meant that absentees from the electoral register included two groups of people whose votes just might – and here the epistemic modality is essential – have cancelled out the 1,269,501-vote margin of Leave's victory.

6

'Free': A little word that did a big job for Brexit

Brexit campaigners presented the referendum debate as an epic battle between on the one hand high-minded principles that we all hold dear – freedom, democracy, independence – and on the other, aspects of EU reality – regulation and bureaucracy, the unelected Commission, impositions from Brussels – that are paltry by comparison and difficult to defend. If Remainers allowed Leave to manipulate the democracy issue as they wished, they did little better at resisting Brexiteers' commandeering of the word *free*.

It is a syntactically flexible word that can be used as an adjective or as a verb, and in the former case combines with a series of nouns in collocations that are highly positive in meaning, such as *free speech*, *free will* and *free-range* (*freeloader* is a rare exception of a negative denotation, while the desirability or otherwise of *free love* is something for each individual to evaluate). Similarly, the related noun *freedom* is nearly always a good thing, unlike its synonym *liberty* which is sometimes diabolical, and in the expression *to take a liberty* refers to disrespectful behaviour.

The Leave argument was that by quitting the EU Britain would be free from European laws, regulations and bureaucracy, which in the tabloids were collectively summed up with metaphors of restraint, in particular the word *shackles*, or terms with military connotations, such as the German loan word *diktat.* The headline of a short article on the website *betteroffout.net* contains a metaphor of restraint and a comparison with the economic consequence of breaking free: *Tied to the EU, growth is 0.3%. Free from the EU it's more* (2016). In the brief (and grammatically clumsy) piece that follows, *tied* is used twice more along with the adjective *trapped.*

Five days before voting day Rebecca Perring and Monika Pallenberg (2016), writing for *The Express*, used the noun *shackles* in both the headline and the lead of their article, then the emotive word *bloc* in their opening sentence. *Free* is also used twice in the headline and lead, and in both cases it is capitalized for emphasis. The nefarious nature of the European Union is made clear in a reference to the strongest member state's concern that the UK could 'go unpunished' if the British people voted to leave the EU. In just sixty-six words the EU is portrayed as an authoritarian institution that puts its members into fetters and would not like to see a rebel escaping punishment.

No more shackles: UK could BREAK FREE of EU laws as early as June 24 if Brexit wins

Germans fear Britain will be able to break FREE from the shackles of European laws on June 23 if the nation backs Brexit

Bundestag experts have expressed concerns the UK will go unpunished if the people vote to quit the 28-nation bloc during next week's EU referendum.

In an article that is considered in more detail in Chapter 13 of this volume, Hawkes et al. (2016) in *The Sun* report on Boris Johnson's urging viewers to 'grab the chance to break free from European shackles' during a televised debate. Never a man to rely exclusively on hackneyed phrases, however, he added that taking back control meant not having to comply with 'every jot and tittle' of EU regulations.

Jots and tittles are irritants, but the farming minister in the Cameron government, George Eustice, is quoted as using a much stronger expression to describe EU policy on the environment (Neslen 2016): 'The UK could develop a more flexible approach to environmental protection free from "spirit-crushing" Brussels directives if it votes to leave the EU, the farming minister, George Eustice, has said.' In the same article Eustice is reported as dismissing EU environmental regulations as 'voluminous documents from Brussels'.

Another frequently used collocation featuring the word *free* was, unsurprisingly, *set Britain free*. It was used in the headline – *SUN ON SUNDAY SAYS A vote for Brexit is all it takes to set Britain free* (2016) – of an unsigned editorial in *The Sun* shortly before voting day, then again in the first sentence of the article along with inclusive *we*. Not content with putting us into shackles, the EU now has us in a 'stranglehold'.

Just four days from now we can set Britain free.

Free from the stranglehold of the EU superstate which, from its modest beginnings 60 years ago, has grown into a monster engulfing our democracy.

For 20 years they would not let us join. Now, with us in, they have progressively tied us up in millions of new regulations.

In an unsigned editorial in the *Daily Mail* entitled *How leaving the EU could set Britain free* (2016), Chancellor of the Exchequer George Osborne's warnings that leaving the EU would be disastrous for the economy are contrasted with the leading Brexiteer Michael Gove's florid rhetoric on the 'galvanising', 'liberating' and 'empowering' effects of a victory for Leave.

After George Osborne's apocalyptic warning that a vote to leave the EU would permanently damage the British economy and cost every family £4,300 a year, Michael Gove struck a markedly contrasting tone yesterday.

In place of scaremongering and despair, here was a message of confidence and optimism. Where the Chancellor had said that saying No in June would be a catastrophe, Mr Gove persuasively argued it would bring 'a galvanising, liberating, empowering moment of democratic renewal'.

How refreshing to hear a politician who so passionately believes in Britain. 'Our best days lie ahead,' he said. 'This country's instincts and institutions, its people and its principles, are capable not just of making our society freer, fairer and richer but also once more setting an inspirational example to the world.'

The 'shackles' and similar metaphors were generally used as shorthand references to what was perceived as excessive EU regulation that created unnecessary costs for businesses and hindered economic growth. Mark Littlewood (2016), director general at the Institute of Economic Affairs, wrote:

> The single market might sound like a wonderful idea in theory, but it has morphed into an obsessive single regulatory area, with a zeal for applying uniform standards for all products and services right across the Continent. The Europhile argument goes that if you're going to have genuine free trade in, say, widgets that you need to have identical rules determining the exact shape, size and definition of a widget in all 28 member states.

Damien Gayle (2016) cites Vote Leave chief executive, Matthew Elliott, also expressing the view that EU regulation creates obstacles to free enterprise: 'Brussels hinders small businesses, particularly those firms who can't afford to lobby Brussels to curry favour.' Similarly, Steve Hilton, a former political adviser to David Cameron, is quoted referring to 'anti-market, innovation-stifling' EU regulations (Slack and Groves 2016).

It is hardly surprising if associations of small businesses and right-wing newspapers are opposed to rules and regulations that make it more difficult for companies to operate and could affect their profits. Regulation *per se* is not necessarily a bad thing, however, nor even a necessary evil, but is entirely positive if it prevents toy manufacturers from using toxic paints and varnishes or obliges the food industry to label products fully and precisely. One might expect the political left to take a very different view of regulation designed to protect workers' and consumers' rights; indeed, some Lexit campaigners argued that, in certain respects, the EU did not have enough regulation, particularly with regard to the banking sector and the tax avoidance schemes operated by the multinationals. Furthermore, the referendum campaign was conducted while the EU was in secret negotiations with the United States over the proposed Transatlantic Trade and Investment Partnership (TTIP) which many leftists opposed energetically, fearing that it would open the European market to American foodstuffs produced without the controls applied in Europe, and would enable multinational corporations to sue governments that threatened their profitability with measures such a national minimum wage or a windfall tax on exceptional profits.

However, just as prominent figures in the Remain camp did not directly challenge Leave's claims concerning the lack of democracy in the EU, so they did not make effective use of the data available to demonstrate that the costs incurred by complying with EU rules were more than offset by the access to markets that such compliance guaranteed. It was (and is) not difficult to find reliable data produced by academics and professionals more interested in the truth than in promoting a political agenda: *Full Fact* (https://fullfact.org) is a factfinding charity with a small team of professional researchers; *Open Europe*, since the referendum *Open Europe Today* (http://openeurope.org.uk), is a non-partisan think-tank with offices in Brussels and London; *The UK in a Changing Europe* (http://ukandeu.ac.uk), funded by the Economic and Social Research Council and based at King's College London, aims to provide evidence-based impartial analysis. To take just one example, two months before the vote *Full Fact* posted a report entitled *EU facts behind the claims: regulation and the single market* (2016), a comparative analysis of Leave's claim that the top 100 EU regulations cost the UK economy £33.3 billion each year, and the Remain counterclaim that the single market of 500 million people means that UK exporters only have to comply with one set of EU regulations instead of twenty-eight national ones. Remain's case does not stand up to analysis since individual member states still have their own contract, transport, competition, labour and planning laws, and oblige foreign businesses to comply with all of them. As for the bill of £33.3 billion per year, *Full Fact*'s study shows that the benefits of EU regulations often outweigh the costs, some of the costliest regulations are part of international agreements that have nothing to do with Brussels (and would therefore remain even after a hard Brexit), and despite the shackles and diktats, 'the UK is still a lightly regulated economy compared to other rich countries'. That final observation comes as no surprise to someone like me – a British citizen living in the heavily regulated society and economy that is Italy – but Britons who have never been resident abroad are generally unaware of how fortunate they are to live in such an uncomplicated country.

Sites like the three indicated in the previous paragraph do an important job but for a relatively small number of visitors. For a wider public to understand that Britain is not paralysed by EU red tape but is actually a low-bureaucracy nation, high-profile Remainers whose faces were known to TV viewers needed to launch a vigorous attack on the claim that having to comply with 'every jot and tittle' was stifling the economy. In general, they did not do so, and, as in the case of the EU's alleged lack of democracy and accountability, Leave supporters were rarely challenged when they talked of setting Britain free from 'the stranglehold of the EU superstate'.

7

Nominalization, presupposition and naturalization

Nominalization is quite simply the formation of a noun or noun phrase from some other word class. In English this conversion sometimes requires the use of a derivational affix, for instance from the verb *develop* to the noun *development*, or from the adjective *safe* to the noun *safety*. With other lexical items there is no morphological transformation: *rise* and *fall* are both verbs and nouns, the adjectives *rich* and *poor* can be used as plural nouns preceded by the definite article (The rich get rich, the poor get children), and *top* can be a noun, an ungradable adjective or a verb.

Sometimes it makes little difference to the overt or implicit meaning of an utterance whether we use a verb phrase – *Fleming discovered penicillin in 1928* – or a noun phrase – *Fleming's discovery of penicillin in 1928*. That is not always the case, however; in the verb phrase *Watson and Crick discovered the structure of DNA*, the focus is on the identity of the discoverers, and begs the question, *And what about Rosalind Franklin?* (the chemist now believed to have been denied the recognition she deserved because she was a woman working in a field that was then an almost exclusively male preserve). In the sentence, *Watson, Crick and Wilkins' discovery of the structure of DNA resulted in their sharing the Nobel prize in 1962*, the focus is on the Nobel prize and the initial noun phrase – *discovery* preceded by three genitive nouns (the names of the scientists) – is taken as given. Since the Nobel Commissions are not known for being duped by impostors or charlatans, the presupposition is that the fact that it was Watson, Crick and Wilkins (and no one else) who made the major scientific breakthrough is not disputed. In the right hands nominalization and presupposition can be very powerful tools in the art of persuasion. As Machin and Mayr put it (2012: 137):

> Nominalisation typically replaces verb processes with a noun construction, which can obscure agency and responsibility for an action, what exactly happened and when it took place. Presupposition is one skilful way by which authors are able to imply meanings without overtly stating them, or present things as taken for granted and stable when in fact they may be contestable and ideological.

A presupposition may be created on a single occasion for a specific issue. Naturalization is when a notion is repeated via various media until it becomes 'common sense', something that appears to be so self-evident that no one would ever challenge it. Or rather, it goes unchallenged by people who do not read between the lines to question whether the notion concerned is really a universally accepted truth and not an ideologically-driven position that does not represent the real interests of the people encouraged to accept it. Lesley Jeffries (2010: 9) offers the following examples: (i) children should not be made to work; (ii) it is a good thing for women to be slim. The first is an ideological stance that enjoys wide consensus in the advanced economies today but would not be shared by families in the developing world who depend on their children's wages, while the second might invite a challenge when stated boldly on-record but when it is implicit in texts of many kinds 'we have trouble rejecting it in our own minds, particularly if we are female' (ibid.). To add a third example, strikes are invariably portrayed as a bad thing in the mainstream media, and news reports refer to the danger of escalation, loss of production, further disruption and the like. Most people would not register anything unusual about the use of the noun *danger* in the previous sentence, but they would certainly sit up and take notice if the newsreader replaced it with the word *hope*. To anyone who has ever been on strike, and therefore knows that it is not a step that workers take lightly, escalation, loss of production and further disruption are the desired consequences.

To return to presupposition, logical presuppositions may be triggered by change-of-state verbs – verbs that indicate a switch from one state to another, one action to another or between action and inaction – and also by temporal adverbs. For example:

> She *quit* as chief executive (Logical presupposition: she was chief executive before)
>
> He *used to* live in Birmingham (Logical presupposition: but now he doesn't)
>
> It doesn't hurt *anymore* (Logical presupposition: but it did before)
>
> I *no longer* trust him (Logical presupposition: in the past I trusted him)

Another trigger of logical presuppositions is the use of factive verbs, such as *know, discover, admit, recognize, confirm, remember, learn, regret* and *realize*. A factive verb presupposes the veracity of its clausal complement, which is usually a that-clause:

> We *know* that the emission of greenhouse gases is causing global warming (Presupposition: the link between greenhouse gases and global warming is not disputed)
>
> My staff have *discovered* a plot to promulgate fake news to undermine my presidency
> (Presupposition: the plot exists and the key information is that it has been discovered)

She never *realized* that her husband was having an affair

(Presupposition: the wife's perspicacity is in doubt, not the husband's infidelity)

Not all climate change deniers are oil lobbyists or Tea Party activists; there are also scientists who genuinely believe that rising temperatures are part of a natural cyclical trend unrelated to human activity. An alleged plot to promulgate fake news might say more about the president's paranoia than the wickedness of his/her political opponents, while it is not at all unusual in a marriage for one partner to imagine that the other is having an affair. However, the verbs *know, discovered* and *realized* in these examples give the impression that the propositions expressed in the clausal complements are established facts. In effect, factive verbs do the opposite of the hedging strategies and use of modality considered in Chapter 2.

A distinction is often made between verb phrases as processes or actions and noun phrases as entities. A verb phrase states or asserts something, and if we don't agree with the proposition we can contest it. An entity, by definition, exists, and the assumption, or presupposition, with a noun phrase is that it is something real or true, so it is far more likely to go unchallenged than a verb phrase is (as we saw with example of the discovery of the structure of DNA). Nominalization is therefore a very useful tool for those in the business of trying to convince people that an ideological stance is actually an objective fact. As Lesley Jeffries (2010: 21) puts it: 'The way in which this basic truth about sentences in English can be exploited for ideological or other effect is by putting the processes/actions and so on into a nominal structure, and thus no longer asserting them, but assuming them.'

Let us consider the following assertions about the European Union:

It is a political project. This project is undemocratic. It is utopian. The project has been advanced by lies and by deceit. The British don't want and don't love this project. Increasingly, most ordinary Europeans don't want and don't love it.

Here we have six short sentences. The first four each contain a finite verb and the fifth and sixth have two. When the assertions are expressed in this way, a well-informed Remainer would have little difficulty in picking them off one by one. Long before we knew there was going to be a referendum, Alison Little (2013), writing for the *Sunday Express*, quoted the UKIP MEP Gerrard Batten, who expressed precisely the same views as follows:

> It is an undemocratic, utopian, political project advanced by lies and deceit – unwanted and unloved by the British and increasingly by most ordinary Europeans.

Now we have just one sentence, and after the copular verb *is* at the beginning there are no more finite verbs. The subject *It* has the subject complement *project*, which is premodified by three adjectives. It is also postmodified by two passive constructions involving three nonfinite verbs, the past participles *advanced*, *unwanted* and *unloved*. The most contentious element is the reference to lies and deceit, but the use of the passive voice means that we do not know who to accuse of lying and deceiving us. The entire subject complement is packaged up as a complex noun phrase featuring both pre- and postmodification. What was asserted in six short sentences is assumed in one long entity.

Obviously this does not mean that Gerrard Batten's position on the EU cannot be contested, but with so many attacks delivered in such a condensed form, and in the context of a debate conducted in real time, it would probably not be possible to counter more than one of them. As it happens, his words were part of a written text, his foreword to a report by the pro-Brexit economist Tim Congdon, so a systematic written rebuttal would be possible, but it would not be equally succinct and punchy.

In Congdon's report (2016) the cost to the UK of EU membership is calculated to be £170 billion a year, and in the same article Alison Little quotes him as claiming that the single biggest cost comes from '120,000 pages of EU law, including job-reducing employment regulations, green energy policies and financial regulations'. The premodifier *job-reducing* applies to all three nominal groups that follow. It is an unusual adjectival form constructed from a noun and a present participle, and appears to have been used to make contradiction less likely. More conventional constructions using the verb *reduce* would invite challenges: employment regulations tend to preserve jobs rather than reduce them, investment in alternative energy probably creates jobs, while it is debatable whether financial regulations have much impact one way or the other on employment.

Moving on to the texts produced once the referendum campaign was under way, we see that the construction of complex noun phrases often entails rather forced premodification involving not only standard adjectives, but also, or mostly, adjectival nouns (a noun used to qualify another noun, as in *university student*), or adjective compounds (noun + an *-ing* or *-en* participle, as in *life-changing*). The compound *job-destroying* and variations upon it appeared repeatedly in attacks on EU regulation. Stevie Beer (2016) reports on Michael Gove, a trained journalist who knows how to manipulate language to good effect, using three adjective compounds in describing the EU as a 'job-destroying, misery-inducing, unemployment-creating tragedy'. That the first and third compounds are actually synonymous is likely to go unnoticed by most readers or listeners, while the gross exaggeration of the second is less susceptible to challenge than the verb phrase *The EU induces misery*.

Allister Heath (2016) also uses *job-destroying* as one of four premodifiers of a powerful noun to describe the EU as 'an ultimately doomed, job-destroying, declining and mismanaged behemoth which stands no chance in an increasingly agile, globalised world'. All four wholly negative adjectival expressions could be contested, most of all the claim that the EU is declining given that it has grown from the six states of the original European Economic Community (EEC) in 1957 to the current twenty-eight, with no fewer than twelve new members joining since 2004. But *declining* is used as an adjective, along with three others, in an entity (a noun phrase with *behemoth* as its head), and our attention is immediately drawn to a comparison with a second entity: 'an increasingly agile, globalised world'. The avoidance of verb processes means that the focus is on that comparison between phenomena that are not asserted but assumed to exist, and the presuppositions in the two noun phrases therefore receive less scrutiny. The essence of that comparison is considered in more detail in Chapter 11, that is, the question of whether Leavers are Little Englanders or genuine internationalists reaching out to a world beyond the confines of the old continent.

Matthew Elliott, the Vote Leave chief executive quoted in the previous chapter (Gayle 2016), used a variation upon *job-destroying* in saying that 'whilst the EU might be good for big multinationals, for smaller businesses it acts as a job destruction regulatory machine'. An adjective followed by three adjective compounds were used in the Sunday Telegraph's unsigned editorial *We must vote Leave to create a Britain fit for the future* (2016), which concludes that the original decision to join the EEC in 1973 'led us into a cul-de-sac, hemmed in by a sclerotic, hide-bound, rules-obsessed, inward-looking institution'. Arguing the Lexit case, Nigel Willmott (2016) also used the adjective sclerotic in correctly predicting that 'on Thursday a majority of working-class people will vote to leave what has become a sclerotic, over-centralised and undemocratic set of institutions, imposing economic austerity and unemployment to pay down the debts of an unregulated and greedy financial system'. Like Allister Heath, Willmott uses two lengthy noun phrases in quick succession ('sclerotic, over-centralised and undemocratic set of institutions' and 'unregulated and greedy financial system'), which directs the reader's attention to the link between the two rather than the presuppositions made in each.

The comments quoted above are attributed to an MEP, an economist, a government minister, a political activist and at least three journalists/writers (we do not know how many pens contributed to an unsigned editorial). What is striking is the recurrence of certain lexical items (*job-destroying, sclerotic*) and, most of all, the repeated use of nominalization featuring strings of premodifiers qualifying the head noun. That those premodifiers often consist of *-ing* or *-en* participles linked to a noun is significant: it is indicative of the systematic avoidance of finite verbs with identifiable subjects. Verb phrases (which must contain at least one finite verb) would oblige greater clarity over who creates the misery or creates the unemployment than Michael Gove offers in his scathing attack on the EU.

Nominalization and presupposition are very effective techniques in deflecting criticism. To find out whether certain views have become naturalized as widely accepted 'facts', we need to look at the language of those who ostensibly have a contrasting view. To an extent we have already done this in Chaper 1 on coordination and the fact that so many Remain supporters conceded that the Leavers had some valid arguments but, on balance, staying in the EU was the lesser evil. Attempts to campaign more vigorously led to Project Fear, which, as we see in Chapter 9, was badly handled and ultimately counterproductive. The party that was most enthusiastic in its support for the EU was the small Green Party whose leader, Caroline Lucas, promised to be 'loud and proud' about backing continued membership and, eschewing fear tactics or a half-hearted preference for the status quo, focused on the positive, on what the EU has actually delivered (Mason 2016):

In a fast-changing world we need international rules to control big business and finance, and to ensure that people's rights are protected – at work and as consumers. The EU has also given us the freedom to live, study, work and retire across an entire continent.

The Green Party is very small, however, and to achieve greater visibility Caroline Lucas elected to team up with the Greek economist and Wolfgang Schäuble antagonist Yanis Varoufakis, the Labour shadow chancellor John McDonnell and other left-wing figures who distanced themselves from Stronger In and formed the *Another Europe is Possible* campaign group to present the radical case for maintaining EU membership. To promote this new movement Varoufakis himself (2016) wrote an article for the Guardian that conceded many of the arguments put forward by Brexit, and most of all Lexit, campaigners. That the European Union has a democratic deficit is acknowledged in his assertion that in the newly formed group 'we stand united in our belief that a democratic, prosperous Britain can only be won in the context of a pan-European struggle to democratise the EU'. He refers to 'the regulatory over-reach of Brussels' and the need to 'keep a check on bureaucrats luxuriating in the power of unelected office'. On the sovereignty issue he sounds almost like a Brexiteer in stating: 'We reject the notion that Britain must settle for diminished sovereignty as the price of global influence in the era of globalisation.' Although he believes that migration has brought 'undisputed net benefits', he concedes that they have been 'asymmetrically scattered' and that the strain on public services in some areas has left 'many with a feeling of having been marginalised in their own country'. He concludes with the choice facing the left:

Progressives must make a judgment call: do they believe that something good may come out of the collapse of our reactionary, undemocratic EU? Or will its collapse plunge the continent into an economic and policial vortex that no Brexit can shield Britain from?

Unlike the passionless, best-leave-things-as-they-are Remain arguments examined in Chapter 1, Varoufakis, McDonnell and Lucas advocate an energetic, proactive approach because the stark choice is either to radically reform the EU or watch it collapse.

Nigel Willmott (2016) sees precisely the same defects in the EU that Varoufakis notes; the essential difference between them is that the former believes, to use his own words, that 'remain and reform is wishful thinking' while the later maintains that another Europe is possible. That the EU has become an unsavoury institution is not in dispute. Of course, Varoufakis is an academic whose position on the Brexit issue is the result of studying the facts and subjecting them to analysis, but when he gives an admirably (or self-defeatingly) honest assessment of the situation even while hoping to persuade people to vote Remain, he also reinforces the public's negative perceptions.

8

The language of racism lite, and not so lite

One of several ironies involving UKIP is the fact that the EU's electoral rules have given the party far more representation than the UK's first-past-the-post system has. Following elections to the European Parliament in 2014, UKIP found itself with twenty-four MEPs (four of whom subsequently left the party), while in the UK general election of 2015 only one UKIP candidate was elected to the Commons (Douglas Carswell, the former Conservative MP for Clacton, who retained his seat after defecting to UKIP, but he too resigned from the party in March 2017).

In France, the Front National made significant gains in the 2014 European elections, a result that encouraged Marine Le Pen to try to form her own European Alliance for Freedom grouping in the European Parliament with – she rather took for granted – the support of UKIP. To the surprise of many, Nigel Farage chose to 'shun Marine Le Pen's advances' (Newman 2016) and instead allied himself with the Movimento Cinque Stelle in Italy, a new political movement that is difficult to pigeonhole as either right or left and, crucially, has none of the embarrassing ideological baggage that the daughter of Jean-Marie Le Pen has to cart around. Ever since its formation the UK Independence Party has faced the accusation that it is little more than a more circumspect version of the unapologetically xenophobic British National Party

(BNP), and Farage's decision to steer clear of any formal alliance with the Front National was clearly another step in his ongoing efforts to rid the party of persistent suggestions of thinly disguised racism.

His job was not made any easier when in February 2015 a YouGov poll commissioned by the *Sunday Times* revealed that only 49 per cent of UKIP voters considered themselves free from racial prejudice (compared with 72 per cent of Labour voters and 73 per cent of Liberal Democrats), 42 per cent described themselves as 'a little' racially prejudiced and 6 per cent admitted to being 'very' prejudiced (Stone 2016). Curiously, many UKIP voters who confessed to having some degree of racial prejudice denied that they were racists; in a separate question 64 per cent declared that they did not hold 'racist' views. It is not clear what criteria they applied to distinguish between racial prejudice and racism, but the figures suggest that the former was seen as something easier to admit to, perhaps a question of choices in personal relations that did not break the laws of the land, while the latter was an altogether more serious matter.

Farage was quick to get rid of people who made racially offensive remarks. When Rozanne Duncan, a UKIP councillor for the Thanet district in Kent, told a BBC documentary-maker that she had a problem with 'negroes' because there was 'something about their faces' (Pitel 2015), she was immediately expelled from the party. Two years earlier Chris Scotton, a prospective UKIP candidate at council elections in Leicestershire, was hastily dropped after it emerged that on his Facebook page he had repeatedly 'liked' inflammatory posts on the website of the far-right English Defence League (EDL) (Hookham and Gadher 2013). In the same period Alan Ryall, a UKIP candidate for Wickham in Suffolk, stood down when it was discovered that he had not declared his previous membership of the BNP. Farage made his position very clear regarding BNP and EDL supporters: 'They are completely on our proscribed list. I have done everything I can to insulate us from this problem' (ibid.).

Two years before the referendum Nigel Farage (2014) drew attention to UKIP's increasing support from ethnic-minority Britons:

I have been noticing for a few months something very encouraging: a surge of support and new members from Britain's ethnic minority communities. In one of my debates with Nick Clegg (bless him) a young woman from an Asian background asked a question about migration and I noticed her nodding as I set out the absurdity of Britain's current immigration policy: to have an open door to more than 400 million people, many unskilled, from more than two dozen countries, while imposing restrictions that made it difficult for a New Zealand surgeon or an Indian engineer to come and make a positive contribution.

Among UKIP's successful candidates in the 2014 European elections was one Amjad Bashir, MEP for the Yorkshire and Humber region, who was eight years old when his family emigrated to Yorkshire from Pakistan in 1960. It was quite a coup for UKIP to have Bashir aboard but less than a year after his election he defected to the Conservative Party.

Despite the determination of Farage and other leading figures to present UKIP as a non-racist, non-sectarian party, accusations of stirring up racial tension continued, not least when in the last month of campaigning Farage himself scored a spectacular own goal by authorizing the use of a poster featuring a long, winding column of migrants – mostly young, male and dark-skinned – with the slogan 'Breaking Point: the EU has failed us all'. Farage's abandonment of his previous commitment to eschewing anything that could be interpreted as racist was seen by many as a last-ditch effort to swing voters with an appeal to the fear factor, and the Breaking Point poster was condemned by Boris Johnson, who pointed out that the official Vote Leave campaign and UKIP were entirely separate entities. In his defence, Farage said that the poster depicted 'an accurate, undoctored photograph' of migrants crossing the Croatia-Slovenia border in October 2015, and that he believed that we 'should open our hearts to genuine refugees' but not to economic migrants (Stewart and Mason 2016).

If the Breaking Point poster used an image to imply that migrants represented a serious danger to our security, many articles in the pro-Brexit media used highly emotive language, in particular metaphors of natural phenomena capable of causing enormous damage – *flood*, *tidal wave*, even *tsunami* – or terms from the semantic fields of military operations – *invasion, army of immigrants* – and great numbers – *hordes, swarms* and the like. Such language implies a degree of risk hardly backed up by hard facts, but professional journalists generally take care not to be too explicit in linking migrants to criminal acts and avoid criticisms of specific ethnic or religious groups likely to lead to legal action. Newspaper readers providing feedback, their identities hidden behind a nickname, have no need to be cautious, and it is here that we find openly racist and Islamophobic attitudes expressed in strong, sometimes vulgar terms. Nick Gutteridge (2016) for *The Express* wrote of the tensions between Angela Merkel and leaders of other member states – notably Austria, Poland and Hungary – who wished to impose strict quotas on the number of migrants they would admit, a policy that contrasted with the markedly more welcoming approach adopted by Germany at the time. Gutteridge focuses on the discord within the EU and resentment at Germany's dominant role. He does not attack Chancellor Merkel, stresses the numbers of migrants ('unprecedented migration' 'vast influx of newcomers') but does not use the word *invasion* and makes no reference at all to the religion of most of those seeking a new life in Europe. His readers do not hesitate to express views that would be actionable if their identities were known and, as the following sample demonstrates, do not merely denigrate migrants, but also recycle old stereotypes about bullying, war-mongering Germans. Graphological deviations have been retained.

Dutchie75

The only one to really blame for this migrant mess is Merkel and nobody else but Merkel she first dropped germany and then the rest of the EU into this disastrous situation of a tsunami of muslims who have no culture and will nev er ever assimilate because of their Islamic attitudes and beliefs which is not even a religion but a terroristic and barbarian behaviour, based on an evil book wqritten by a man in 632 called mohammed who 'married' 11 wives the youngest being 9 years old thus he was a pedophile.

Kipper4u

If these filthy invaders are such a benefit,,
WHY DOESNT SHE WANT TO KEEP THEM ALL?????

method man

this is a real easy problem to solve just take the muslim refugees to a muslim country, all of them

Doug82

Ya! You vill obey der fuhrer – resistance is futile!.

Botley Mike

Austria, be careful or Fuhrer Merkel will be sending the panzers in again for another take over of your country.

When President Hollande and Chancellor Merkel commemorated the centenary of the Battle of Verdun, one of the bloodiest episodes of the First World War which, over a period of ten months, claimed 300,000 French and German lives, the former declared: 'Our sacred destiny is written in the ravaged soil of Verdun. It can be stated in a few words: we should love our country, but we should protect our common home, Europe, without which we would be exposed to the storms of history.' Patrick Maguire (2016) interpreted this as a coded message to British electors to vote to remain in the EU (a 'thinly-veiled ATTACK on Brexit'), but after an initial reference to 'grovelling heads of state' his language is restrained and much more in keeping with the solemnity of the tribute to the men who lost their lives at Verdun. Indeed, the thinly veiled attack is later referred to as a 'passionate appeal'. Readers' feedback was much less restrained, with Islamophobia again accompanied by Second World War stereotypes of German bullying and French pusillanimity.

RegKing

Germans destroyed two generations of young British men, which led to us having to import foreigners from the commonwealth to do menial work following WW2 –this led to the multi-culti invasion which has destroyed the country.

Marmaduke

Germans caused two wars, France ran away from 2 wars and sent jews to the Germans to be exterminated, they only want to be liked lol, and they are telling us the EU is vondvar.Brexit

middleengland

Thirty years from now this pair of idiots will be dead and buries, leaving behind a Muslim Europe if they get their way. Think about that before doing as poodle Cameron tells you on the 23rd of June.

BEARLY ALIVE

IF I WAS IN DANGER OF SEEING MY HOUSE OF CARDS COLLAPSE I'D BE WORRIED TOO . . . ESPECIALLY MERKEL, HAVING OPENED THE DOOR TO THE MIGRANT LOCUSTS . . .

As we see in Chapter 13, the pro-Brexit press did distort the facts on occasion, particularly with regard to the number of migrants entering the UK, and during the referendum campaign *The Telegraph*, *The Mail* and *The Express* were all reported to the Independent Press Standards Organisation (IPSO). This resulted in the newspapers concerned having to publish corrections, but the language used was not sufficiently direct to be deemed an incitement to racial hatred, and thus in breach of UK law (although Dave Prentis of the Unison trade union reported the Breaking Point poster to the Metropolitan police).

What was left implicit in an article became explicit and somewhat nauseating in feedback on it.

No British newspaper is detested by the left quite as much as the *Daily Mail*, and its editor-in-chief, Paul Dacre – a man with a predilection for calling his staff 'a load of cunts' (Addison 2017, Kindle edition: position 3772) – has acquired a notoriety rarely achieved by members of his profession. The *Mail's* great rival, the *Daily Express*, is similar in terms of ideology and style but has never acquired the same level of opprobrium, partly because it does not have a similarly unwholesome history. Today the *Daily Mail* flaunts its patriotism but during the 1930s its owner, Lord Rothermere, praised Oswald Mosley and his British Union of Fascists, was on friendly terms with both Hitler and Mussolini, published scare stories about German Jews flooding into Britain, and in 1938 sent Hitler a telegram of support for the annexation of Sudetenland. Only when armed conflict was imminent did the editorial line turn 180 degrees, by which time it was clear to Lord Rothermere that a war-time government would not hesitate to use emergency powers to close down his newspaper. Since the war it has consistently espoused right-wing economic policies, praised the monarchy and promoted 'family values' (thus opposing abortion, same-sex marriage and the feminist movement), and has opposed the trade unions, immigration and, since the days of the EEC, Britain's involvement in greater European integration.

Because of these last two characteristics, the *Daily Mail* actually spent decades preparing for the 2016 referendum with a series of articles intended to raise fears about immigration and resentment towards European institutions. Three of the more recent pre-2016 headlines are sufficient to illustrate the approach: 'By 2066, white Britons "will be outnumbered" if immigration continues at current rates' (Shipman 2010); '4,000 foreign criminals including murderers and rapists we can't throw out . . . and, yes, you can blame human rights again' (Shipman and Doyle 2013); 'Wish you were here? Refugees are taken on jollies to zoos, theme parks and even to the beach to help them "integrate" into British life . . . and guess who's paying for it all' (Tonkin 2015).

The three themes of these headlines – the threat to traditional British culture and identity posed by immigrants, compliance with the European Convention on Human Rights which often prevents the UK from deporting foreign criminals, and the money spent on welcoming refugees that could be used for more worthy causes – were recycled on an almost daily basis once the referendum campaign got under way. The *Daily Mail* gave considerable coverage to the so-called Calais Jungle, the inadequately equipped camp on the outskirts of Calais for migrants who wanted to reach Britain but were denied admittance by the UK government. The majority were Syrians, and therefore were legitimate asylum seekers rather than economic migrants, and they included unaccompanied children. *The Mail*'s focus, however, was not so much on the humanitarian issues as on episodes of violence, such as clashes with the French police and threatening behaviour towards lorry drivers in an attempt to secure a lift through the Channel Tunnel. When the British actors Jude Law and Toby Jones, the comedian Shappi Khorsandi and the singer Tom Odell visited the camp to draw attention to the plight of people who had got so frustratingly close to their objective, *The Mail* dedicated most of its report to a heavily hedged account of an alleged attack on the celebrities' security team (Linning 2016):

> Security guards hired to protect Jude Law when he visited the 'Jungle' migrant camp were reportedly targeted by rock-pelting migrants just moments after the actor boarded the coach home.
>
> The star made the journey to northern France last week to highlight the plight of child refugees who are being evicted under a move by French authorities to demolish the southern part of the camp.
>
> He was joined by Tom Odell and a film crew, who captured him on camera as he urged David Cameron to let the hundreds of children at the camp come to the UK.
>
> But moments after the celebrities boarded the production team coach back to Britain, their security team was ambushed, according to the *Sunday People*.

The attackers reportedly hurled stones at the men before stealing their mobile phones.

A source told the newspaper: 'We were shocked to see some of the migrants acting like football hooligans. The security team had stones thrown at them and two had phones smashed and stolen.'

The hedging techniques we investigated in Chapter 2 with regard to Remain's cautious approach are here used by a committed pro-Brexit newspaper to pre-empt questioning of the factual accuracy of the piece. The adverb *reportedly* appears in the first and fifth of the quoted paragraphs, which allows *The Mail* to shift potential challenges to the unidentified reporter. Similarly a *source* is cited in the last paragraph, but his/her identity is not revealed. The most obvious hedge is the journalist's confession that she is writing of events she had not witnessed, so any comeback should be directed towards the *Sunday People*.

The original *Sunday People* article (Boyle 2016) is available on the website of its sister newspaper, the *Daily Mirror*, which, as already noted, supported Remain and had little in common with *The Mail* or *The Express* on the immigration issue. Apart from the unidentified *source*, there is no hedging. A somewhat surprising similarity between the two reports concerns readers' feedback, which on *The Mirror* site looks for the most part as if it had been posted by *Mail* readers.

GeorgeTyrebyter

Celebrity slumming. What a stupid gat this idiot is. You are not gaining anything in proving your liberal weeper credentials. These are still illegal scum. You're lucky to get away. Better luck, migrant scum, next time.

CdricBallet

Those well thinking libnuts millionaires are a danger to our societies. They have not a single idea about what they are doing, never had to live with migrants and islam and criminality. Pathetic

The predictability of *The Mail*'s treatment of immigration – catastrophe precipitated by invading Muslims and the cost to the long-suffering tax payer – lends itself to parody. A brilliant spoof of a *Daily Mail* front page, with the headline *Terror as Gigantic Muslim Spiders Bring Deadly Ebola to UK* (2014), is available on the democraticunderground.com site. A bizarre image of giant spiders in burqas attacking a passenger train illustrates a text in which the capitalized words are almost obligatory lexemes used in every edition of the *Daily Mail*:

> Swarms of giant, MUSLIM spiders illegally entered the country yesterday, bringing TERROR and DEATH – and although there is no evidence to support it, we're going to say that they are BENEFIT SCROUNGERS.
>
> The arachnid army, which will probably force your local shop to make all your pasties HALAL, arrived in the UK via Folkstone and was no doubt helped by the bloody FRENCH.
>
> Although scientists have said categorically that the huge bugs definitely do not carry the deadly ebola virus, we're going to put EBOLA in block capitals anyway, because they help to increase unwarranted FEAR.
>
> The creepy crawlies, wearing BURQAS, have no sexual interests beyond the evolutionary desire to reproduce but we're still going to speculate that they are PAEDOPHILES because nonces sell papers to people like you quicker than PRINCESS DIANA headlines do these days.

Democraticunderground.com's hoax makes us smile, but other observers of *The Mail*'s treatment of the refugee crisis focused on parallels with that newspaper's inglorious past.

Sophie Brown (2015), writing for the *Huffington Post UK*, referred to a *Daily Mail* headline from 1938 – *German Jews Pouring Into This Country* – and cited the opening paragraphs of the relevant article:

'The way stateless Jews and Germans are pouring in from every port of this country is becoming an outrage. I intend to enforce the law to the fullest.'

In these words, Mr Herbert Metcalde, the Old Street Magistrate yesterday referred to the number of aliens entering this country through the 'back door' – a problem to which The Daily Mail has repeatedly pointed.

The number of aliens entering this country can be seen by the number of prosecutions in recent months. It is very difficult for the alien to escape the increasing vigilance of the police and port authorities.

Similarities with the same newspaper's attitude to those wishing to enter Britain from the Calais Jungle are impossible to ignore: switch *asylum seekers* for *Jews*, *migrants* for *Germans*, *illegal immigrants* for *aliens* and *Home Secretary* for *Old Street Magistrate* and the parallels are disquieting.

However distasteful we might find the 'tidal wave' metaphors of the pro-Brexit press, and however much we abhor the explicit racism and Islamophobia of readers' feedback, the fact remains that in the first half of 2016 in certain areas of England medical, educational and social services were struggling to cope with the influx of EU migrants. The Lexit argument that the availability of labour from Portugal, Romania and the Baltic states had driven down wages to an unacceptable level could also be supported by statistics.

The example often cited in the media of a town in crisis is that of Wisbech in Cambridgeshire, once a tranquil market town that grew rapidly following the expansion of the EU in 2004. Today approximately one third of its 31,000 inhabitants are EU migrants, mostly from Poland, Lithuania, Romania and Latvia, while staffing levels in education, medical services and the police have remained largely unaltered. When John Harris (2014) of *The Guardian* visited the town two years before the referendum, he learnt of piece-work and zero-hours contracts in agriculture and food processing, recruitment from eastern Europe controlled by shady gangmasters, illegal distilling of vodka, clashes between Lithuanians and Latvians and, between 2010 and 2012, an unprecedented five murders (all the victims were East Europeans). Most disturbingly, he spoke to an unemployed 45-year-old man who was born and brought up in Wisbech, whose application for agency work in agriculture had been rejected on the grounds that his lack of knowledge of a Baltic language meant that he would be unable to communicate with workmates.

A tactical error by the Remain campaign was not to engage with people who expressed their concerns about the impact of immigration from the EU in rational, non-racist terms, and instead to adopt a self-righteous attitude in accusing all Leavers indiscriminately of racial prejudice. As noted in Chapter 2, the Labour MP and chair of Vote Leave, Gisella Stuart (2016), went so far as to say that by showing little interest in people's worries about immigration, her party was turning itself into 'the biggest recruiting agent for Ukip I can think of'. She added:

> [People] feel there are legitimate concerns they have, and Labour are not even responding to it. If you're an MP in a big city, immigration matters, and it is first and second generation immigrants who are concerned about immigration. Families of second and third generation immigrants from the Indian subcontinent find it really difficult: they say, why do we have to jump so many hurdles just to bring in relatives for a wedding?

The Conservative Party was split over Brexit, which meant, perversely, that it remained representative of its equally split electorate. Polls prior to 23 June indicated that people from the lower socio-economic classes, Labour's traditional electors, were those most likely to vote to leave the EU, while the overwhelming majority of Labour MPs were encouraging their constituents to vote Remain. In the final weeks before voting day, a number of commentators noted that, on immigration as well as other issues, the working class felt that Labour was no longer listening to them. Owen Jones (2016) stated bluntly: 'If Britain crashes out of the European Union in two weeks, it will be off the backs of votes cast by discontented working-class people.' Lisa Mckenzie (2016) also felt that the working classes were being ignored, and that within working-class communities the main concern was not immigration in itself, but the steady erosion of their security and living standards over a thirty-year period:

> Working-class people in the UK can see a possibility that something might change for them if they vote to leave the EU. The women in east London and the men in the mining towns all tell me the worst thing is that things stay the same. The referendum has become a way in which they can have their say, and they are saying collectively that their lives have been better than they are today. And they are right. Shouting 'racist' and 'ignorant' at them louder and louder will not work – they have stopped listening.

Suzanne Moore (2016) saw a great deal of sanctimonious anti-racism from the bourgeois left and a total lack of communication with those living with the day-to-day reality of competing in the labour and housing markets with migrants from EU states, and the consequent crisis of the Labour Party.

> That immigration issue that we never talk about? We talk about it *all the time* – just in different tongues. What we don't do is listen. If we did, then the crumbling of the Labour remain vote would not be surprising. What did we see happening at the last election? What do we think happened in Scotland? The complacency of thinking that you can take working-class votes for granted is absolute condescension.

Fundamental to UKIP's aim to take back control was the desire to make the right of residence in the UK dependent upon a demonstrable ability to contribute to the British economy, with an Australian points system often proposed as a fair method of selecting worthy candidates. This must have struck a chord with unqualified Britons competing for unskilled jobs and rented accommodation with EU migrants, and that Remain in general, and the Labour Party in particular, failed to address their concerns – or just dismissed them as the complaints of ignorant racists – was without doubt a significant factor in Leave's victory.

Right-wing Brexiteers and their supporters in the media tended not to make too much of the issue of EU migrants, who are, of course, a source of cheap labour for employers, and focused instead on asylum seekers and other would-be migrants from outside Europe, the very immigrants that working-class Britons were less concerned about. Newspapers like *The Mail* and *The Express* endeavoured to keep their racist and Islamophobic language just the right side of the boundary leading to prosecution for incitement to racial hat-red – racism lite for want of a better term – while, as we have seen, their read-ers' feedback was anything but lite.

The foreign-born population of the UK is not evenly distributed through-out the land. Vargas-Silva and Rienzo (2017) report that in 2015 Northern Ireland had the lowest percentage of inhabitants born abroad (1.4 per cent) and Scotland had a lower percentage (4.3 per cent) than all English regions except for the North East. To say that this accounts for the fact that a majority of voters in Northern Ireland and Scotland opted for Remain would be ridicu-lously simplistic, however, given that London, where 36.8 per cent of residents were born outside the UK, also voted to stay in the EU.

Scotland is a special case, of course, since the binary choice between remain-ing in the EU or leaving was bound to be conditioned by the country's rela-tionship with another supranational union, the United Kingdom. Like many others, I expected June 2016 to produce a cautious endorsement of the status quo as had happened in Scotland two years earlier. Why that did not occur is considered in the next chapter.

9

Comparison with the Scottish independence referendum of 2014: How Project Fear worked in 2014 but not in 2016

Although the Scottish National Party (SNP) was founded in 1934, it really emerged as a major player after the Scotland Act of 1998 and the subsequent establishment of the Scottish Parliament as a devolved legislature. A turning point was the Scottish election of 2007 when the SNP finished with one seat more than Labour and thus became the largest party in the Holyrood Parliament. Four years later it added twenty-two more seats, which gave it an overall majority. At the time the SNP still only sent six MPs to Westminster, but its success in elections to the Scottish Parliament meant that the British government could hardly refuse to allow a referendum on independence even though the Conservative, Labour and Liberal Democratic parties had no wish at all to see Scotland break away from the Union.

UKIP's electoral breakthrough came in the 2015 general election when Britain's first-past-the-post electoral system restricted it to just one MP but it won 12.6 per cent of the votes cast, which under the proportional representation system would have given it eighty-two seats (Dathan 2015). In terms of popular vote but not number of seats, it had become the UK's third largest party, and had pushed Labour into third place in many Conservative seats and the Tories into third place in many Labour-held constituencies. Just as the SNP had done in Scotland, UKIP had shaken up the traditional parties. It had taken votes from both Labour and the Conservatives, and was sufficiently irritating to David Cameron to induce him to gamble on a referendum that he, much of his party, most Labour MPs and all Lib Dems fervently hoped would not go the way Nigel Farage wished.

In 2014 the expression *Project Fear* was not yet in general circulation even though it was first coined by Rob Shorthouse, director of communications for the Better Together anti-independence campaign group (Gordon 2014). Eric Shaw (2014: 64–68), writing before the independence referendum and with specific reference to the Scottish Labour Party (SLP), referred instead to *anxiety-arousal* as one of the SLP's three negative strategies in the campaign (the others being *critical*, critical scrutiny of arguments and claims made by Yes Scotland, the umbrella campaign group for independence, and *attack*, disparagement of opponents' honesty and competence). Shaw's description (ibid. 67) of the SLP's creation of anxiety is representative of the approach adopted by the Better Together group in general, but Labour had some particularly authoritative voices arguing for maintaining the union, including the former prime minister, Gordon Brown, and his chancellor of the exchequer, Alistair Darling, both Scots.

> Labour has used an anxiety-arousal strategy to foster a mood of disquiet, worry, even apprehension about the prospect of independence. Its campaign has revolved around the frequently-reiterated theme that independence constituted a perilous leap into the unknown; a gamble, a reckless step to take in an unpredictable and threatening world.

The Scottish independence debate was necessarily conducted in relation to the European Union once Brussels had clarified that a newly independent Scotland would not be able to make an immediate switch from sterling to the euro, indeed would not even be a member of the EU and would have to apply to join in the normal way. Better Together seized upon the currency issue as a key element in its anxiety-arousal strategy with warnings that it might not be feasible for Scotland to continue to use sterling while it awaited membership of the EU.

In the referendum of 18 September 2014, 55 per cent of those who voted opted for remaining part of the UK. In his analysis of the results, James Kirkup (2014) noted that a significant percentage of the SNP voters who had given the party control of the Scottish Parliament in 2011 must have voted against independence in the referendum, although he was only half convinced that the currency question was the clinching argument.

> One explanation is that SNP voters took heed of chilling warnings that an independent Scotland would be unable to keep the pound and so face economic turmoil. Another is that they never wanted independence, but simply voted for the SNP at Holyrood because they believed a nationalist administration in Edinburgh would get the best deal for Scotland within the Union.

However, a Lord Ashcroft Poll, summarized by the Guardian on 20 September 2014 (*Scottish independence: poll reveals who voted, how and why*), revealed that 57 per cent of those who had voted against independence considered the currency question one of the two or three most important issues and that no other aspect of the debate had swayed no voters to the same extent.

Yes Scotland in 2014 had all the political parties except the SNP lined up against it, along with the financial, business and administrative establishment of the UK, and indeed Europe given that Brussels did not wish to see Scotland break away. Given the circumstances, it is perhaps surprising that as many as

45 per cent of Scots defied the anxiety-arousal strategy. In 2016 Vote Leave was a little less isolated in that, in addition to UKIP, part of the Conservative Party also campaigned vigorously for Brexit, and while the Confederation of British Industry was firmly on the side of Remain, other business leaders argued that leaving the EU would benefit medium-sized and small firms. A coordinated and continuous attempt to arouse anxiety was made, however, and Rob Shorthouse's Project Fear label soon became a fundamental element of the language of Brexit.

During the referendum campaign the Treasury published a series of forecasts of the economic consequences of leaving the EU, all of them bleak and some bordering on the apocalyptic, which were seized upon by Remain campaigners, dismissed as scare tactics by Leave, and in the final analysis failed to instil fear in the hearts and minds of voters. The strategy backfired because it focused exclusively on worst-case scenarios, glossed over the fact that trying to predict how markets will react to a major political upheaval is anything but an exact science, and once translated from economic to political discourse, was expressed with a level of hyperbole that provoked more mirth than anxiety. Six months after the referendum, the Centre for Business Research at the University of Cambridge published its analysis of the Treasury's assessments: the study found that the forecasts regarding employment, wage levels, affordable housing and the prospect of reduced immigration were unduly pessimistic, while on the issue of trade deals the Treasury's warnings had been 'very flawed and very partisan' (Hope 2017). Leavers also had the advantage of being able to remind everyone that in 1998 gloomy predictions had been made about the consequences of Britain's decision to keep sterling, but by the spring of 2016 not even the most enthusiastic Remainer proposed joining the eurozone.

Early on in the referendum campaign Martin Temple, chairman of the Engineering Employers Federation (EEF), warned that leaving the EU would be tantamount to stepping into an 'abyss of uncertainty and risk' (Watt

2016). Anatole Kaletsky (2016), chairman of the Institute for New Economic Thinking, then pitched in to say that what Boris Johnson was pleased to call Project Fear was actually just common sense. When in February 2016 the government published a document entitled *The process for withdrawing from the European Union* on negotiation procedures in what was still considered the unlikely event of a vote to leave the EU, the *Daily Mail* was quick to rename the report 'Dave's Dodgy Dossier' (though it was signed by the then Foreign Secretary, Philip Hammond) and to describe its content as 'lurid claims' and 'cynical scaremongering' (Doyle 2016).

As opinion polls showed that support for Brexit was gradually increasing, attempts to generate fear intensified, from a prediction that leaving the EU would result in a £3 rise in the price of a packet of cigarettes (Tapsfield 2016) to a shift in emphasis from economics to security, and rather hysterical warnings about the danger of war in Europe. In a speech delivered on 9 May, David Cameron (2016) cited the Treasury's estimate that leaving the EU could cost every British household up to £4,300 by 2030, but later switched to 'the strength and security of our nation', 'the character of an island nation which has not been invaded for almost a thousand years', and after references to Blenheim, Trafalgar, Waterloo, the Great War, 'our lone stand in 1940' and 'the Few who saved this country in its hour of mortal danger', advised voters that 'when terrorists are planning to kill and maim people on British streets, the closest possible security cooperation is far more important than sovereignty in its purest theoretical form'. Unfortunately for Mr Cameron, details of his speech had been leaked to the *Daily Mail* some hours beforehand, which allowed Slack and Peev (2016) to lampoon the content in an online article warning that 'Europe risks war and genocide if Britain votes to leave EU'. Shortly after the speech, the *Daily Mirror* used the headline 'Brexit could trigger World War Three, warns David Cameron' (Glaze and Bloom 2016), while Philip Johnston (2016) in *The Telegraph* noted that the prime minister's 'warnings of European disintegration and evocations of Churchill and Marlborough' were an attempt to mobilize the 15–20 per cent of the electorate who, according to the polls, had not yet decided how to vote.

In the final run up to voting day Stephen Pollard (2016) for *The Express* could amuse himself with ironic comments upon the escalation of Project Fear now that leading figures in European institutions had entered the fray.

> Forget David Cameron's warning that we would cause World War Three if we leave the EU, bonkers as that scare tactic was. Forget the idea that we would suddenly be plunged into a recession from which there will be no escape. In fact, forget all the nonsense the Remain camp have spouted as they desperately try to stop the British people voting to leave.
>
> Because according to Donald Tusk, the former Polish prime minister who is now president of the European Council, if we dare to leave the EU we will destroy civilisation itself. Speaking to a German newspaper, he said: 'As a historian I fear Brexit could be the beginning of the destruction of not only the EU but also Western political civilisation in its entirety.' Yup.

In the same article Pollard claimed to have learnt that David Cameron had secured an assurance from the gaffe-prone Jean-Claude Juncker that he would not make any public pronouncements on the Brexit debate, and that the president of the European Commission had agreed to hold his tongue but with the caveat that he would intervene if the polls indicated that Leave were in front during the final week. For Pollard this held out the prospect that 'however bonkers Project Fear's warnings may have been to date, the next week is likely to make even Mr Tusk's words seem sane'.

In this book I have repeatedly argued that Remain campaigners – with the notable exception of the Green Party – hedged and side-stepped and generally did not make their case with great vigour or passion. They tended to be pushed onto the defensive on matters such as the alleged lack of democracy in the EU instead of adopting a pro-active approach and pointing out the positives deriving from EU membership rather that the risks entailed in leaving. They did not do enough to mobilize young voters who had the biggest stake in maintaining freedom of movement within the Union and, as it later transpired, were less keen to splash through puddles to get to the polling station than elderly Brexit supporters were (David Cameron [2016: 4, 5] used the very last paper edition of *The Independent* on 20 March 2016 to explain that his greatest fear was low turnout). Ironically, when the polls started to suggest that a victory for Leave could not be ruled out, the reaction was to turn up the heat of Project Fear to such an extent that the apocalyptic warnings and hysterical rhetoric were in the end not taken too seriously.

Six weeks before voting day, Allister Heath (2016) observed that the policy was proving to be counterproductive.

> Behind the scenes, there is now real worry on the Remain side. But it is so wedded to its elite-driven fear campaign – getting powerful people or institutions to warn of Armageddon – that its answer is simply to do more of the same, albeit even more aggressively. It hopes and believes that most people haven't switched on yet, and that they eventually will as the referendum nears and the volume is turned up ever further.
>
> This is a dangerous strategy. Apocalyptic claims from endless grey-suited figures may come to sound like old news. Hysteria only works when it is seen as plausible and dispassionate. Barack Obama's heavy-handed intervention backfired, while the prime minister's claim that a Brexit would increase the risk of war was so over the top that it will have encouraged many undecided voters to switch off altogether.

Charlie Cooper (2016) for *The Independent* noted that Remain started the referendum campaign well as 'warnings of the economic consequences of Brexit had an effective shock and awe quality to them', but as the weeks and months passed and the polls showed that Leave were winning over more voters, the public seemed to give less and less credence to more and more dubious claims and began to seek, not facts, but a vision, or for Cooper, a 'story'.

In this feverish post-truth atmosphere, facts and reason go out the window as effective political arguments. Many voters simply don't trust anything anyone says on the EU anymore. The eventual winner in this referendum therefore won't be the side with the best facts, it will be the one with the best story to tell.

Cooper also noted that in an interview lasting less than an hour, Michael Gove had managed to use the word *control* thirty-five times, and that those who had not benefitted from globalization felt that what they had lost most of all was control over their destiny. Gove, therefore, was telling the story that people wanted to hear, albeit a story (anyone who has studied his political career would be sceptical about his willingness to cede real control to the populace).

Project Fear was effective in Scotland largely because the main warning was not a worst-case scenario but an objective fact; independence would have left the country without a currency, unable to adopt the euro and dependent on the Westminster government's good will for continued use of sterling. No one could predict with much confidence the immediate and mid-term consequences of the UK leaving the EU, so the 2016 version of Project Fear was much more a question of interpretation, and Leave's attempt to terrify voters with a vision of catastrophic fallout lacked credibility, and sometimes descended into silliness.

In some ways we should not compare the two referenda of 2014 and 2016, but the general election of 2015 and the Brexit referendum the following year. In 2015 the polls predicted a close result and another hung parliament, so it came as a surprise – not least to the Tories – when the Conservative Party finished with an overall majority of twelve seats in the Commons, though with a popular vote of only 36.9 per cent. Since MPs of the Northern Irish Sinn Fein party never take up their seats at Westminster, the Conservatives actually had a working majority of seventeen. Labour was generally viewed as having performed badly even though it had slightly increased its number of votes compared with 2010. However, the party lost forty of the forty-one Scottish seats it had won in both 2010 and 2005; in 2015 the SNP won fifty-six of the fifty-nine seats in Scotland, with the Conservatives and Liberal Democrats emulating Labour in securing just one seat each. The extraordinary success of the SNP was the single biggest cause of Labour's poor return, and with the main party of opposition in such a weak state, and with the Tories freed from the obligation to consider the views of the Lib Dems, it is hardly surprising that the newly re-elected David Cameron felt he could do as he liked, and even take the enormous gamble of authorizing a referendum that most of Parliament did not want. Faced with a stronger and more united Labour opposition still led by Ed Milliband, Cameron would not have been quite so cock-a-hoop. SNP MPs, pro-EU to a (wo)man, had by their own electoral success weakened the party most capable of leading opposition to the very idea of holding a referendum on continued membership of the European Union.

10

Leave's appointment with history and Remain's another day at the office

Had the referendum produced a 52-48 per cent victory for Remain, on 24 June 2016 we would all have gone about our business as usual, and after two or three days we would have turned our minds to other matters. David Cameron would still be prime minister with George Osborne in charge of the economy, Theresa May would still be pretending that she had always been in favour of staying in the EU, and Nigel Farage would be getting a little tedious in his insistence that the fight would go on.

The dilemma for Leave campaigners was the fact that all they could promise voters was an anticlimax, the prospect of more of the same. Brexiteers, in contrast, promised a once-in-a-generation opportunity to change the course of history, correct the errors of the last four decades and liberate Britain from a role in Europe with which she had never felt comfortable. It was not about petty details of tax rates or tariffs, but the much bigger picture of the UK's position on the international scene and our relationship, not just with Europe, but also with the United States, the Commonwealth and the BRIC countries.

This meant considering the referendum in the context of Britain's ongoing search for an appropriate role since 1945, an approach that sometimes resulted in historical overviews being somewhat distorted by a touch of journalistic spin. Evocations of the Second World War were common, with references to 'our finest hour' and other examples of Churchill's stirring rhetoric. What was often lost in the historical analysis was a realistic assessment of Britain's greatly diminished clout on the world stage since 1945.

On 4 February 2016, when the referendum campaign was still building up steam and a number of high-profile figures had yet to commit themselves one way or the other, *The Mail* published an unsigned editorial with the headline *Who will speak for England?* The question is not a direct quotation but it refers to the imperative – 'Speak for England!' – that the Conservative MP Leo Amery shouted across the floor of the Commons at Labour deputy leader Arthur Greenwood on 2 September 1939, the day after Hitler invaded Poland. According to *The Mail*, the prime minister, Neville Chamberlain, had shown reluctance to abandon his policy of appeasement despite the fact that Britain was guarantor of Poland's independence, but Amery's challenge sparked Greenwood into launching a spirited attack on the prime minister, which led to a heated debate in the Commons, and resulted in Chamberlain declaring war on Germany the next day.

As we noted in Chapter 8, in 1938 the *Daily Mail* used the front-page headline *German Jews Pouring Into This Country*, and Lord Rothermere left it rather late before distancing himself from Adolf Hitler, so it required a certain chutzpah for *The Mail* to evoke the House of Commons on one of its better days as MPs obliged the government to stand up against a racist tyranny. The editorial writer denies that the intention is to suggest that 'there are any parallels whatsoever between the Nazis and the EU', then immediately makes it clear that (s)he sees the choice facing Britain in 2016 as comparable to the momentous decision the nation had to make on the eve of the Second World War, a choice that would have profound consequences for future generations.

But as in 1939 we are at a crossroads in our island history. For in perhaps as little as 20 weeks' time, voters will be asked to decide nothing less than what sort of country we want to live in and bequeath to those who come after us.

Are we to be a self-governing nation, free in this age of mass migration to control our borders, strike trade agreements with whomever we choose and dismiss our rulers and lawmakers if they displease us?

Or will our liberty, security and prosperity be better assured by submitting to a statist, unelected bureaucracy in Brussels, accepting the will of unaccountable judges and linking our destiny with that of a sclerotic Europe that tries to achieve the impossible by uniting countries as diverse as Germany and Greece?

Up to this point the piece is clearly aimed at the paper's entire readership, but as the editorial proceeds it becomes increasingly obvious that other, much more specific readers are being indirectly addressed, that is, those leading Conservatives with a track record of Euroscepticism who, *The Mail* clearly believes, should have the courage to stand up to the party leader and put principle before political expediency. Just as Amery's shouted challenge to Arthur Greenwood in 1939 set in motion a revolt that shamed the prime minister into honouring Britain's commitment to Poland, so *The Mail's* provocative headline was intended to shame leading Tories into rebelling against David Cameron.

Names are named. Boris Johnson – still to declare his position and therefore not yet good old BoJo – is 'happy to play flirtatious footsie with the 'out' campaign' but is likely to support Cameron 'at the first whiff of a plum Cabinet job'. Former Tory leader William Hague is another 'Eurosceptic leopard to change his spots', Foreign Secretary Philip Hammond is a 'once outspoken Eurosceptic' backing Cameron, and Home Secretary Theresa May 'appears to have been bought off by the EU's professed willingness to crack down on sham marriages and make it easier to turn away criminal migrants'. That leading Conservatives are suspected of 'finding the allure of office more appealing than the duty to speak up for their country' is presented as morally reprehensible since it leaves the Brexit case to people of questionable competence outside the party, including 'the dismal ratbag of policy-wonks, cranks and nonentities (almost all male) in the feuding factions of the 'out' camp'. For *The Mail* the only people who can be entrusted to lead the Battle of Brexit are senior Conservatives willing to stab their leader in the back.

The message to voters is that the referendum represents a defining moment in British history, and the parallels with 2 September 1939 remind prominent Conservative MPs that their duty is to defy their leader just as the Commons once challenged Neville Chamberlain. The *Daily Mail*, always among the Tory Party's most reliable supporters, now takes on the role of kingmaker, using allusions to a literal war to incite a metaphorical civil war and the overthrow of the party leader.

The day before *The Mail* editorial *The Sun* also evoked the Second World War with the headline *Who do EU think you are kidding Mr Cameron?* (Newton Dunn 2016). The headline is a reference to the song *Who do you think you are kidding, Mr Hitler?* (composed by Jimmy Perry and Derek Taverner, and performed by the Second World War comic Bud Flanagan), the signature tune to the BBC sitcom *Dad's Army*, which is about the war-time Home Guard. This consisted of volunteers who were either too young or too old for the regular army, whose main role was to patrol places where the Germans might try to infiltrate troops, either on coastal sites or by parachute drops. The comedy series is about the bungling exploits of men who meant well but whose existence probably did not unduly worry the Third Reich, and Newton Dunn's headline portrays David Cameron as incompetent rather than wicked after he had failed to secure significant changes to immigration policy following lengthy negotiations with EU partners. This impression of bumbling ineptitude is reinforced by a photo montage of the khaki-uniformed cast of *Dad's Army* with the superimposed faces of Cameron and his better known ministers.

Two years earlier *The Sun* had used almost the same headline (Wooding 2014), the only variation being the conventional pronoun *you* instead of the *you/EU* pun. On that occasion the link to *Dad's Army* was occasioned by Nigel Farage's description of Cameron as a 'stupid boy', the epithet regularly applied to the sitcom's youthful Private Pike by his commanding officer, Captain Mainwaring. In 2014 Cameron's alleged stupidity was evident in his futile attempt to block the nomination of Jean-Claude Juncker as president of the European Commission when, according to Farage, the appointment was already a done deal. As it turned out, twenty-six member states voted for Juncker, with only Hungary joining Britain in opposing his nomination. For Farage this had exposed the prime minister's lack of influence in Europe and had made him look 'like Private Pike, the stupid boy, and everyone's laughing at him'. Not content with using practically the same headline twice, *The Sun* then updated the 2014 article on 6 April 2016.

The appointment with history was bound to generate appeals to voters to make Britain great again, and Emma Pullen (2016), CEO of The British Hovercraft Company, duly provided a headline, lead and opening paragraphs that linked the country's wartime spirit with the interests of British businesses today.

Leaving the EU will make Britain great once again

The British showed the world what we are made of in 1940.

I believe that fire still burns in our hearts and I pray that June 23 will be the day when Britain once again becomes Great Britain. I'm passionately excited about this huge opportunity we have to take back control of our country, take our place on the world stage and build a bright future for British businesses to flourish outside the EU.

But it is not just my business head that wants to leave the EU – my heart does too. I'm extremely proud of my late father, who fought at Tobruk,

Libya, in 1941. He wasn't a hero, just a lad from Chatham who knew what had to be done and got on with it in that stolid way his generation did.

When the head and heart have a shared objective, and the owner of said organs is 'passionately excited' and motivated by the fire of 1940 that 'still burns', the reader might expect the road to renewed greatness to be a well-lit highway. Reading on, however, it turns out to be the familiar path of liberating British businesses from EU regulations.

As noted earlier in this work, the right-wing *Daily Express*, which in normal circumstances cannot find even the most grudging word of approval for anything the Labour Party does, was quite willing to let the Lexit voice be heard. Brendan Chilton (2016), leader of the Labour Leave campaign, seized the opportunity to make an impassioned appeal in *The Express* for a return to the values of a historical period the country can be proud of, not the Second World War, but the post-war Labour governments of Clement Attlee and Harold Wilson that created the National Health Service and enacted enlightened legislation in such areas as workers' rights, equal pay and race relations before Britain joined the EEC. In contrast the EU, which imposes austerity upon Greece, Portugal and Italy and conducts secret negotiations with the United States over the TTIP, is presented as a reactionary institution intent on reversing the hard-won reforms of the twentieth century. Where the top-down mindset of the *Daily Mail* urges senior Tories to replace Cameron with one of their own, Chilton's bottom-up view of things leads him to use imagery of class struggle in correctly predicting Labour voters' drift towards Leave and deploring the party hierarchy's loss of contact with the base.

Up to 40 per cent of Labour voters are set to vote Leave on June 23 – and this figure will rise. It is extremely embarrassing to see senior Labour figures bowing to the EU as if it were a compassionate deity handing out rights to grateful serfs.

In doing so, these grandees are blindly ignoring the history of the British Labour and trade union movement and all that it has achieved for working people in the UK and abroad. It was Labour and trade union figures who won the rights for working people in this country – not the EU.

It is unlikely that Richard Desmond, owner of *Express Newspapers*, and his editor, Hugh Whittow, have particularly fond memories of the Labour and moderate Conservative governments between 1945 and Thatcher's victory in 1979, but Brendan Chilton's anti-EU stance evidently overrode certain ideological differences.

On the eve of voting day *The Sun* reported on leading Brexiteers' final efforts to drum up support (Hawkes et al. 2016) and, predictably, it was Boris Johnson who found the most grandiloquent terminology to describe the pivotal moment in history and, less predictably, heap praise upon the wisdom and courage of *Sun* readers.

Sun readers have the future of our country in their hands. They represent the best of Britain, the best of British instinct, and I know they believe in our great country and I hope very much they want to take our country forward tomorrow on a path toward greater democracy, greater openness to trade with the rest of the world and a more dynamic future for Britain.

They know the brave cross they put on the ballot paper can make the difference between restoring democracy to Europe or remaining shackled to Europe. It will be a historic moment.

It is time to take the chains off the giant, unshackled Britannia and let the Lion roar again!

In the same piece, Priti Patel is reported as warning in rather less bombastic terms that the referendum represents the 'last chance to keep our democracy' and Michael Gove is cited proclaiming that a victory for Remain would be 'game over' for Britain since the EU would never reform itself. But Hawkes et al. return to BoJo for his assurance that voting Leave, far from being a leap into the dark, was actually a 'stride into the light' because beyond the confines of the European Union there was 'a great sunlit meadow'.

As noted above it was difficult for Remain campaigners to produce inspirational rhetoric when their message was essentially that it was better to just leave things as they were. A notable exception was *The Mirror*'s unsigned editorial on 18 June 2016 headlined *Make the EU Referendum Victory in Europe Day and vote Remain for the sake of the future*, which also refers to the Second World War but focuses less on Britain's victory than on the subsequent peace in Europe. Below the headline and lead is a republished cartoon by Philip Zec (1909–1983) depicting a wounded soldier before a ruined landscape handing over a laurel representing 'victory and peace', and saying 'Here you are. Don't lose it again!'. The *Daily Mirror* published it twice in 1945, once on Victory in Europe Day on 8 May, then again on 5 July, the date of the first post-war general election, with an editorial urging people to vote on behalf of the men who had given their lives in the conflict and opt for the Labour Party's commitment to building a more just society.

In June 2016 Zec's cartoon is compared with an image of someone in a similar pose to that of the wounded soldier and bearing a laurel representing 'stability and a place in Europe'. There are fundamental differences, however, for in the updated version the person depicted is a healthy young woman who, in a society that offers far greater equality of opportunity, is dressed as a construction worker with overalls, helmet, goggles and fluorescent jacket, while in the background there is a well-maintained housing estate and a sunny sky. It is perhaps no coincidence that the woman in the second cartoon bears a certain resemblance to Jo Cox, the Labour MP murdered four days earlier by Thomas Mair, a man with a history of involvement with far-right nationalist groups.

The juxtaposition of the two cartoons is most effective, and the conclusion to the fairly short editorial proves that Remainers could also claim to have an appointment with history.

The referendum is not just about our previous history. Where you put your X on the ballot paper is about making our own history.

It is not about our past but how we forge our future. And it is a once in a lifetime opportunity.

This is truly the battle for Britain. Make Thursday Victory in Europe Day.

Where both the pro-Remain *Mirror* and the pro-Leave *Mail, Express* and *Sun* ignored recent history was in claiming that the 2016 referendum represented a once-in-a-lifetime opportunity for the public to have a direct say in their country's destiny. As Denmark demonstrated in 1992 and 1993 over the Maastricht Treaty, and Ireland in 2001 and 2002 over the Treaty of Nice, a referendum result could trigger further negotiations and agreement upon opt-out clauses, followed by a second referendum and a different outcome. In Britain's case the time span between the two referenda was much longer, and the voting switch was in the opposite direction from that in Denmark and Ireland, but there were notable similarities in some of the issues discussed in the two campaigns.

11

Little Englanders or reaching out to the world beyond Europe? Comparison with the 1975 referendum on remaining a member of the European Economic Community

Remainers often portrayed Brexit supporters as Little Englanders nostalgic for a Britain that was militarily and economically powerful enough not to need to pay much heed to anyone else. Leavers retaliated with the claim that it was the EU that had a self-absorbed perspective, an almost provincial approach, while Brexit meant reaching out to the world beyond the 28-nation bloc. Comparisons were made between the 2016 referendum and that of 1975 on whether to remain a member of the European Economic Community (EEC), at the time usually called the Common Market. Remain supporters hoped that, as in 1975, common sense and realism would prevail over isolationism

and self-delusion, while Leavers argued that the EU had become a very different animal from the free-trade zone that was the old EEC.

On 31 July 1961, Prime Minister Harold Macmillan announced to the
House of Commons that Britain was to apply for membership of the EEC,
which then consisted of six states: West Germany, France, Italy, Belgium, the
Netherlands and Luxembourg. This marked quite a turnaround on the part
of the Conservative government, which just four years earlier had declined to
sign the Treaty of Rome. Macmillan appointed Edward Heath, who had been
several years ahead of the party in advocating EEC membership, as chief negotiator with Brussels.

Labour's conversion came a few years later and was never as wholehearted
as the Tories' desire to get Britain into the Common Market. A little over a
year after Macmillan's announcement, the leader of the Labour Party, Hugh
Gaitskell (1962), speaking at the party conference, noted that the EEC's
Common Agricultural Policy would oblige Britain to import food from member states at higher prices than those offered by Commonwealth nations, but
saved his strongest attack for the question of sovereignty. The basis of his argument was that the EEC was far more than a customs union but was actually the
first step leading towards a political federation in which the UK would be no
more than a state within a United States of Europe, just as Texas and California
were states belonging to the United States. It would mean 'the end of Britain
as an independent nation state', and would inevitably result in the collapse of
the Commonwealth.

> We must be clear about this: it does mean, if this is the idea, the end of
> Britain as an independent European state. I make no apology for repeating
> it. It means the end of a thousand years of history. You may say 'Let it end'
> but, my goodness, it is a decision that needs a little care and thought. And
> it does mean the end of the Commonwealth. How can one really seriously
> suppose that if the mother country, the centre of the Commonwealth, is a

province of Europe (which is what federation means) it could continue to exist as the mother country of a series of independent nations? It is sheer nonsense.

The parallels with UKIP's continual references to the EU superstate are obvious; Gaitskell warned of the dangers of ceding sovereignty and losing control while the Brexiteers campaigned on a platform of regaining both. Gaitskell's choice of the word *province* drew attention to the UK's loss of international stature in a European federation while the pro-Brexit press imagined a confident, independent Britain assuming a leading role on the world stage once again. By 1962 it was already clear that the newly independent nations of the Commonwealth did not feel that they had to defer to 'the mother country'; in the previous year they had expelled South Africa's apartheid regime without worrying too much about what the Westminster government thought. In 2016 Brexiteers' were confident that Britain would have no difficulty negotiating deals with the Commonwealth nations despite the fact that they had for decades been trading with the rest of the world.

President Charles De Gaulle of France was suspicious of Britain's close relationship with the United States – Hattersley (1998: 144) goes so far as to talk of his fear of 'an Anglo-Saxon conspiracy to rule the world' – and not everyone was surprised when in January 1963 he vetoed the UK's first attempt to join the Common Market. Momentum was not lost, however; after Labour narrowly won the general election of 1964 and increased its majority seventeen months later, Prime Minister Harold Wilson and most of his cabinet had come round to the view that Britain's future was as part of the EEC. The second application to join the Common Market was made in 1967, and de Gaulle again used his veto. By this time, however, becoming a member of the EEC was favoured by nearly all of the Conservative Party, a majority of Labour MPs (although a significant number, mostly but not exclusively on the left wing of the party, continued to oppose entry), all the newspapers with the exception of the low-circulation *Morning Star*, the CBI and an increasing number of trade unionists. It was just a question of waiting until de Gaulle departed from the scene, and he duly obliged by resigning from office in 1969 and dying shortly afterwards. His successor, Georges Pompidou, did not oppose British entry, and when the Conservatives led by the committed European, Edward Heath, won the general election of 1970, there was little doubt that the EEC was soon to expand. The Treaty of Accession was signed in January 1972, Parliament passed the necessary legislation during the course of the year, and on 1 January 1973 the UK, the Republic of Ireland and Denmark become full members of the EEC.

This was not the end of the story, of course. When Harold Wilson returned to Downing Street in 1974 his main concern was a domestic economy reeling from the effects of the decision by the Organization of Petroleum Exporting Countries (OPEC) to raise the price of oil by 400 per cent, and the split within his party over Europe was something he wanted to deal with once and for all. He opted for the strategy of opposing Britain's membership of the EEC 'on Tory terms', engaging in renegotiations with Brussels, then allowing the British people to vote in a referendum on whether they wished to stay in the Common Market under what he would present as significantly improved terms. It was far less of a risk than David Cameron's gamble in 2016 in that a series of opinion polls indicated that in the 1960s and early 1970s EEC membership was not something the electorate had particularly strong opinions about, and most 'were disposed to take their cues on the Market from the political party they currently supported' (King, 1977: 30). With a majority of Conservative voters already likely to vote to remain in the EEC, Wilson was confident that he and leading figures in the party, backed by the media, would be able to persuade a sufficient number of Labour supporters that the renegotiated terms were right for Britain. He had calculated correctly: after negotiations involving, among other things, changes to the Common Agricultural Policy and certain exclusions for Britain regarding value added tax, continued membership of the EEC was approved by 3,724,000 voters against 1,986,000 wishing to leave.

An obvious similarity between the two referenda was the fact that the vast majority of the electorate was incapable of making an informed choice. When the evolutionary biologist Richard Dawkins (2016) wrote that David Cameron was 'recklessly playing Russian Roulette with our future' by allowing 'ignoramuses' like himself to have a say in such a complex issue as membership of the EU, he was unconsciously echoing King's (1977: 93) comment upon the 1975 result that 'the details of the new terms were far too complicated for most voters to grasp; indeed, there were probably not more than two or three hundred people in the entire country who could describe them in detail, even in outline'. In 1975, voters were influenced by the politicians they most trusted (or mistrusted least), and the campaign to leave the EEC was led by left-wing MPs like Tony Benn and Michael Foot, who were viewed as less authoritative than Wilson and Heath and who also suffered the embarrassment of being on the same side as the right-wing, anti-immigration former Conservative minister Enoch Powell. In 2016 the sober, authoritative figures were again on the side of Remain, but the more swashbuckling approach and colourful language of Nigel Farage and Boris Johnson evidently had more impact on voters who, lacking the competence to make rational decisions based on evaluation of technical details, were bound to follow their gut feelings.

From Britain's first attempts to join the EEC, there were some who portrayed anti-Common Marketeers as Little Englanders out of touch with the post-war zeitgeist and the emerging generation of young and youngish Britons who felt European and had an internationalist outlook. Richard Weight (2002, cited by Dominic Sandbrook 2007: 389) quotes Lord Chalfont, Wilson's chief negotiator during the ill-fated bid to join the EEC in 1967, reassuring the Council of Europe that public support for the whole European project was strengthening:

I hope no one will be deceived by the trivialities of Carnaby Street and much of 'Swinging London'. Behind all this there is, rising in my country, a generation of young men and women, tired of humbug, angry with social inequality, sickened by war, and resolved to do something about it. To these young people the future that lies within . . . the European idea is as exciting as anything that has happened in the long and vivid history of Britain.

Anthony King (1977: 38), referring to the Labour Party's divisions over Europe in the early 1970s, oversimplifies the issue as follows: 'The anti-Europeans, in one way or another, resisted the modern world; the pro-Europeans, by contrast, accepted it.'

As noted in Chapter 5, four decades later the former president of the National Union of Students, Megan Dunn (2016), identified the Remain stance with youth and the modern world, presenting her own generation as internationalist by nature, scarcely conscious of national frontiers and hard-wired to think globally (Dunn's demographic and their reactions to the referendum result are considered in Chapter 14).

Brexit supporters did not meekly accept the accusation that they were old-fashioned, inward-looking Little Englanders. Indeed, as we saw in Chapter 3, among the slogans used by the Better Off Out campaign, one of the most effective turned the accusation on its head and claimed that it was the Leavers who were the real internationalists: 'No to the European Union, Yes to the Wider World'.

Similarly, in 1975 a black-and-white poster used by anti-Common Marketeers featured Barbara Castle, the secretary of state for health and social services, shopping baskets comparing grocery prices in London and Brussels, and the slogan 'Out & Into the World'.

If Leave stressed the momentousness of the choice facing the British people in June 2016, in June 1975 it was Harold Wilson, urging the public to vote to stay in the EEC, who alluded to an appointment with history, a decision that would have profound consequences for generations to come (*The Times*, 5 June 1975, cited by King 1977: 117).

> Tomorrow is the decisive day in the affairs of our people. When all the arguments have died down and this campaign comes to an end and when the dust has finally settled, tomorrow's decision will be seen not just as a vote, but as a vote about the future of our young people, our children and those who come after them.

As noted earlier, in 1975 the national newspapers with significant circulation figures were all in favour of staying in the EEC. King (ibid. 134, 135) gives a summary of press reaction when the decisive vote to stay in Europe was announced. Headlines included:

YES! MILLION TIMES YES (*Evening Standard*)
MESSAGE RECEIVED (*Daily Mirror*)
EUROPEANS! (*Daily Express*)
YES! (*Daily Mail*)
GOOD! NOW LET'S ALL GET CRACKING (*The Sun*)

The Times quoted the home secretary and future president of the European Commission, Roy Jenkins, who made the kind of reference to the Second World War that in 2016 was more characteristic of the Leave camp. He described the referendum result as 'a second D-Day for British resurgence in Europe based not on sulky acquiescence but on enthusiastic cooperation'.

In an untypical display of fair play, the Conservative *Daily Telegraph* congratulated the Labour prime minister, whose referendum gamble had 'paid off handsomely', producing a result that was 'quite frankly, a triumph for Mr. Wilson'.

King did not have the benefit of hindsight when he reached a conclusion that proved to be spectacularly mistaken (ibid. 137):

The most important single consequence of Britain's 'yes' vote on June 5, 1975, was to place Britain's membership of the Common Market beyond any doubt. The fact that the vote was a democratic one, together with the size of the pro-European majority, gave Britain's membership in the EEC a legitimacy that nothing else could possibly have done. The question of British Common Market membership had been on the agenda for nearly a generation. Suddenly, and permanently, it was struck off.

What King could not possibly predict was that well before the end of the century a British prime minister would have a bitter, long-lasting confrontation with the president of the European Commission, and that this conflict would sow the seeds for a rift within the Conservative Party that would culminate in the blue-on-blue clash of the 2016 referendum campaign. It was under Jacques Delors' presidency that the Exchange Rate Mechanism (ERM), the first stage of a process intended to lead to monetary union, was created. Margaret Thatcher, much to the chagrin of her own cabinet, made it abundantly clear that the UK would never sign up to a single European currency under her watch. But there was something about Delors' vision of Europe that antagonized Thatcher even more than the ERM. For Roy Hattersley (1998: 356, 357), a committed European and a leading figure in the Labour opposition of the 1980s, the conflict was ideological and had at its core Jacques Delors' concept of a social Europe.

> Monetary union was not his only ambition. He came to represent the aspiration for a 'people's Europe'. The idea was French as well as socialist. At the 1989 meeting of European socialist leaders, President Mitterrand had told the British delegate that he would veto the implementation of the Single Market in 1992 if Margaret Thatcher refused to accept the Community's 'social dimension'. Predictably, she would not endorse and he did not veto. But at the Trades Union Congress on 9 September 1988, Jacques Delors set out a vision of Europe that earned him a standing ovation and confirmed

the Tory leadership's worst fears. European union might one day become a vehicle for reinstating all the apparatus of socialism – consultation, consensus and regulation – which Margaret Thatcher had laboured for ten years to dismantle in the United Kingdom.

Thanks to Delors the Labour Party became enthusiastically pro-European as its leaders came to see Brussels as a bulwark of social justice against the onslaught of Thatcherism. In the Conservative Party, on the other hand, a Eurosceptic faction emerged, grew rapidly, made life a misery for Thatcher's successor, John Major, and made it impossible for the party to present a coherent approach to Europe up to and beyond the referendum of 2016. Certain newspapers that had had a pro-EEC stance in 1975 enthusiastically backed Thatcher in her confrontation with Delors, and continue to attack Brussels to this day. Among them is *The Sun*, which has gone from 'GOOD! NOW LET'S ALL GET CRACKING' to headlines of a very different nature.

12

From 'Up Yours Delors' (1990) to 'Stick it up your Juncker' (2016). Was it *The Sun* wot won it once again?

In a previous chapter it was noted that the *Daily Mail* today flaunts its patriotic credentials and makes frequent references to the armed services' heroics during the Second World War, studiously avoiding any reminder of its owner's admiration for Adolf Hitler in the 1930s. It is equally ironic that *The Sun* has for decades been a powerful voice for the right even though it began life in 1964 as a relaunch of the left-wing *Daily Herald*. The *Daily Herald* was originally only published intermittently to support strikers during periods of industrial action; then in 1922 it became the official newspaper of the Trades Union Congress (TUC) and was published daily. It continued to support the Labour Party after the TUC sold 51 per cent of its stake to Odhams Press, and at its peak was the UK's most popular newspaper, selling up to two million copies a day. In 1961 Odhams was taken over by Daily Mirror Newspapers Ltd, who then formed the International Publishing Group (IPC). In 1964 the TUC sold its 49 per cent, which gave IPC total control and allowed it to rebrand the newspaper as *The Sun*. *The Sun* originally aimed to be an independent, non-partisan paper, and it remained politically neutral for a few years after its acquisition by Rupert Murdoch's News Corporation Group in 1969 (although the switch to tabloid format was immediate, and the first page-3 girls appeared shortly afterwards).

The real change came in the late 1970s when *The Sun* openly supported Margaret Thatcher and contributed to her first general election victory in 1979. *The Sun* approved of all aspects of Thatcherism, including the policy of confrontation with the unions, and during the long and bitter miners' strike (March 1984 to March 1985) made no pretence of giving balanced reporting of the frequent clashes between pickets and the police. On 14 June 1984, the successor to the TUC's *Daily Herald* attempted to use the punning headline 'Mine Fuhrer' above a photo of Arthur Scargill, the leader of the National Union of Mineworkers, as he waved to a group of strikers, a wave that was interpreted by *The Sun* as a Nazi salute. Neither the headline nor the photo were seen by the public because the newspaper's unionized printers refused to handle them, but the front page article went ahead with the alternative, and untypically wordy, headline: 'Members of all The Sun production chapels refused to handle the Arthur Scargill picture and major headline on our lead story. The Sun has decided, reluctantly, to print the paper without either' (Montague 2012).

During Thatcher's eleven years and seven months in Downing Street, the circulation of *The Sun* was around the four million mark, so its influence on public opinion was much appreciated by the prime minister. Her successor, John Major, unexpectedly won the 1992 general election with a majority of just twenty-one seats. *The Sun* had no doubt about its own role in tipping the balance sufficiently to secure Major's narrow victory; on the day after the election its front page boasted 'It's the Sun wot won it', a headline that twenty years later even Rupert Murdoch admitted was 'tasteless and wrong' and for which the News Corporation boss gave his editor at the time, Kelvin MacKenzie, 'a hell of a bollocking' (Dowell 2012). Tasteless and wrong it may have been but it also proved to be memorable, and variations upon it were still in use in analyses of *The Sun's* influence on David Cameron's victory in the general election of 2015. It exhibits two typical features of *Sun* headlines: simple, monosyllabic vocabulary plus slang and/or deliberately ungrammatical English intended to present Britain's best-selling tabloid as the voice of ordinary working people.

Puns are another characteristic of *Sun* headlines and Thatcher's confrontation with the president of the European Commission, particularly her hostility towards the ECU (European Currency Unit) as a key step in the direction of monetary union, inspired a play on the surname Delors that has also entered the annals of tabloid journalism. In November 1990 the president of the European Commission was told 'UP YOURS DELORS' and treated to a photo of two raised fingers, a front page that an unrepentant *Sun* republished twenty-five years later (Parsons 2015) and in April 2016 updated on its website when the referendum campaign was heating up. Many Britons no longer in their first flush of youth remember the infamous headline, but the offensiveness and explicit racism of the lead and the article itself may not be so readily recalled. In the lines quoted below, the graphological features of the original text have been retained.

UP YOURS DELORS

At midday tomorrow Sun readers are urged to tell the French fool where to stuff his ECU

The Sun today calls on its patriotic family of readers to tell the feelthy French to FROG OFF!

They **INSULT** us, **BURN** our lambs, **FLOOD** our country with dodgy food and **PLOT** to abolish the dear old pound.

Now it's your turn to kick **THEM** in the Gauls.

We want you to tell Froggie Common Market chief Jacques Delors exactly what you think of him and his countrymen.

At the stroke of noon tomorrow, we invite all true blue Brits to face France and yell 'Up Yours, Delors.'

The ear-bashing from our millions of readers will wake the EC President up to the fact that he will **NEVER** run our country.

Racial slurs for Delors and the entire population of France include the traditional insults *frog* and *froggie*, *feelthy* as a derisive imitation of French speakers' pronunciation of English vowels (in contrast, mispronouncing the name *Delors* to produce the rhyme in the headline is all right), and the crude pun associating *Gauls* with *balls*. Later in the article a pun on *bastards* and *Bastille* is used to warn us that after completion of the Channel Tunnel 'the garlic-breathed bastilles will be here in droves'.

Two of the four words printed in bold capitals in the second paragraph require some explanation: *burn* is a reference to a demonstration by French farmers against imported British livestock in which a lorry transporting lambs from the UK was torched; *flood* exaggerates the quantity of unpasteurized French cheese exported to Britain, some of which had been found to contain listeria bacteria (Belam 2007). Naturally, *The Sun* also goes much further back into history to include the obligatory references to Waterloo and the France that surrendered in the Second World War 'when we stood firm'.

Many would say that the article amounts to incitement to racial hatred. Twenty-five years later, however, Parsons (2015) is anything but apologetic and states that the 1990 front page could just as easily have been headlined 'Frog Off'. He argues that history has shown that Jacques Delors was utterly wrong while Margaret Thatcher 'was right too soon' in that she had correctly seen that the European Community was heading for disaster long before the less presentient cabinet colleagues who plotted her downfall.

Delors won his feud with Thatcher but the ultimate Little European has, in the end, lost the argument. Like many bad ideas, the European Union has been found to be a running sore on the face of humanity.

Obviously the description of Delors as 'the ultimate Little European' seeks to turn on its head the Little Englander jibe frequently aimed at Brexit supporters. Parsons concludes by informing us that the 90-year-old Delors 'is still a familiar face at swanky Paris restaurants and clubs' whose think-tank, the Jacques Delors Institute, 'is gobbling up vast sums of public money'.

Marwick (1996: 487) reports that on 6 June 1994, the fiftieth anniversary of D-Day, a *Sun* leader entitled *We're Still Fighting in Europe* presented Britain's relationship with Europe as a continuation of the war-time struggle to preserve our independence and democracy:

> Our role in Europe in 1994 may not be as it was in 1944.
>
> But we are still fighting dictators – the Eurocrats who want us to bow to their laws and life-styles.
>
> Your vote in Thursday's Euro elections is a blow in the battle to keep our country British.
>
> Not a suburb of Brussels.

Over four decades racial abuse aimed at French politicians, and by extension all of France, has not only been prompted by Britain's uneasy relationship with the European Community/Union. *The Sun* supported George W. Bush's decision to invade Iraq in 2003 and praised the British prime minister, Tony Blair, for having committed British troops to the 'coalition of the willing'. President Jacques Chirac's strong opposition to this military intervention led *The Sun* to produce a special edition with a front page in French bearing the headline 'CHIRAC EST UN VER' along with a photomontage of the French president's head superimposed upon the body of a giant worm (Byrne 2003). Two thousand copies of this special edition were distributed in Paris on 20 February 2003, so that Parisians could read, in their own language, what *The Sun* claimed was the opinion of the British people:

Greetings to the people of Paris from the Sun newspaper, which is read by 10 million people every day.

We think your president, Jacques Chirac, is a disgrace to Europe by constantly threatening to veto military action to enforce the will of the UN against Iraq.

British people feel M Chirac, who in the UK is known as the 'worm', is arrogantly strutting about trying to make France seem more important than it really is.

On behalf of our ten million readers, we say to you today: are you not ashamed of your president?

That President Chirac was ever nicknamed the worm in the UK will come as a surprise to all British residents other than those directly involved in designing the provocative front page distributed on 20 February 2003. Having coined the moniker, however, *The Sun* went on to use it forty-nine times over the following twelve months (Chovanec 2010). Less surprising is the reference to Chirac's 'arrogantly strutting about', arrogance being one of the character traits traditionally ascribed to the French according to the negative stereotype constantly recycled by all of Britain's right-wing tabloids. To claim that the president wants to make France seem more important than it is in reality is breathtakingly hypocritical coming from a paper that frequently evokes the UK's finest hour and sees Britain as having lasting clout on the world stage by virtue of its involvement in US-led military operations. The sheer effrontery of *The Sun*'s headline is matched only by its counterproductivity; the insult prompted French people who had not voted for Chirac to rally to his defence.

Although Rupert Murdoch's *Sun* became a right-wing, anti-Brussels newspaper that adored Margaret Thatcher, it also supported Labour's pro-Europe Tony Labour during his ten years as prime minister. This was partly because Murdoch likes to back winners, and after Blair's landslide victory in 1997 it was clear that he was likely to be in power for a considerable time. In addition, his strongly pro-Washington foreign policy and his business-friendly economic strategy meant that he was anything but a socialist. The main consideration, however, was the fact that Tony Blair, having seen the way *The Sun* had demonized the Labour Party leader Neil Kinnock in 1992, had no intention of antagonizing Rupert Murdoch or any other newspaper proprietor. Labour's 1992 election manifesto included the promise to trigger an investigation into media concentration by the Monopolies and Mergers Commission; Tony Blair made sure that his party did not go into the 1997 campaign handicapped by a manifesto commitment that was sure to provoke the hostility of the head of News Corporation (Freedman 2015).

The 'Calais Jungle' gave *The Sun* the opportunity to attack the incompetent French and their 'soft' president (François Hollande this time), laud the vastly superior law enforcement measures on the British side of the Channel and join the other right-wing tabloids in talking up the danger posed by migrants hoping to find a way to enter the UK. In a piece first published in 2015 but updated in April 2016 for the referendum campaign, Matt Wilkinson sees French ineptitude as a threat to Britain's security. Naturally, the headline contains a pun: an allusion to the invented word *Supercalifragilisticexpialidocious*, the title of a song written by Richard M. and Robert B. Sherman for the 1964 film *Mary Poppins*.

Softy Calais goes ballistic . . . Frenchies are atrocious
MIGRANT CRISIS: Call to send in our Army

A Police boss last night called for the British Army to be sent in to halt the flood of migrants trying to swarm through the Channel Tunnel at Calais.

It came as the French government, led by Francois Hollande, was accused of going soft on thousands who have laid siege to the train terminal, breaking through fences and fighting running battles with police.

An extra 150 riot police were drafted in as the Home Secretary Theresa May met her French counterpart and held a Cobra meeting to discuss the crisis, which saw a migrant killed beneath a truck on Tuesday.

But police in France have been accused of driving captured migrants a mile from the terminal and freeing them for new border assaults.

As more illegal immigrants massed last night, Kevin Hurley – the police and crime commissioner for Surrey – called for Gurkha soldiers based at Folkestone's Shorncliffe barracks to be sent in.

Mr Hurley, whose area includes a services where he claims 100 migrants recently tried to get off lorries, said: 'The Gurkhas are a highly respected and competent force and just around the corner. They could help to ensure that our border is not breached.'

Reactions to the puns used by *The Sun* are necessarily subjective and the headline to this article might draw a smile even from people who despise the paper's portrayal of the Calais migrants. The humour is not extended beyond the headline, however, as in the first two sentences of the article we have the usual image of natural disaster ('flood of migrants'), the dehumanizing of the asylum-seekers ('swarms') and quasi-military terms ('laid siege', 'running battles'). The main target of Wilkinson's attack is, of course, the incompetence of the 'Frenchies', whose government is accused of 'going soft' and whose police are presented as weak. The solution proposed by Kevin Hurley – the deployment of British troops on foreign soil – would be little short of an act of war, and to a moderately reflective reader the fact that a senior police officer could say something so ridiculous is more worrying than the alleged shortcomings of law enforcers in France.

While always quick to draw attention to French inadequacy, *The Sun* has never neglected the danger within, and in November 2015, days after coordinated terrorist attacks in Paris killed 130 people and injured many others, the threat represented by British Muslims was announced by the headline *1 in 5 Brit Muslims' sympathy for jihadis.* The article has since been taken down from *The Sun*'s site after an investigation by the Independent Press Standards Organisation (IPSO) found that it was based on wilful misinterpretation of poll findings (Worley 2016). The newspaper was instructed to publish IPSO's adjudication, which it duly did in March 2016. It is unlikely that the editor of *The Sun* was particularly bothered about having to do this; as we noted with Matt Wilkinson's article on the Calais Jungle, *The Sun* sometimes updated an article published in 2015 or earlier if it was relevant to the 2016 referendum campaign, so IPSO's ruling, which was widely reported in other newspapers and on various websites with an image of the original front page, meant that the November 2015 article received a second airing just as the Brexit debate was becoming intense. For a newspaper that thrives on notoriety and controversy, it is often – though not quite always – the case that there is no such thing as bad publicity.

Jean-Claude Juncker ticks most of the boxes to be a prime target for *The Sun* except for the fact that he is not French, although as a French-speaking Luxembourger he is the next best – or next worst – thing. In June 2014 Emily Ashton used the headline *Stick it up your Juncker*, an obvious pun on the idiomatic expression *stick it up your jumper* in which *jumper* substitutes for a more vulgar term. The occasion was the need to choose a successor to José Manuel Barroso as president of the European Commission and Angela Merkel's backing of Juncker's candidature. Ashton writes: 'Eurocrat Mr Juncker is viewed as the heir to Jacques Delors – who infuriated Margaret Thatcher by trying to force closer EU integration, inspiring our famous 1990 headline "Up Yours Delors!"'. In addition she gives an unflattering summary of Juncker's record as prime minister of Luxembourg, notes his declared preference for secret talks rather than public debates and cites rumours about his heavy drinking. David Cameron strongly believed that making Juncker president of the European Commission would weaken his own position and, according to Ashton, issued a warning to the German chancellor that turned out to be prophetic.

Mr Cameron is said to have told the German leader Angela Merkel last week that it would force him to bring forward his in-out referendum from 2017 to calm his Eurosceptic MPs.

This would likely lead to Britain voting No to EU membership as the PM would not have had time to show he can reform Brussels from within.

Ashton's article was updated on *The Sun*'s site in April 2016 and its headline was immediately taken up by Leave campaigners, was used by other Brexit-supporting newspapers and frequently reused by *The Sun*, and became the caption to a poster showing Cameron and Juncker with their arms raised as if about to come to blows. Jean-Claude Juncker had indeed become the heir to Jacques Delors as *The Sun*'s favourite target.

So was it *The Sun* wot won it in 2016 as it claimed to have done for John Major in 1992? As soon as the result was known Jane Martinson (2016) for *The Guardian* addressed this question, noting that a similarity between the two votes was a relatively high turnout of over 70 per cent. During the long referendum campaign there had been a lively debate, though necessarily an ill-informed one given the complexity of many of the issues involved. The pro-Leave press sometimes distorted the facts, particularly with regard to EU regulations – indeed the European Commission set up and still maintains its *Euromyths* website to set the record straight – and Martinson cites a survey showing that British readers trust their newspapers much less than their European counterparts do. However, she also refers to evidence that the newspapers still tend to set the agenda and other media then respond: 'Where the newspapers lead on issues, far more trusted broadcasters follow.' Remain campaigners wanted to focus on the economy and the benefits of tariff-free trade, but the pro-Brexit press were successful in keeping immigration high on the agenda, thus ensuring that the subject had to be discussed on television. Martinson quotes David Deacon, professor of communication and media analysis at Loughborough University, neatly summarizing the impact of the press and television on how people vote: 'The media has more influence in telling people what to think about than in what to think.' *The Sun* set out to make sure that people gave considerable thought to Britain's history of fighting to preserve liberty, the democratic deficit in the EU, allegedly excessive regulation, the danger represented by both the Calais Jungle and British Muslims, and, of course, the nefarious ways of the French.

The Sun certainly believed that it had played a crucial role in securing a no vote in the referendum and drew a parallel with the defeat of Neil Kinnock's Labour Party in 1992 that had prompted the original claim that it was *The Sun* wot won it. In January 2017, after the German newspaper *Die Welt* had used the English headline 'Little Britain' in its reaction to a speech by Theresa May on her government's Brexit strategy, *The Sun*, somewhat illogically addressing Angela Merkel rather than *Die Welt*, produced a special front page and hand-delivered it to the German Embassy in London (Gysin 2017).

A MESSAGE TO MERKEL Little Britain? We've got a simple message for the critics who ridiculed the 17.4 million of you who voted Leave for daring to dump the EU

Would the last country to leave the EU please turn out the lights

The Sun last night turned the tables on the Germans who dubbed our great nation 'Little Britain'.

In a remake of one of our most famous front pages we ask: 'Would the last country to leave the EU please turn out the lights'.

And to drum the message home, Sun man Patrick Gysin went to the German Embassy in central London to deliver a personalised front page.

The message to Merkel includes the image of a light bulb with an unflattering photo of the German chancellor inside it. The original front page from 9 April 1992 is reprinted, with its image of an unflattering shot of Neil Kinnock inside a light bulb and its message to voters: 'If Kinnock wins today will the last person to leave Britain please turn out the lights'. Neil Kinnock, the favourite according to the polls, did not win that day, and twenty-four hours later *The Sun* proudly and ungrammatically claimed credit for having engineered his defeat. Although *The Sun*'s circulation is now less than half what it was in the early 1990s, it is difficult to believe that its relentless attacks on EU institutions and leading figures, along with its stoking of anti-French sentiments, did not exert some influence on voters in 2016.

13

Dirty tricks: Lies, personal attacks and the Queen supports UKIP

For Oxford Dictionaries the Word of the Year 2016 was *post-truth*, defined as 'relating to or denoting circumstances in which objective facts are less influential in shaping public opinion than appeals to emotion and personal belief'. Coined in 1992 by the Serbian-American playwright Steve Tesich in his reflections upon the Iran-Contra scandal and the Persian Gulf War, it was chosen as the Word of 2016 because two events of that year – the US presidential campaign and the Brexit debate in Britain – led to a huge increase in frequency of use, particularly in the months from May to October. Among the shortlisted contenders for Word of the Year that *post-truth* fought off was the term *Brexiteer* (Midgley 2016).

As noted previously, only a very small percentage of the electorate possessed the knowledge and expertise to make an informed evaluation of the advantages and disadvantages of EU membership, so 'appeals to emotion and personal belief' were bound to have more impact on voters than facts and technical details that were beyond the grasp of most people. That does not justify, however, Leave's biggest lie that the UK gives the EU £350 million each week since it is quite simply dishonest accountancy to quote one side of the balance sheet and disregard the other. Similarly, Remain's dodgiest dossier of all, the White Paper entitled *The long-term economic impact of EU membership and the alternatives*, which stated that leaving the European Union would cost every British household £4,300 a year, was put together by Treasury officials and approved by the chancellor of the exchequer, so it was hardly a case of errors committed in good faith by the insufficiently informed (Congdon 2016).

In addition to the truth-checking charity *Full Fact*, *The UK in a changing Europe* project and the European Commission's site dedicated to correcting inaccurate claims promulgated in the media – all of which are mentioned earlier in this work – individual journalists also attempted to verify the credibility of assertions boldly made by both sides in the Brexit debate. John Rentoul (2016) for *The Independent* considered Remain to be more wrong than right in warning that Brexit would mean holidaymakers having to get a visa to go to Spain or claiming that outside the EU Britain would still have to absorb just as many immigrants as before, but was correct in stating that British exports would be subject to tariffs; ex-mayor of London, Boris Johnson, was correct to say that two of our EU partners have delayed the introduction of safer tipper trucks that pose less of a risk to cyclists, but was wrong to claim that German demands had held up the construction of Crossrail tunnels.

Lies often have a core of veracity in them but that truth is obscured by selective omissions or excessive emphases, exaggeration or understatement. In an interview with *The Telegraph*, Boris Johnson, never a man to avoid hyperbole, began with the reasonable observation that since the collapse of the Roman Empire the history of Europe has been characterized by attempts to unify the continent under a single government. He then threw caution to the winds with a comparison between would-be unifiers of the past and the EU's current vision of ever greater integration (Ross 2016).

Napoleon, Hitler, various people tried this out, and it ends tragically. The EU is an attempt to do this by different methods. But fundamentally what is lacking is the eternal problem, which is that there is no underlying loyalty to the idea of Europe. There is no single authority that anybody respects or understands. That is causing this massive democratic void.

In the early chapters of this book it was argued that Remain campaigners tended to hedge and use modality, and generally present their case more timidly than their Leave counterparts. Two days after Johnson's controversial interview – which was dismissed by many in Britain as just typical Johnson bombast but was viewed more seriously in Brussels – David Cameron attempted to match his old friend's rhetoric by stating that a vote to leave the EU would be welcomed by Vladimir Putin, Isis and Abu Bakr al-Baghdadi (Cooper and Wright 2016). Not for the first time Cameron had shot himself in the foot as attention was diverted from Johnson's histrionic remarks to his own no less preposterous thesis that Islamist terrorists were following the Brexit debate and rooting for Nigel Farage.

The *InFacts* website does not claim to be neutral on the EU question; during the referendum campaign its writers aimed to present the fact-based case for Britain's remaining in the EU and after the vote maintained the same approach in describing the damaging consequences of a hard Brexit. To take just one example, with the campaign in full swing the *InFacts* editor-in-chief, Hugo Dixon (2016), published a very short but persuasive piece countering Leave's insistence that the City of London would continue to thrive outside the EU, and the Mythbust and Fake News pages of the site seek to expose misleading or plainly false claims made by Brexiteers. In the final weeks of the campaign *The Guardian* twice allowed Dixon and Luke Lythgoe (2016) to reach a wider readership, first in a piece about the eight 'most toxic tales' in *The Telegraph*, *The Mail* and *The Express* that *InFacts* had reported to IPSO, then two weeks later in a follow-up article about six more claims unsupported by hard facts. In the second piece the offending articles were: a story in *The Times*, and repeated in *The Mail* and *The Express*, about secret plans to set up an EU army, a claim that was refuted by the Ministry of Defence; misquotation in *The Express* from a report by the Chartered Institute of Public Finance and Accountancy to make it appear that a £10 billion shortfall in the National Health Service budget was the consequence of immigration; a *Daily Mail* front page in which an EU *recommendation* concerning Britain's housing policy is converted into a *demand*; *The Sun's* manipulation of statistics to claim that in 2014 '4 in 5 British jobs went to foreign nationals' when the true figure was 17.5 per cent; *The Telegraph's* misquotation of a Home Office official to make the entirely false claim that Brexit would result in the deportation of three million EU citizens; misuse of the term 'migrant children' in *The Express* to denounce the soaring costs of educating '700,000' such pupils, when the figure of 700,000 actually included children born in the UK who had at least one parent from a European Economic Area (EEA) country (like Nigel Farage's offspring by his German wife).

From the above it appears that the pro-Brexit newspapers were far more likely to play fast and loose with the facts than their pro-Remain counterparts, and when it came to unequivocal falsehoods the Leave-supporting press was indeed more culpable. Project Fear, the dodgy dossiers and the dire warnings issued by political figures like Lord Mandelson and Tony Blair generally involved not outright lies but an exclusive focus on worst-case scenarios, outcomes that were conceivable but by no means probable. That is not the same thing as wilfully misquoting a report or misinterpreting statistics.

IPSO is not without its critics. On its website it describes itself as 'the independent regulator for the newspaper and magazine industry in the UK' and sees its mission as 'to support those who feel wronged by the press, to uphold the highest professional standards in the UK press, to determine whether standards have been breached and provide redress if so'. Redress typically comes in the form of obliging errant newspapers to publish corrections or adjudications. A criticism sometimes levelled at IPSO, particularly by the press campaign group *Hacked Off*, is that since it is financed by member publications, that is, by the very papers and magazines it regulates, it tends to be too tolerant of misconduct. Indeed, shortly after Leave's victory an unsigned article entitled *Brexit and the newspapers – where was IPSO?* (2016) on the *Hacked Off* website reported on a number of offensive pieces in the right-wing press that were not investigated by IPSO, and noted that even readers of *The Sun* and *Daily Mail* had complained that their own newspapers had misled them.

There is no doubt that the pro-EU press, while not impeccable, behaved much better during the campaign. However, it should also be noted that three pro-Remain newspapers – *The Independent*, *The Guardian* and the *Financial Times* – could not be reported to IPSO anyway because they had not signed up to be regulated by that organization.

Turning our attention to personal attacks, we find that here Remain supporters did not comport themselves significantly better than their adversaries. Indeed, because they directed their attacks not just at politicians and public figures who expect to be subject to rough treatment in the media, but also at the ordinary men and women who intended to vote to leave the EU, it could be argued that they were nastier.

Images, whether traditional posters or .jpg files posted on the internet, featured prominently in both sides' personal attacks. Leave tended to target Juncker and other leading figures in the Brussels establishment, sometimes naming them, often referring only to their roles. Remain preferred to attack the leading Brexiteers, evoking the disquieting prospect of a Britain in the hands of such (usually) men and (very occasionally) women. Both sides portrayed their adversaries as the kind of people you'd rather not have anything to do with.

Ironically, *The Sun*, by frequently reusing its 'Stick it up your Juncker' jibe in the run-up to the referendum, probably did far more than the Remain camp to make the president of the European Commission known to the British public. His name rarely appeared without premodification, recurrent epithets being *unelected, arrogant, Brussels bigwig, chief Eurocrat, EU boss* and *heavy drinking.*

The website of the Leave.EU movement, on the other hand, refers merely to the 'Belgian immigration minister' rather than Theo Francken in a downloadable poster that asks 'Do you really want to be a part of this club?'. The rhetorical question follows a quotation by Mr Francken which, given the ministry he heads, is particularly insensitive towards an EU partner that is doing more than its fair share to deal with a problem that involves the whole continent: 'The Greeks now need to bear the consequences of being unable to stop the migrant flow.'

Tim Martin, chairman of the J D Wetherspoon pub chain and an active Brexit supporter, addresses by name Christine Lagarde, managing director of the IMF, in an open letter published not in a poster but in a form more in keeping with the nature of his business, that is, on a beer mat. Martin distances himself from *The Sun*'s approach by beginning with a respectful 'Dear Madame Lagarde' and the polite preamble 'At Wetherspoon, we sincerely respect and admire the French people and your country', but then notes that she is due to stand trial on corruption charges, her predecessor, Dominique Strauss-Kahn, resigned in disgrace, then asks her directly why anyone should trust the IMF. The implicature is that before Madame Lagarde's trial begins, she is already as good as convicted and sentenced, and that she is in any case guilty by association with her predecessor. On the other side of the beermat more direct questions culminate in a not unreasonable enquiry as to whether the IMF thought to inform the EU that no currency in history has survived without a single government. Given that there are nearly 1,000 Wetherspoon pubs in Britain, plus the fact that beer drinkers rarely have other reading material with them, Martin's chosen medium has its merits.

Most British people can name very few European heads of government but Chancellor Merkel has held power for so long, and her country has become so dominant, that she has entered the public consciousness as no other EU leader has managed to do since Silvio Berlusconi's bunga-bunga days. Precisely because she is so recognizable, she too was targeted in poster attacks. In 2015, when the referendum was still expected to be held in 2017, thus giving David Cameron time to convince the public that his renegotiations with Brussels had addressed Eurosceptics' concerns, UKIP asked supporters to distribute a poster featuring a stern-faced Angela Merkel and the question 'What EU concessions will David Cameron win for Britain?', followed by the answer 'Whatever Angela Merkel lets him have'. Thus, with one image and fifteen words the poster presents the British prime minister as totally devoid of influence and the German chancellor as totally in command. Cameron is weak and self-deluded, Merkel strong and dictatorial.

One of the most effective images used by Remain first appeared with an article by Brian Reade (2016) for *The Mirror*, and was then downloaded from *The Mirror*'s site and widely reposted. It is a mock-up of a poster promoting Quentin Tarantino's Western movie *The Hateful Eight* with the heads of eight leading Brexiteers superimposed upon the bodies of the film's main characters. The new hateful eight are the UKIP leader Nigel Farage, the Conservative MPs Michael Gove, Boris Johnson, Iain Duncan Smith, Jacob Rees-Mogg, Chris Grayling and Priti Patel (the only woman of the odious octad), and the Labour maverick George Galloway. Reade notes that the day after the referendum, 24 June, will be the hundredth anniversary of the start of the Battle of the Somme in the First World War in which '420,000 of our troops were sent over top to be slaughtered'. Picking up on Boris Johnson's suggestion that if Leave win 24 June should be known as UK Independence Day, he feigns agreement, writing that it 'would be a perfect day to celebrate yet another occasion when this country let donkeys blindly lead lions into No Man's Land'. Thus far thus fair in that professional politicians expect to face heavy criticism and all eight of the 'Tarantino-esque' figures have been called worse things than donkeys in their time. But Reade also imagines the nature of Independence Day celebrations and evokes an image of xenophobic drunks causing mayhem.

What better than a new national holiday, kicked off with a Full English Brexit, before getting tanked up on Taunton cider and rampaging all the way to Dover, tossing Colman's mustard jars through tapas bar windows and then holding a massive two-fingered salute towards France?

In *The Independent* Paul Beaumont (2016) explicitly linked Brexit sentiments with football hooliganism. The UEFA Euro 2016 football championship was held in France from 10 June to 10 July of that year, and after England's first match against Russia, English fans clashed with riot police in Marseille. He argues that both football and the Brexit debate are about tribalism and anger, and sees the referendum as 'designed to help us choose between the Big Tribe of Europe and Little Britain'. He concludes his article as follows:

> Football gives us something to fight over, an environment in which to experience triumph and tragedy, without actually fighting; without actually going to war. But it's the same emotion that is fuelling the Brexit debate. No wonder, then, that it is boiling over into violence on the streets of Marseille.

What is interesting is the readers' feedback to Beaumont's article. One reader says *The Independent*'s linking of practically everything with Brexit is 'laughable', another states that the paper is 'beyond the pale now, akin to the *Daily Mail* but with your blind prejudices in reverse', a female reader objects to the notion that she and friends intending to vote out are like hooligans, and another states that the pro-EU *Independent* and *Guardian* are just as 'entrenched when it comes to their own ideological agenda' as *The Sun*, with the aggravating circumstance that their views come with 'a special odour of snobbery'.

Some days after the referendum Helene Guldberg (2016), co-founder and director of the online magazine *Spiked*, decided to test the stereotype of the Leave voter.

> The EU referendum result exposed the enormous disconnect between the pro-EU views of the political class, and its affluent, metropolitan supporters,

and the anti-EU views of the rest of the UK. It also exposed an enormous amount of elite snobbery towards ordinary voters. Many Remainers have been quick to dismiss those who voted to leave the EU as ignorant, foreign-hating, nationalistic bigots. They have also suggested that the issues at stake were too difficult for ordinary voters to comprehend. It's clear that many Remainers have never stepped foot in strongly pro-Brexit areas, let alone tried to find out what Leave voters really think.

So, being based in the West Midlands, an ethnically diverse region in which almost 1.8 million people voted to leave the EU compared to 1.2 million who voted to remain, I decided to meet with Brexit supporters from Birmingham, Coventry and the Black Country. I discovered that the Remainers' caricature of the Leave voter as a racist ignoramus was very far from the truth. The Leavers I spoke to were reasoned, sensible and motivated primarily by a desire for more control over their lives and more of a say on political issues.

Guldberg's interviewees were particularly indignant about the accusation of racism and all insisted that the referendum campaign had not stirred up racial tensions in their area. She quotes Richard from Birmingham, who has a French partner, describes himself as 'a big black man with dreadlocks' and believes linking Brexit to racism is 'all propaganda'. Similarly, Tanveer Khan insists that there is no more racism today than when he came to Britain twenty years ago and blames the media for 'creating divisions'.

It is possible that Remain's stigmatization of Leavers as racist chavs eventually made Brexit supporters even more determined to send a clear message to those telling them how they should think, and if that was the case it was yet another tactical error committed by the pro-EU side. *Campaign* is the trade journal of the advertising industry, and shortly after the referendum a number of advertising agencies took the unusual step of using this journal to publish a series of adverts that the Britain Stronger In Europe group had commissioned but then elected not to use. Claire Beale (2016) for *Campaign* notes that Stronger In 'had some of the country's best creatives and stategists to hand' and then chose to ignore their ideas. While the experts urged a switch to more positive campaigning, Stronger In was reluctant to abandon the Project Fear approach that had worked so well in Scotland but was clearly losing credibility in the EU debate. The result, according to Beale, was that, 'While the Leave campaigners were able to talk up all the good things about quitting the EU, Stronger In's agenda was unrelentingly negative and undynamic'. She also quotes an unnamed creative saying that there were too many decision-makers within Stronger In, too many opinions, with the consequence being 'a complete clusterfuck'.

Two days later, *The Mirror* gave further examples and details of the rejected adverts (Mullin 2016). Some were negative in the Project Fear tradition, such as a photo of a girl standing on the edge of a cliff with the question 'What will life be like, if we leave?' Others, however, reflected the focus on positives that the advertising agencies recommended; to present EU membership as beneficial to future generations, one advert showed a pregnant woman with a speech bubble coming out of her swollen tummy saying 'I'm in'.

One poster that was used, and used extensively, was produced by the pro-EU campaign group *We Are Europe*. It portrayed two men with idiosyncratic hairstyles engaged in a passionate kiss, and the style was sufficiently realistic for us to recognize them as caricatures of Donald Trump and Boris Johnson. A similar personal attack on a less robust operator than Johnson might have provoked outrage, but BoJo's reputation as a political bruiser meant that he was considered fair game, and he was frequently presented in cartoons and photographic mock-ups as a buffoon, while in his case typical premodifiers were *joker* and *clownish*.

The Kiss of Death poster attack on Johnson was effective; verbal attacks on him were liable to backfire because he tended to turn them to his own advantage. In a televised debate in June 2016 Johnson had three feisty women lined up against him: the energy secretary Amber Rudd, the leader of the SNP Nicola Sturgeon and the Labour MP Angela Eagle. *The Sun* called them 'the Gang of Three' and used the ambiguous headline 'Fighting Off The Girls' (Hawkes et al. 2016) to report on their strategy of attacking Johnson's character and motives. They accused him of having belatedly converted to Brexit as a tactic he hoped would enable him to replace Cameron in 10 Downing Street, while Rudd said that although he was the life and soul of the party he was 'not the man you want to drive you home at the end of the evening'. The strategy failed: Johnson, clearly enjoying the verbal tussle, used their attacks to adopt an untypically statesmanlike style as he warned against the danger of resorting to personal jibes.

Both sides in the referendum campaign sought celebrity endorsements, and on 9 March 2016 *The Sun* claimed to have the biggest British celebrity of all on its side when it used the headline 'Queen Backs Brexit'. Buckingham Palace tends to avoid getting involved in controversies with the media but in this case a complaint was lodged with IPSO, which was duly upheld in July of that year. The full text of the adjudication is available on *The Sun's* website, along with the original article and the political editor's defence of its publication (Newton Dunn 2016). The article refers to a lunch at Windsor Castle during the 2010–2015 Conservative-Liberal Democrat coalition government, and quotes 'a highly reliable source' and 'a parliamentary source' claiming that the Queen made her views known at length and with great passion to Nick Clegg, at the time Lib-Dem leader and deputy prime minister. IPSO ruled that the headline breached Clause 1 (Accuracy) of the Editors' Code of Practice; while the content of the article is conjecture based on unnamed sources, the headline presents the Queen's pro-Brexit position as a hard fact.

It is quite possible that Queen Elizabeth has her doubts about the EU – if anyone should be concerned about the question of sovereignty it is surely the sovereign – but it is difficult to believe that a monarch with her long record of correct observance of protocol would commit the crass error of expressing her views in public. *The Sun's* headline falls into the category of dirty tricks because the Queen, unlike a Boris Johnson who can and does respond in kind, is bound by her constitutional role to be above politics and to avoid controversy. *The Sun* made a claim about her that she was powerless to refute personally. When her grandson, Prince William, referred in a speech to Britain's tradition as 'an outward looking nation', Victoria Murphy (2016) for *The Mirror* had the good sense to include a verb in her headline that made it clear that she was not stating boldly on record that he wished people to vote to remain in the EU: 'Prince William wades into the EU debate by hinting Brits should vote to stay In'. Unlike Victoria Murphy, *The Sun*, as we have already seen, is not unduly concerned about incurring the displeasure of IPSO.

And UKIP did not hesitate to make use of *The Sun's* dirty trick. Among the campaign posters the party invited supporters to print and distribute or download and repost was one featuring a photograph of the Queen with the caption 'I'm voting UKIP'.

The closer we got to voting day the more the polls indicated that the Leave camp had chipped away at Remain's early lead. A close result was predicted, but when 23 June came round, many people, myself included, still could not really imagine that a majority of voters would choose to leave the EU. And when it sank in that they had done precisely that, the country was revealed to be even more divided than we had thought.

14

The Day After: How could this happen?

The headlines and leads in the 24 June predawn editions of the three most committed pro-Brexit tabloids were predictably triumphant and linguistically predictable: *The Sun* used a pun, the *Daily Mail* recycled the shackles metaphor and the *Daily Express* remained true to the theme of an appointment with history.

SEE EU LATER!

Britain waking to an EU exit   *Leave claims win in huge poll*

(*The Sun*)

WE'RE OUT!

• After 43 years UK freed from shackles of EU • PM in crisis as voters reject Project Fear • Leave surge sends pound to a 31-year low

(*Daily Mail*)

HISTORIC DAY FOR BRITAIN

Nation decides as Boris and Gove ask Cameron to stay on

(*Daily Express*)

The Sun's front page featured an image of Leave supporters celebrating their victory, underlined the legitimacy of the vote by drawing attention to the size of the turnout and also promised readers a 'big brexfast' of eight more pages of referendum coverage.

A fall in the value of sterling in the event of a vote for Brexit had been predicted by both sides and the Leave camp, judiciously selecting economists to cite, had maintained that a weaker pound would give a boost to Britain's economy, so in its lead the *Daily Mail* did not try to hide or downplay the markets' reaction to the referendum result. The 'We're out!' headline was accompanied by a photograph of Nigel Farage with arms raised in triumph.

The *Daily Express* showed Chelsea pensioners in full uniform queuing to enter the polling station, an image of tough old patriots determined to play their part on the historic day for Britain. The headline about the historic consequence of the result was juxtaposed with a lead about the internecine struggle within the Conservative Party and Gove and Johnson's improbable hope that David Cameron might continue as prime minister even with their knives still buried in his back.

Although the *Daily Telegraph* energetically supported the Leave campaign, on 24 June it differed from the pro-Brexit tabloids in that it acknowledged that the voters had 'upset predictions' and used the word 'shock', which, as we will see, was a lexeme that frequently occurred in the Remain-supporting newspapers' reports of the referendum result. Over the following days, prominent Leavers did indeed give the impression that they had not really expected to win and were not quite sure what to do with their victory, but on their front pages immediately after the result was known the three tabloids neglected this aspect.

A fourth pro-Brexit tabloid, the *Daily Star*, has rarely been cited in this work since it is primarily concerned with celebrity gossip, breasts and buttocks, the royal family, UFOs and the supernatural, with its minimal coverage of politics scarcely worth commenting upon. Its headline and lead of 24 June are given below for contrastive purposes; unlike its tabloid competitors, it went to press before the result was known, so, lacking the one news item everyone wished to know about, had to resort to a ludicrous story about an MI5 plot to erase the pencilled crosses for leaving the EU from ballot papers. A photomontage shows David Cameron holding a gigantic and decidedly phallic-looking pencil.

Britain backs Brexit

Shock for Cameron as Labour heartlands upset predictions to leave country facing the exit door

(*Daily Telegraph*)

BREXIT FIX FACTOR

Pencil conspiracy as result is neck and neck

(*Daily Star*)

The pro-Remain press opted for stark headlines and leads that focused on the fall in the value of the pound and the likelihood that the prime minister would resign.

UK out. PM out

• Cameron to quit by October after Britain votes by 51.9% to 48.1% to leave EU • £120bn wiped off shares as pound sinks to 31-year low • Johnson and May favourites to lead Brexit negotiations

(*The Independent*)

Cameron faces fight for survival as Britain sets course for Brexit

• Pound plunges by 9% to lowest level since 1985 • Farage claims victory as leave stretches ahead • Tory leave MPs pledge to back PM come what may

(*The Guardian*)

WE'RE OUT

» Britain votes to quit the EU » Pound goes into freefall

(*The Daily Mirror*)

Britain's Brexit revolt

• Huge gains for Leave campaign in referendum • Nail-biting finish as Farage warns 'genie out of bottle'

(*The Times*)

OUT Global shock as Britain quits EU

» Britain votes to leave EU in stunning blow to Europe » Sterling suffers sharpest fall since 2008 financial crisis » Pressure on PM to quit despite support from Eurosceptics

(*The i*)

The pro-Remain *Times* used a photograph of jubilant Brexit supporters very similar to that on the front page of its fellow News Corporation newspaper *The Sun*, as did *The Telegraph*. In keeping with its headline *The Independent* published a photograph of a glum-looking David Cameron while *The i*, a newspaper not cited previously, gave us a satellite image of Great Britain and north-eastern France in which the former's literal insularity could be interpreted as a visual metaphor for its post-referendum political isolation. *The i* aims to adopt a politically neutral stance (in the 2015 general election it did not advise readers on how to vote) but on the morning after the referendum manifested the same surprise and disappointment as the overtly pro-Remain press.

When Leave's victory was not yet confirmed but looking highly probable, *The Guardian*'s 4.45 am edition had a front-page photograph showing three people before empty wine glasses with expressions of dismay tinged with disbelief. The occasion is a results party organized by Stronger In at London's Royal Festival Hall, and the photo was obviously taken when results from around the country were making it clear that the expected celebrations would not happen. It is an image that encapsulates the division that post-referendum analyses examined in detail: wine-drinking metropolitans at a venue that symbolizes high culture in the capital city who were totally unable to comprehend why working-class beer drinkers in the north and midlands had decided to ignore their Labour MPs' advice and vote to leave the EU.

Throughout the referendum campaign the *Daily Mirror* was the pro-Remain newspaper that made the most creative use of visual metaphors. After the early results suggested a narrow victory for Remain, it produced a front page showing a young woman with the EU flag superimposed upon her face kissing a young man with a Union Jack face. The only text was the headline 'Project Reunite' (2016) plus a wish for an end to the bitterness of the preceding months: 'As Farage all but concedes defeat . . . and after the fear & hate . . . Britain needs Remain & Leave supporters to start the healing process. . .' (*The Mirror*'s ellipses). When subsequent results showed that it was actually Leave who had secured a narrow victory, *The Mirror* published its 'historic 5am edition' with its 'We're Out' front page (2016) – *The Mail* used the same headline with the addition of an ecstatic exclamation mark – with an image of just the young man with the Union Jack face. This time the flag is in a less than pristine state, the flaking blue and red paint symbolizing different things to different people but, given *The Mirror*'s clear pro-Remain stance, unlikely to be interpreted in a positive way.

What the referendum made abundantly clear was that Great Britain and Northern Ireland was a kingdom that was far from united. Even before all the votes were counted, *The Economist* spelt out the divisions in the country in an unsigned article entitled 'The Brexit vote reveals a country split down the middle' (2016):

First returns and television interviews with voters and (slightly shell-shocked) political grandees painted a picture of a United Kingdom divided sharply along lines of region, class, age and even – in the case of Northern Ireland, where such Roman Catholic areas as Foyle voted Remain while Protestant areas like North Antrim went for Leave amid much higher turn-out – by religious denomination. If the public had quietly weighed the costs and benefits of EU membership, it was often hard to hear that analysis through a din of stuff-the-lot-of-them rage from the Leave camp, and the first growls of mutual recrimination among Labour and Conservative politicians backing Remain.

The 'stuff-the-lot-of-them rage' described in *The Economist* was more conventionally termed 'a popular revolt' by Elliott and Coates (2016) in *The Times* in an article depicting a nation with such deep divisions that it risked disintegration:

> Britain is heading out of the European Union today after a referendum result that remakes the country's political landscape and shatters the continent's post-war settlement.
>
> Swathes of England and Wales ignored David Cameron's warnings on the economic consequences of Brexit to express their anger over immigration and inequality in a popular revolt that has left the country deeply divided.
>
> The pound plunged to a 31-year low as global markets reacted to the prospect of years of uncertainty, including over the future of the UK itself.
>
> Alex Salmond, the former Scottish first minister, said he was certain that his successor, Nicola Sturgeon, would demand a second independence referendum.

Nicola Sturgeon did indeed call for a second referendum on Scottish independence, the future of the open border between Eire and Northern Ireland became an issue, while the strong Remain vote in London highlighted the rift within England itself. On this third point, Lara Prendergast (2016) for *The Spectator* noted that two days after the referendum more than 120,000 signatures had been added to a petition circulating on Facebook calling for London to become an independent city state within the EU (which Prendergast considers a 'Little Londoner mindset').

Throughout this work it has been argued that the pro-EU camp did not match Leave's passionate campaigning and powerful language but when the final result was known Remainers seemed to find their voice at last, and it was an angry one. A number of polls showed that young people had voted overwhelmingly to remain in the EU, and as soon as they realized what had happened they bombarded social networks and microblogging services to express their anger and their sense of having been betrayed by middle-aged and elderly people. From early morning on 24 June the hashtags #NotInMyName and #WhatHaveWeDone were trending on Twitter, with the past participles *shafted* and *screwed* among the politer terms to describe what had been done to young people by those who had far less of a stake in the future. *The Guardian* used the Tumblr platform to set up *75percent* (so-named because a YouGov poll indicated that 75 per cent of 18- to 24-year-olds had voted to stay in the EU), and collected the distraught, embittered and often genuinely fearful complaints of both young voters and those 16- and 17-year-olds who had not been permitted to vote on an issue of such importance for their future. The under-18s were well represented in a hastily organized but peacefully conducted anti-Brexit demonstration outside the Houses of Parliament on the day after the momentous vote.

Discontent among young people did not suddenly emerge after the referendum. They were already bitter about university tuition fees, zero hours work contracts, high rents and the impossibility of getting a foot on the property ladder, and they had every reason to be resentful towards a generation who, in their eyes, had had it easy with student grants, secure employment and guaranteed pension rights. Amid the precariousness of their lives, the one positive thing they took for granted was that they lived in a continent with open borders where they could go where they liked to study or seek work, and when even this seemed to be snatched from them by the votes of the over-50s, it came as a kick in the teeth. Families were split as Brexit-supporting parents stood accused of having voted selfishly and against their own children's future.

Rhiannon Lucy Cosslett (2016), a young freelance writer and co-founder of the feminist online magazine *Vagenda*, wrote two articles for *The Guardian*, one on 24 June with a selection of tweets and posts, the second three days later focusing on the mixed emotions of young voters whose parents had voted Leave. In the first acrimony towards the baby boomer generation was expressed in hard-hitting terms:

> 'I'm so angry,' wrote one Twitter user. 'A generation given everything: free education, golden pensions, social mobility, have voted to strip my generation's future.' Another statement, from a commenter on the *Financial Times* website that has been widely shared, summed up the sense of furious betrayal among the young: 'The younger generation has lost the right to live and work in 27 other countries. We will never know the full extent of lost opportunities, friendships, marriages and experiences we will be denied. Freedom of movement was taken away by our parents, uncles and grandparents in a parting blow to a generation that was already drowning in the debts of its predecessors.'

Three days later, after young people had had time to talk (or try to talk) to older relatives, the initial anger was tinged by profound sorrow at the tensions created in family relationships, and often by difficulty in accepting the fact that their parents harboured racist or nationalistic sentiments they considered abhorrent. Among Cosslett's collected quotations, a young woman says, 'As much as I love my parents, this referendum has made me see them in a different light', while a young man's enormous admiration for his single mother does not blind him to a distasteful aspect of her personality:

> I've always been so proud of her for all the things she sacrificed for us. She's warm, kind, generous and funny. She has such acute sympathy that she's been known to cry hearing about the illness of other people's relatives. Oh, and she also hates immigrants.

The figure of 75 per cent of 18- to 24-year-olds initially reported as having voted Remain was only a slight exaggeration. When YouGov pollsters had had more time to analyse their data, it was revealed that 71 per cent of 18- to 24-year-olds and 54 per cent of the 25–49 age group had voted Remain, while 60 per cent of 50- to 64-year-olds and 64 per cent of over-65s had voted Leave (Moore 2016). The statistics are clear: those who had most of their lives in front of them had been outvoted by people whose best days were behind them, and this was not something the pro-Brexit press could brush aside.

On the day after the vote Adam Boult (2016) for *The Telegraph* made no attempt to distort the figures, and of the enormous number of tweets available chose to quote one posted by someone whose surname was, in the circumstances, somewhat poignant; Chai Cameron had written: 'I'm scared. Jokes aside I'm actually scared. Today an older generation has chosen to ruin the future for the younger generation. I'm scared.' Four days later, however, the same newspaper published a piece by an Oxford undergraduate whose parents had voted Leave, Bethany Kirkbride (2016), who urged her demographic to understand that 'older generations are just as frustrated as young people', and to direct their anger not at mum and dad, but at young friends and acquaintances who had not bothered to vote.

Alex Matthews (2016) for the *Daily Mail* quoted the YouGov statistics but in reporting on the hastily organized anti-Brexit demonstration in London the day after the referendum chose certain words that implied that the protest was not entirely peaceful: 'Millennials have slammed baby boomers for voting Britain out of the EU as furious crowds of young people protest in London'. Young Britons are reported as having 'voted in droves in favour of the Remain campaign'; today the word *drove* is used generally for a large group of people acting together, but it originally referred to a herd of cattle being driven (a drove-road was an ancient cattle track), which implies that young Remain voters had not exercised free will but had been driven by a herdsman. Unlike other witnesses to the event, Matthews saw that many of the protesters 'wore face paint and ignited flares' (in reality a small minority had painted their faces and hardly any lit flares), and from the Houses of Parliament, Downing

Street and London Bridge they did not walk but 'marched towards the Shard'. Of the many and varied placards in evidence, Matthews quoted two slogans guaranteed to be provocative for *Daily Mail* readers: 'no borders' and 'refugees welcome'.

On *The Mail*'s website the updated version of Matthews' article on 25 June includes no fewer than twenty-four photographs. Remarkably, the first of them shows a group of male demonstrators with, in the foreground, a young man dressed entirely in black (including cap and gloves), wearing a face mask and holding a flare in each hand. It is not clear whether he and his friends are genuinely part of the anti-Brexit protest or are using the event to promote some other agenda. Several photographs feature police officers as well as the protesters, although none shows them struggling to maintain order. Others clearly have the *Daily Mail* readership in mind as they focus on the more provocative gestures or the physical appearance of individual protesters: three show a young woman drenched in fake blood and carrying a placard reading 'Brexit: What a Bloody Joke', while another features a young person who appears to be male wearing lipstick and nail varnish.

The article contains no reference to property being damaged, people intimidated or arrests made.

In the days following the referendum several writers and bloggers referred to Sky Data figures suggesting very low turnout of young voters, which meant that not everyone felt sorry for those whose future prospects had been damaged by the baby boomers. The severest critics were young people who had braved the rainy weather to get to the polling station, such as Bethany Kirkbride cited above. Anna Rhodes (2016) for *The Independent* had little doubt that the young had dug their own grave.

Swaths of young people in this country have been lamenting at the fact that our futures have been 'ruined' by selfish older voters who probably won't live to see the full extent of the damage they have caused.

It has been estimated that only 36 per cent of people in the 18–24 category voted in the referendum. 62 per cent of young people did not bother to take themselves down to the polling station and cast their ballot.

Turnout in areas with a higher proportion of young residents was lower across the country. So, it is rather hypocritical for the young to chastise older Brits when less of us voted than those who did not.

It subsequently emerged that the Sky Data statistics were very wide of the mark. Research conducted by the London School of Economics (LSE) found that 64 per cent of registered 18- to 24-year-olds voted, almost double the figure originally reported on Sky News although still significantly lower than the overall turnout of 72.2 per cent announced by the Electoral Commission. The same LSE study put turnout figures at 65 per cent for 25- to 39-year-olds, 66 per cent for the 40–54 demographic, 74 per cent for 55- to 64-year-olds and an astonishing 90 per cent for those aged 65 or over (Yeung 2016). Young Britons clearly did themselves no favours by not making it to the polling station in sufficient numbers but the youngest voters of all were nowhere near as culpable as the original dodgy datum suggested. Full Fact investigated the hopelessly inaccurate statistic of only 36 per cent of 18- to 24-year-olds casting their ballot and discovered that it did not refer to actual votes cast in the referendum; it was 'based on likely turnout for the 2015 election' (Milne 2016) and misleadingly reported on Sky News.

The referendum showed that Britain was also split down the middle in terms of the winners and losers in a post-industrial and globalized economy, with the latter having used the EU vote as an opportunity to send a powerful message to a political class they perceived as indifferent to the difficulties of their daily lives. One of the first to provide an in-depth analysis of the result was David Runciman (2016), professor of politics and international studies at the University of Cambridge, who compares Cambridge, where 74 per cent of voters opted for Remain, with the nearby city of Peterborough, where 61 per cent voted Leave, to exemplify the winners and losers in the global economy. With eight science parks, two universities and one of the most important hospitals in Europe, Cambridge thrives in the knowledge economy and many of its well-educated, mobile and thoroughly networked inhabitants have undoubtedly been economic winners in the globalized world. Peterborough has relatively low unemployment but also wage rates that are below the average for eastern England, its economy still involves the production of physical goods, and over the last decade the city has absorbed a considerable number of EU immigrants, particularly from Eastern Europe. Its inhabitants are precisely the sort of people likely to feel that globalization in general and European integration in particular are processes they have been subject to but had never chosen. As Runciman puts it:

> The digital revolution has opened up the prospect of a future in which knowledge is the primary currency, connectivity the primary asset, and physical geography is at best a secondary concern. People who are rooted in particular places, who work in industries that produce physical goods, and whose essential social interactions do not happen online are the ones who wanted Out. They have glimpsed a future in which people like them are increasingly at the mercy of forces beyond their power to control. And they are right.

For Runciman the referendum result means that 'the economic winners find themselves on the losing side, for what is effectively the first time in the modern political history of this country'.

David Goodhart (2017) explores a similar distinction at book-length and sees the socioeconomic right–left dichotomy of a manufacturing economy as having been superseded in the knowledge economy by a sociocultural division: 'The Great Divide' between 'Anywheres' and 'Somewheres'.

Anywheres have no great sense of attachment to nation or place. They usually did well at school, often left home to go to university, have 'portable "achieved" identities' (ibid. 3) and tend to support economic and social liberalism. They have come to dominate the political agenda in the developed world, their rise to prominence coinciding with the decline of solidarity-based social democratic parties.

In contrast, Somewheres 'usually have 'ascribed' identities – Scottish farmer, working-class Geordie, Cornish housewife – based on group belonging and particular places' (ibid.). They are usually less well-educated, have been adversely affected by the loss of secure employment for the unskilled and have generally fared badly out of globalization. Somewheres have a sense of having been excluded from the decision-making process, of looking on impotently as the Anywheres call the shots. For Goodhart the Brexit vote, the election of Donald Trump and the rise of populism all over Europe are symptoms of frustrated Somewheres fighting back.

In the specific case of the EU referendum, analysis of the results from over a thousand local government wards revealed a strong correlation between educational attainment and how people voted; graduates and people with good qualifications from school were significantly more likely to vote Remain (Rosenbaum 2017).

We saw in Chapter 4 how old Etonians leading the pro-Leave campaign managed to portray themselves as champions of the common man as the tabloids railed against lobbies, vested interests, the banks, the multinationals, the metropolitan elite and even the luvvies of the acting profession. After the referendum, the unapologetically anti-intellectual approach continued as *The Mail*, *The Express* and *The Sun* attacked the Remainers – renamed Remoaners – for their reluctance to accept defeat, making fun of their inability to comprehend the common sense values of the ordinary people who had not been intimidated by Project Fear. On 5 October 2016 the *Daily Mail* leaked the contents of Theresa May's planned speech at the Conservative Party conference (Slack 2016).

May savages the liberal elite: PM will use keynote speech at the Tory conference to condemn those who sneer at ordinary Britons' worries and reach
out to millions of blue-collar workers

- Prime Minister to criticise people who have 'sneered' over
  immigration

- Theresa May to condemn those who dismiss voter concerns as
  'parochial'

- Set to pledge to lead Government that will intervene on
  workers' behalf

- It follows Sunday's speech in Birmingham where she outlined
  Brexit plan

Theresa May will today condemn the metropolitan elite for sneering at
millions of ordinary Britons over immigration.

In words that will resonate across the country, the Prime Minister
will criticise those who try to dismiss the concerns of many voters as
'parochial'.

And she will savage the political and chattering classes who think the
public's patriotism is 'distasteful' and their views on crime 'illiberal'.

For 'ordinary Britons' and 'blue-collar workers' we could substitute
'Somewheres', while 'the metropolitan elite' and 'the political and chattering
classes' are clearly 'Anywheres'. The words *sneer, parochial, distasteful* and *illiberal* imply that the elite consider themselves morally and intellectually superior to the 'millions of ordinary Britons' who have legitimate concerns about
immigration and whose patriotism is the product of Somewheres' attachment
to place. Blue-collar workers, particularly those who are members of a trade
union, may not be wholly convinced by Theresa May's and the *Daily Mail's*
new-found concern for the well-being of the proletariat, but the anti-elite

stance doubtless struck a chord with many people who resented being constantly portrayed as ignorant racists.

John Longworth (2017), co-chair of a pressure group called *Leave Means Leave*, used the word *elite(s)* no fewer than eight times in a short article in *The Sun* claiming that in 2016 working people were robbed of £35 billion 'to fund vanity projects for the wealthy chattering classes'. The collocations are:

... they were exercised by the plain ignorance of the left-liberal elite...

... this privileged elite had 'lost the plot'...

... the people on 23rd June burst the elite bubble...

... exemplified by the obsessions of the elite...

... easier for the elite to chat at the Hampstead dinner table...

... the elites are well-healed...

... nicer for the elite to be part of a superior and technocratic club (the EU)...

... elites are the lucky ones, with no idea of problems plaguing the masses...

Like the *Daily Mail*, *The Sun* is not particularly credible in the role of defender of the *sansculottes*, but Longworth (who was director-general of the British Chamber of Commerce between 2011 and 2016) refers directly to the Peasants' Revolt, then obliquely to the French Revolution in his assertion that the attitude of the elite 'is not so much "let them eat cake" as we will steal your cake and give it away without shame and then ridicule anyone who dares to complain!'. Like James Slack in *The Mail*, he attacks what he perceives as the contempt displayed by the haves towards the have-nots, referring to the 'sneering superiority' of a ruling class preoccupied with abstract affairs and unable to relate to 'the grubby reality of the practical and all too proximate needs of their fellow countrymen and women'. If some of Longworth's lexical choices are not typical of *The Sun* – 'the nonchalant urbanity that precedes decadence and, eventually, social dissonance' – his conclusion is crystal clear, and evocative of the great lie of the £350 million Britain allegedly sends to Brussels each week: if the £35 billion wasted on the chattering classes' vanity projects were reallocated, we could 'increase NHS funding by a quarter and Defence spending by a third and there would be change'.

Less than a month after the referendum, Nick Gutteridge (2016) in *The Express* used the word *elite(s)* in both the headline and the lead, and then five times in the body of his report of comments made by the Lebanese statistician and academic, Nassim Taleb. The collocations are:

... a revolution against 'stupid' Brussels elite...

... people's revolution against the bumbling Brussels elite...

... the posturing of unaccountable elites...

... the entire world has grown tired of a sneering elite...

... have just realised that these elites don't know what they're talking about...

... that elite doesn't have the intellectual level that you would expect...

... With the elite we're not talking about people with huge intellect...

The last three of these usages are direct quotations of Taleb's words and the third and fourth are indirect reports of his comments during an interview on the CNBC channel.

This article differs from those from *The Mail* and *The Sun* in that Nassim Taleb, and in imitation Nick Gutteridge, portray the EU elite as consisting of individuals who are not particularly cerebral and therefore have not yet understood that the European project in its present form is destined to fail. However, like James Slack and John Longworth, Taleb uses – or is reported as using – the word *sneering* with reference to how the elite see the rest of us: 'He said the entire world has grown tired of a sneering elite which has spent the last few decades "patronising the bottom 30 per cent" whilst vastly enriching itself'. Furthermore, the political editor of the *Daily Mail* and the former director-general of the British Chamber of Commerce appear to have a comrade in Nick Gutteridge, who reports approvingly of Taleb's assessment that a revolution is in progress: 'And he hailed the Brexit result as kicking off a revolutionary "wave" that is "spreading", adding that working class people "are intelligent . . . and they realise globalisation doesn't pay for them, it pays for someone else".'

Like the regional and generational divides in the UK, the class division between the winners and losers in the globalized, knowledge economy emerged long before the EU referendum was held, but the unexpected result shone a very bright light upon an issue that the winners had been happy to leave undiscussed. As noted earlier in this work, in the final days of the referendum campaign journalists like Suzanne Moore and Owen Jones had sensed that enough working class people were sufficiently disenchanted to wish to stick two fingers up at a political class they felt did not care about them. Moore and Owen were right; it was the results in the Labour heartlands that gave Leave their victory. A pyrrhic victory perhaps, for many would argue that for ordinary people the only consequence of the Brexit vote was to replace one elite with another.

From a purely semantic point of view, David Runciman, Nassim Taleb and others misuse the word *elite*. An elite should be relatively small in number but disproportionately strong in terms of power and influence, but the 48 per cent who voted Remain were numerous (16,141,241 to be precise) and during a tense night in 2016 suffered a painful defeat. As Nick Cohen (2017) ironizes:

> At 48 per cent, Britain now has the largest elite in political history. This supposed elite breaks with another precedent. Uniquely, it is an elite which is everywhere except the one place an elite needs to be: in power. A powerless

elite is not much of an elite at all. It exists only as a propaganda target for the holders of real power.

Whether we call them the elite, Anywheres or simply the winners, the referendum gave them the novel experience of suffering a defeat. Not everyone accepted that defeat with good grace. Predictably, there were calls for a second vote, and equally predictably both the government and the main opposition party knew that such a proposal was not politically feasible. However, the British people would not have to wait very long before going to the polling booths again.

15

The issue that would not go away: The general election of 2017

After repeatedly saying that her government would serve its full term until 2020, on 18 April 2017, Theresa May surprised many people by announcing that there would be a 'snap' general election on 8 June. In some ways the timing was odd since just twenty days earlier she had triggered Article 50 of the Treaty of Lisbon, which set the clock ticking on the two-year period that the UK had to negotiate with Brussels and reach an acceptable exit deal. Hammering out an agreement in just two years was never going to be easy given the complicated nature of the issues involved plus the fact that whatever terms were negotiated would have to be ratified by twenty-seven national parliaments, each of which would have a veto over the conditions. The decision to permit the distraction of an election campaign when there was so much work to do struck some people (though not an enormous number) as capricious, if not downright irresponsible. By April 2019 Britain would be out of the EU, deal or no deal, and the government already had a working majority of seventeen in the House of Commons.

Theresa May's view was that going on the stump for fifty days was not time wasted at all since re-election with a significantly improved majority would show that the public trusted her, which would strengthen her hand when dealing with Brussels and allow her to conduct talks more effectively. At the time hardly anyone questioned her confidence that her party was heading for an emphatic victory. Polls showed the Conservatives twenty or more points ahead of Labour while the smaller parties had little reason to welcome new elections: UKIP was struggling to find a purpose now that the referendum had been won; the Liberal Democrats had still to win back their traditional supporters who had punished the party in 2015 for having entered into a coalition with the Tories; the SNP, after their extraordinary success two years earlier, knew that they could not improve upon that triumph and were more likely to shed a few seats. But what really convinced the prime minister that she must seize the day was the fact that her personal approval ratings were very high while those of Jeremy Corbyn, the Labour leader, were abysmal. Corbyn was immensely popular with the rank and file who had elected and re-elected him party leader but was held in contempt by a great number of Labour MPs who considered him far too left-wing ever to be elected; many feared losing their seats in the upcoming election because of the ineptitude of their leader, and when Corbyn himself oozed quiet confidence in welcoming the prime minister's decision, this merely confirmed suspicions that he was living on a different planet.

With Jeremy Corbyn apparently such a liability to his party, one might have expected the right-wing press to lay off him in the hope that he would remain Labour leader until 8 June, thus ensuring a Tory landslide. Not a bit of it. From the moment Mrs May announced her decision to go to the country, the *Daily Mail*, the *Daily Express* and *The Sun* launched a campaign of daily attacks on Corbyn and his two best-known colleagues, shadow chancellor John McDonnell and shadow home secretary Diane Abbott. The two key accusations were that they were Marxists whose plans for the economy would ruin the country, and that all three had a history of being unhealthily friendly with terrorists, from the Irish Republican Army (IRA) decades ago to the Islamists of today.

The day before the vote *The Sun* featured a photomontage of Jeremy Corbyn peering out from a dustbin and a dire pun in the headline to its unsigned editorial: *THE SUN SAYS Don't chuck Britain in the Cor-bin – vote Tory unless you want a friend of terrorists who's ready to open borders and hike up taxes as our next PM* (2017). Ten of the Labour leader's vices are then listed: 'terrorists' friend, useless on Brexit, destroyer of jobs, enemy of business, massive tax hikes, puppet of unions, nuclear surrender, ruinous spending, open immigration, Marxist extremist'. Many Britons would have difficulty accepting the opening sentence as a description of the UK in 2017:

> He would chuck our spectacular progress and prosperity over the last 35 YEARS in the bin.
>
> Only a vote for the Conservatives – not Ukip or any other – will keep Corbyn and his sinister Marxist gang away from power.
>
> If enough people vote Labour, Britain faces a nightmare beyond anyone's experience.

An unsigned editorial in the *Daily Mail* – *Labour's apologists for terror: The Mail accuses Corbyn troika of befriending Britain's enemies and scorning the institutions that keep us safe* (2017) – begins with the generous assumption that the Labour leader was sincere in expressing sympathy for the victims of an ISIS-inspired attack on London Bridge days before the election, then signals a change of direction with a highly significant *but*.

> But the ineluctable truth is that the Labour leader and his closest associates have spent their careers cosying up to those who hate our country, while pouring scorn on the police and security services and opposing anti-terror legislation over and over and over again.

Yes, Mr Corbyn has impressed some with his quiet composure under hostile questioning. But he personally has spent a political lifetime courting mass murderers in the Middle East, Ireland and elsewhere in the world, affronting the party and its decent traditional supporters, while voting on 56 occasions against measures aimed at containing the terrorist threat.

Meanwhile his closest ally, the Marxist shadow chancellor John McDonnell, has called for MI5 and armed police to be abolished, while saying that the IRA murderers of men, women, children, British servicemen and police officers should be 'honoured'.

As for Diane Abbott, the clueless and incoherent woman in charge of the security brief, she has voted against anti-terror measures 30 times, while declaring in the past that any defeat of the British state by IRA terrorists was a 'victory'.

The headline contains the term *troika*, a Russian loan word that has acquired negative connotations since it began to be used to refer collectively to the IMF, the European Commission and the European Central Bank, the triumvirate that has imposed stringent austerity measures upon indebted eurozone states, most savagely upon Greece. If Corbyn, McDonnell and Abbott formed a trio, they would be entertaining; as a troika they are dictatorial and heartless.

In the first and second paragraphs Corbyn is accused of first 'cosying up to' and then of 'courting' disreputable individuals who are not identified precisely, but are described as 'those who hate our country' and 'mass murderers' respectively. The Labour leader is also accused of affronting his party's 'decent traditional supporters', with the implicature that the adjective *decent* cannot be used for Corbyn himself.

It later emerges that the main mass murderers are the IRA, and interspersed between the paragraphs of the online version of the editorial are three photographs of Corbyn with Gerry Adams, leader of Sinn Féin, a party that presses for Northern Ireland to leave the UK and be reunited with the Republic of

Ireland. *The Mail* neglects to remind us that Adams was a Westminster MP from 1983 to 1992 and again from 1997 to 2011 (although he always refused to sit in the Commons), so it was really not that scandalous for one elected representative of the people to talk to another. Since the Good Friday Agreement of 1998 brought an end to sectarian violence, Sinn Féin has participated fully in the power-sharing Northern Ireland Assembly. Reconciliation was symbolized in 2015 when Prince Charles, during an official royal visit to Ireland, met Adams and shook his hand.

There are more ways to represent other people's words than through conventional direct or indirect speech. Mick Short (1996: 288–325) identifies a number of alternative methods, including free indirect speech, the narrator's representation of speech and the narrator's representation of speech acts. Departures from conventional direct speech in inverted commas give the narrator greater scope to put a spin on what others said, but ostensibly verbatim quotes can also be misleading if they are incomplete or not clearly embedded in the original context. The *Daily Mail* editorial assigns one-word quotes to each of Corbyn's comrades: 'honoured' for John McDonnell and 'victory' for Diane Abbott. There can be few anglophone adults who have not uttered those two words at some time in their lives, so in theory we could all be quoted in the same way. In both cases the alleged quotation comes at the end of a paragraph containing only the leader writer's words (it is unlikely that Diane Abbot would describe herself as clueless and incoherent), so the contextless one-word citations are associated in the reader's mind with things not uttered by McDonnell or Abbott, but written by an employee of the *Daily Mail*.

The Mail did at least acknowledge Jeremy Corbyn's 'quiet composure', and during the seven-week campaign the Labour leader did indeed earn respect for his repeated assertion 'I don't do personal' and his refusal to respond in kind to those who attacked his character rather than his policies. In addition, for the first time the public began to learn something about the man behind the politician, and discovered that he used public transport, grew vegetables on his allotment and made his own jam. Martin Townsend (2017), editor of the *Sunday Express*, was not taken in by that image of Corbyn as a friendly, good-natured sort of chap; on the contrary, he was a very dangerous individual whose reptilian qualities were extreme even for a Labourite.

> Politicians are chameleons. They can be all things to all people, able to shape-shift effortlessly from suited authority in the House of Commons to 'down with the people' salt-of-the-earth charm out in their constituencies.
>
> But even by the lower-than-a-toad's-belly standards of the usual Labour Party lizards, Jeremy Corbyn has waged a seamlessly cynical campaign.
>
> On Sky last week, the man whose policies place him far further to the Left than any Labour leader in living memory had morphed himself into an avuncular 'Grandad' figure.
>
> A man of smiling, aged charm who used the same tone of voice to explain how he'd dither and dance around any decision to kill a terrorist in a drone strike (thereby saving hundreds of innocent lives) as he would to explain fly-fishing techniques to a wide-eyed grandson.
>
> Can anyone even half-consider putting this man in charge of our nation's security? Corbyn, once a joke figure, has become a deeply dangerous threat to us all.

Apart from his evident fascination with reptiles and amphibians, Townsend also displays a penchant for alliteration ('seamlessly cynical', 'shape-shift', 'dither and dance'), a love of four-hyphen compound adjectives ('salt-of-the-earth', 'lower-than-a-toad's-belly), and an apparent inability to recognize ambiguity ('down with the people') or an unfortunate juxtaposition ('avuncular "Grandad" figure') in his own prose.

As always with nasty attacks of this nature in the right-wing tabloids, one has to ask whether they actually influenced floating voters or merely reinforced the beliefs and prejudices of readers who would never dream of supporting

Jeremy Corbyn anyway. Post-election analyses revealed that young people had learnt their referendum lesson and turned out to vote in far greater numbers than they had done a year earlier, and that a clear majority of the 18–24 age group voted Labour. That demographic category probably does not form part of the Tory-supporting tabloids' core readership, but some obviously had a look at the online editions and used Twitter and humour to respond to the demonization of the Labour leader. The hashtag #LastMinuteCorbynSmears allowed people to poke fun at the hysterical attacks by posting parodies of the more ridiculous accusations, often by questioning Corbyn's gardening and jam-making skills, but also by lampooning his portrayal as an unpatriotic Marxist and law-breaker. Tom Stevens (2017) collected some of the wittier examples, including:

- Corbyn buys jam at Waitrose and steams the stickers off to pretend he made it.

- He bludgeons strawberries to death and boils them with sugar.

- Corbyn's shared allotment turns out to be a socialist plot.

- Jeremy Corbyn reheats tea in the microwave, and thinks 'Snickers' is a far better name than 'Marathon'.

- Jeremy Corbyn eats After Eights at 7.59.

- Corbyn has done a secret deal with FIFA to declare the 1966 World Cup Final ball did not cross the line.

Returning to *The Mail* and *Sunday Express* editorials cited above, a look at readers' feedback reveals that a significant minority were willing to be quite vehement in expressing their dissent. *The Mail's Labour's apologists for terror* editorial prompted one reader to point out that during the Troubles in Northern Ireland, the Conservative prime ministers Edward Heath, Margaret Thatcher and John Major all took part in negotiations with the IRA but, in contrast with Corbyn's open talks with Gerry Adams, did so in secret. Others attacked the *Daily Mail* head-on:

- Far right propaganda, trying to confuse voters the day before the election. Exactly like how the media lied and tricked us into voteing to leave the EU!

- Unbelievable crap from the desperate DM. I'd be ashamed if I was a journalist in its employ. And if you believe the crap instead of truly educating yourselves on the issues and the policies then you don't want a fair and decent society.

- Why would anyone want to vote for may?You [*sic*] people want the NHS privatised,you [*sic*] really don't know what ur getting yourselves into.

- Shows how desperate the paper has become, worried now that it's tax avoiding days may be over.

- No mention of May doing £ multi billion arms deals with the Saudis, who arm ISIS financially, ideologically and militarily.

Similarly, a minority of *Sunday Express* readers were unimpressed by Martin Townsend's alliteration and reptilian metaphors.

- I smell your fear Martin Townsend, your woman of straw Mrs May is snatching defeat from the jaws of victory, May the U –Turner who has overseen the decimation of the police and armed forces who won't face Mr Corbyn in debate but we are expected to believe she will stand up for Britain over Brexit.You [*sic*] and your paymasters are starting to panic and I like it.

- He has been positive. I like him. Theresa May has been negative. End of story. Goodnight and bless you all.xx [*sic*]

- Third attempt to get through your censorship of comments…. Fake news – beware of Tory sponsored smear tactics.

- The only people that are waging a seamlessly cynical campaign are the Tory lead media and and [sic] their newspapers on Jeremy Corbyn, the spineless editor of this piece of fake news knows which way his bread is buttered

Townsend's editorial was published three days before election day and *The Sun* and *The Mail* pieces just one day before the vote. What is evident in all three is that Brexit is not the main issue. Although May had said that she had opted for an early election in order to secure a strong mandate to lead Brexit negotiations as she saw fit, in practice she immediately turned the poll into a vote of confidence in her own leadership qualities. Her message to the electorate was very simple: vote for me because I am a leader while Jeremy Corbyn most definitely is not. Her key soundbite was 'strong and stable leadership' and one had the impression that she would have been content to say nothing else at all throughout the election campaign. Her friends in the popular press duly made Corbyn's lack of leadership qualities their main focus, at first portraying him as almost comically inept, then, as some (but not all) polls showed Labour closing the gap, turning up the heat to present him as an evil communist with a history of supporting terrorists. Brexit, including immigration, was not what the election was about.

Like her predecessor, May took a gamble on a totally unnecessary vote and was left looking rather foolish, in Britain and in the whole of Europe. As soon as the full results were in, there was general consensus among commentators as to the reasons for the Conservatives' poor performance. During the election campaign May had been reluctant to stray too far from her alliterative 'strong and stable' soundbite as she insisted that the key issue was her decisive leadership, but her refusal to take part in televised debates plus an embarrassing U-turn on her party's manifesto proposal for funding residential care for the elderly (dubbed the 'dementia tax') made her look anything but a second iron maiden. Indeed, George Osborne, whom she had fired from the cabinet, coined the expression 'weak and wobbly', which was immediately seized upon by her opponents. In contrast, Labour switched the agenda to their popular manifesto and plans to improve NHS funding, build council houses and scrap university tuition fees, all proposals that appealed to millions who were weary of years of austerity. In addition, Jeremy Corbyn's greatly increased TV exposure enabled the public to discover that he was not the three-eyed monster portrayed in the right-wing tabloids, while Momentum, a grassroots campaigning organization, mobilized thousands of volunteers who targeted marginal constituencies with a combination of old-fashioned door-to-door canvassing and very modern use of social media. Emma Rees (2017), Momentum's national organizer, believes their work countered the political apathy that had taken root in many communities: 'By running a nimble, creative campaign with a youthful staff we connected with those who were new to the Labour party, new to campaigning and often new to politics.'

But if Europe was not the word on everyone's lips during the election campaign, it was always present as a subtext, and when it emerged that May, far from securing a convincing victory to strengthen her hand in talks with Brussels, had instead lost her overall majority in the Commons, the impact of the changed political landscape on Brexit negotiations was the subject of considerable speculation. On a turnout of 68.7 per cent, the Conservative Party lost thirteen seats to finish on 318, eight short of the number needed for an overall majority, while Labour gained thirty seats to end up with 262. Results for the other parties were SNP 35 (-21), Liberal Democrats 12 (+4), the Northern Irish Democratic Unionist Party (DUP) 10 (+2), Northern Irish Sinn Fein 7 (+3), the Welsh nationalist Plaid Cymru 4 (+1) and the Green Party retained its single seat. The new parliament was significantly different in ways other than the party allegiances of its members: of the 650 MPs, a record 208 (32 per cent) were women, 52 were from ethnic-minority backgrounds and 45 openly declared themselves to be LGBT (lesbian, gay, bisexual or transgender), a rise of 40 per cent compared with 2015 (Wilson 2017).

A fair number of Labour's thirty gains involved constituencies where a year earlier a majority of voters had opted for Remain, which led Laurence Dodds (2017) for *The Telegraph* to ask, 'Was this the revenge of the liberal metropolitan elite?' Professor John Curtice, who achieved a degree of celebrity status literally overnight during the BBC's coverage of the results as they came in, noted that in constituencies where more than 55 per cent had voted Remain in the referendum there was a seven-point swing to Labour, while in seats where 60+ per cent had voted Leave there was a 1 per cent swing to the Conservatives (Barford 2017). In 2016 Londoners had bucked the trend in most of England by voting Remain, and a year later they switched to Labour in considerable numbers; of the seventy-three constituencies in Greater London, forty-nine were won by Labour, including such unexpected gains as Hampstead and Kilburn after a 12 per cent swing, and Kensington by just twenty votes after three recounts.

Since Labour had supported the government's decision to trigger article 50, for Remainers still hopeful of overturning the referendum result it would have been more logical to vote for more committed pro-EU parties like the Liberal Democrats or the Greens. For those for whom the priority was to unseat a Conservative MP, however, a vote for the second largest party was the sensible choice, while for people in multicultural London who had accepted that the referendum result could not be wished away, there was the consolation of knowing that negotiators chosen by Jeremy Corbyn would aim to achieve a soft Brexit that respected acquired residence rights. The Labour Party manifesto, *For the many not the few* (2017: 24), was bound to be more appealing to London's multiethnic population than the Tories' courting of UKIP voters.

We will scrap the Conservatives' Brexit White Paper and replace it with fresh negotiating priorities that have a strong emphasis on retaining the benefits of the Single Market and the Customs Union – which are essential for maintaining industries, jobs and businesses in Britain. Labour will always put jobs and the economy first.

A Labour government will immediately guarantee existing rights for all EU nationals living in Britain and secure reciprocal rights for UK citizens who have chosen to make their lives in EU countries. EU nationals do not just contribute to our society: they are part of our society. And they should not be used as bargaining chips.

It is shameful that the Prime Minister rejected repeated attempts by Labour to resolve this issue before Article 50 was triggered. As a result three million EU nationals have suffered unnecessary uncertainty, as have the 1.2 million UK citizens living in the EU.

In contrast, during the election campaign the Tories promised to reduce immigration and did not explicitly rule out expulsions, while Theresa May's second-favourite soundbite – 'No deal is better than a bad deal' – suggested that she would not be averse to a very hard Brexit indeed. Although it was Labour's anti-austerity policies that most appealed to the younger voters responsible for the party's revival, the generation that had not wanted Brexit also knew that Labour would not go into talks in Brussels with sleeves rolled up and wielding a broken bottle.

So Brexit, an issue of enormous importance for the future of Britain, disappeared off the radar in the weeks before the election, but as soon as the result was known immediately re-emerged as a hot topic as it seemed unthinkable that a weakened government could persevere with its declared approach to negotiations with Brussels, that is, driving a hard bargain and being ready to walk away if necessary. On the morning after the vote Andrew Grice (2017) saw the debacle of the early election as signifying the end of a hard Brexit negotiated by a handful of May loyalists without consulting Parliament or the other parties.

The Remainers have an unexpected spring in their step today. May has paid a very heavy price for ignoring the 48 per cent. The hard Brexiteers, who always feared the prize would somehow be snatched from them even after the referendum, are re-living their worst nightmare.

Brexit will still go ahead, since the Conservatives and Labour, who won more than 80 per cent of the votes between them, both promised that. But it could now be a very different Brexit, a much softer version than the one May wanted. Membership of the single market and customs union, ruled out by May, are now back on the agenda. She wanted to marginalise Parliament in the Brexit process; if she had won a majority, the House of Lords would not have blocked leaving the single market and customs union as this was in the Tory manifesto.

Instead, Parliament will now play a more important role. Pro-European Tory MPS may well link up with like-minded MPs in other parties to push for a soft Brexit. Some MPs and peers will argue that May's plan for hard Brexit has been rejected.

Emily Allen (2017) for *The Telegraph* also felt that the result made a hard Brexit less probable and noted that to secure a majority in the Commons, Theresa May was expected to seek an agreement with the Democratic Unionist Party of Northern Ireland, which was pro-Brexit but was also anxious to avoid a hard border with the Republic of Ireland and therefore wanted a soft Brexit.

Like Andrew Grice, John Rentoul (2017) focused on the difficulty the government was likely to have getting its Brexit terms through the House of Lords, a problem exacerbated by the failure to win a clear mandate for its election manifesto, but unlike Grice he did not see Brexit in one form or another as inevitable: 'I now wonder whether Britain really will leave the EU at midnight on 29 March 2019 after all.'

The only good news for the Conservatives from the election results was the party's much improved performance in Scotland, something that was accredited to the communication skills of Ruth Davidson, leader of the Scottish Conservative Party. With regard to Brexit, however, winning seats in pro-Remain Scotland piled more pressure upon May, for Davidson could speak from a position of strength when she urged her party to seek a deal that entailed staying in the EU single market and retaining freedom of movement. Other senior Tories who had never wanted Brexit also emerged from the shadows to press for a soft version. Beneath a headline in *The Mail* that wondered whether Brexit was 'a giant stitch-up', Sofia Petkar (2017) raised doubts as to whether the start of official negotiations, scheduled for Monday 19 June 2017, would actually begin on time. In the wake of the 'shambolic general election', there was something sinister about the Tory Remainers' assertiveness.

> It was the first concrete sign that Brexit is being deliberately delayed, or worse, as part of a broader political agenda. One senior EU official gleefully claimed that Theresa May has 'lost control over her own government', adding: 'It's like waiting for Godot.'

Petkar prefers implicature to unambiguous statements, flouting the maxims of quantity and manner with her brief and insufficiently defined allusions to 'or worse' and 'broader political agenda'. That the unnamed EU official is reported as having spoken 'gleefully' is indicative of hard Brexiteers' resentment of the fact that the UK's self-inflicted disarray had generated amusement in some circles. The reference to Beckett's *Waiting for Godot* implies that Petkar fears (where Rentoul hopes) that Brexit may never happen.

British politicians who shared Rentoul's hope, wary of being accused of disregarding the will of the electorate, kept their views to themselves. When both the newly elected president of France, Emmanuel Macron, and the German finance minister, Walter Schäuble, intimated that the door had been left ajar should Britain have second thoughts about leaving the EU, there was little response.

The Mail was more explicit in using the words 'Cabinet Remainers plot with Labour to 'soften' Britain's departure from the EU' as part of its headline to an article about Ruth Davidson's 'newly-enhanced influence' (Tapsfield et al.

2017), but also quoted the Brexit Secretary, David Davis, insisting that although official talks might not begin on Monday 19 June as scheduled, they would definitely start later that week. Furthermore, he did not budge from the position that 'the UK would still have to leave the single market, customs union and jurisdiction of the European court' (ibid.). Despite the widely held view that the election result indicated the electorate's preference for a soft Brexit, the man charged with leading Brexit negotiations – presumably with his prime minister's approval – showed little inclination to make a radical change in approach. Indeed, *The Sun* reported him refuting speculation that the government had softened its Brexit stance and insisting that he was still prepared to walk away without a deal if talks did not make satisfactory progress (Clark 2017). Theresa May also signalled that she had no intention of changing course when in her post-election cabinet reshuffle she recalled arch-Brexiteer Michael Gove.

Theresa May and David Davis could talk as tough as they liked but they could not deny the arithmetic of the post-election House of Commons; even with an agreement with the ten DUP MPs, it would not need much of a rebellion by Tory Remainers to defeat the government. Hamish McRae (2017) argued that the election had made the political situation more uncertain but, paradoxically, had actually clarified the economics of Brexit since, whatever May and Davis said days before the start of official talks, two facts had emerged.

> One is that the option of walking away without a deal will be strongly and vigorously opposed by the business establishment – and the power of business to shape policy will be much greater than before. The other is that the Government will adopt some form of collegiate approach to the negotiations, with greater input from Scotland and Northern Ireland, as well as from finance.

It is difficult to argue with these observations: if the CBI and the City insisted that a deal with Brussels had to be struck, the government would be most unlikely to abandon the negotiating table, and since preliminary talks with the

DUP had already opened the door to one Northern Irish party, other parties from the six counties would insist upon equal treatment, which in turn would make it impossible to exclude Scotland. McRae, who understands the complex technicalities of Brexit better than most, also pointed out that something else that was obvious, and 'screamingly so', was that there wasn't time to negotiate a definitive deal before March 2019, which meant that an interim agreement had to be reached to avoid the risk of crashing out of the EU without a deal. His proposal – the 'off-the-shelf solution in the European Economic Area, the Norway relationship' – is anathema to hard Brixiteers but McRae's argument is that it could buy time to permit a permanent deal to be agreed upon.

He was not alone in believing that the government was underestimating the magnitude and the complexity of the forthcoming negotiations. Six days before the general election, when Mrs May was still saying that only she could be trusted to deliver the best Brexit deal for the country, Schona Jolly (2017) noted that with more than two months gone since the triggering of Article 50 the government had done next to nothing 'to prepare us for the Herculean task that lies ahead', was led by someone who 'refuses resolutely to tell us how she envisions Britain after Brexit', had sacrificed time it could ill afford to lose by calling an election, and seemed not to understand how difficult the whole process was going to be.

Lawyers have been warning since before the referendum of the unprecedented legal, constitutional and regulatory complexities that lie ahead. There is no sight of the government's preparation for any of that. Unpicking 40-plus years of frameworks, even if possible, requires a level of skill and resource that simply hasn't been made available to the civil service. This week, the *Financial Times* splashed on the 759 treaties that Britain will need to renegotiate after Brexit 'just to stand still', spanning 168 non-EU countries and covering almost every aspect of a modern economy including customs, trade, fisheries, transport and financial services.

Almost one year after the referendum, there is literally nothing to show in terms of preparations except for a unilateral decision by the PM to pull us out of the single market and customs union. The government refuses to produce a costing or analysis for this. Similarly, it refuses to set out, or even engage with, the disastrous impact of what leaving without a deal will mean. For all May's talk of strength and clarity, her words and actions have revealed neither. Fighting rhetoric might win votes, but it is damaging and useless in real terms; when the horseplay is over, Britain deserves to know its politicians considered all the possible positions and adopted the most sage.

There is no hedging here, no use of epistemic *might* or *could* regarding the consequences of failed Brexit talks. On the contrary, Britain *will* need to renegotiate 759 treaties and leaving the European Union without a deal *will* mean a disastrous impact. Adverbs are used not to hedge but to reinforce ('there is literally nothing to show') or to underline the plain truth of her words ('simply hasn't been made available'). Schona Jolly does not think or believe that May and her government are incompetent; she knows this to be the case, as is immediately evinced from her headline: 'The government has no clue how to deliver Brexit.'

An equally blunt headline – *The Guardian view on Brexit Britain: a clown not a lion* – introduced an unsigned editorial in *The Guardian* three days before talks were due to start, and the editorialist's contempt was aimed not only at Theresa May (accused of 'wooden-headedness' and of refusing 'to allow herself to be deflected by facts'), but also at her chief negotiator.

Next week David Davis, the Brexit secretary, will travel to Brussels to begin talks with the EU. Mr Davis said last month he would be wrangling with Europe all summer over the sequencing of the talks. On Friday, with barely a whimper it emerged that he had accepted Brussels's timetable. Britain will now settle the exit bill and discuss what to do with EU citizens before talking about a future trade deal. Mr Davis has roared like a lion, only to end up looking like a circus clown. It's not just that we look ridiculous, it is that we act ridiculous. Britain is going into talks about how to enact one of the biggest geopolitical shifts this country has ever attempted with no government and no plan.

Returning to Hamish McRae (2017) and his proposal for an interim agreement along the lines of the Norwegian or Swiss models, he concedes that his suggestion presupposes a cooperative attitude on Europe's part, something he believes would be forthcoming provided that Britain addressed its own attitude problem.

> Of course, what really matters here is not so much what we want but Europe wants. Common sense suggests that an interim deal would make sense for Europe as well as the UK. A little less arrogance on our part – and given the mess of the past week I don't think we have much cause to be arrogant – would lead to a more acceptable deal for all. Then the longer-term future of the relationship will be determined by economics and not by politics.

After rescheduling of the Queen's Speech, which had originally been timetabled to coincide with the start of Brexit talks, David Davis was able to fly to Brussels on Monday 19 June to begin negotiations. He did so when talks with the Democratic Unionist Party had not yet produced a formal agreement, and the leader of Sinn Féin, Gerry Adams, was saying that a Conservative-DUP pact was in breach of the Good Friday agreement for Northern Ireland. The Queen's Speech – which is read by the Queen but written by ministers, and sets out the government's agenda at the formal State Opening of Parliament each year – had not yet been delivered, which meant that the government's programme, including its Brexit strategy, had not been revealed to Parliament, discussed and voted upon. Within Davis's party there was a seemingly irreconcilable rift between hard Brexiteers who would countenance no compromise and Remainers – notably the chancellor of the exchequer, Philip

Hammond – tempted to put country before political loyalty and make it clear to the government that the majority of MPs of all parties wanted a soft Brexit and were prepared to use their numerical strength. More mental pabulum for David Davis came from a poll commissioned by none other than the *Mail on Sunday* which showed that two-thirds of voters also favoured the soft option (Owen and Carlin 2017). Speculation was rife as to how long Theresa May could survive as prime minister, with some predicting the party conference in the autumn as the occasion to replace her and others saying that she could, and should, go much earlier. The Labour Party, which was expected to be humiliated on 8 June 2017, had instead been revitalized by its support among the young, and was chomping at the bit to get started on the next election campaign, while its supposedly unelectable leader was talking like a prime minister in waiting.

As David Davis set off for Brussels for the start of talks, Britain did indeed have little cause to be arrogant.

THE EPILOGUE SO FAR

The *Oxford English Reference Dictionary* offers the following definitions of *epilogue*: the concluding part of a literary work; an appendix; a speech or poem addressed to the audience by an actor at the end of a play; a short piece at the end of a day's broadcasting. Britain's decades-long struggle to achieve a satisfactory relationship with Europe is, of course, neither a literary work nor a play, although it does share certain characteristics with a soap opera: it just goes on and on seemingly with no end scheduled, it has moments of melodrama and some of its protagonists risk coming over as caricatures. As things stand at the time of writing, at midnight on 29 March 2019 the UK will be out of the EU whether a deal has been thrashed out or not, but only the most blinkered of Brexiteers believe that that will be the end of it. Indeed, if there is one word we cannot use with reference to Britain and the EU it is *end*: there is no end in sight, nor the prospect of one, hence the oxymoron *The Epilogue So Far*.

I had originally intended to end this work with the result of the referendum of 23 June 2016, and would certainly have done so had there been a victory for Remain. That would not have been the end of the story either – nothing less than a crushing defeat, which was never on the cards, would have persuaded UKIP and Tory Brexiteers to lay down their arms – but the issue would have faded into the background for a while, at least until David Cameron's government had completed its five-year term in 2020. Instead the voters surprised us, although as Jay Elwes (2016) stated with admirable conciseness, what they sprung on us was more a start than an ending.

The European Union referendum delivered a startling result – but not a conclusion. Having voted to leave the EU, Britain faces more questions and uncertainty than it has for a generation and the drive to find solutions to those challenges has only just begun.

The state of our not very United Kingdom that the unexpected result laid bare, plus the national soul-searching that followed, made it impossible not to add one more chapter. Then Theresa May decided that she was not going to let David Cameron outdo her in the hubris stakes, and yet another chapter was required. A book, unlike the UK-EU soap, must, sooner or later, come to an end, and this one ends precisely when talks to decide what kind of Brexit emerges are just beginning. There is no right time to key in the final full-stop when further twists in the plot are sure to come, but not to do so at all would render the whole enterprise futile.

Of the many variables responsible for the unpredictability of future developments, there are some that I cannot comment upon with any authority because I do not have access to the necessary information. These include the behind-the-scenes wheeling and dealing in both Westminster and Brussels, and the true health of the European Union given the level of indebtedness of certain member states, notably the one in which I live. Sticking to what I know, or can at least inform myself about, I'll conclude this work with a look at demographic factors before returning to my comfort zone of language.

YouGov figures quoted in Chapter 14 indicated that 71 per cent of 18- to 24-year-olds voted Remain while 64 per cent of people aged 65 or over opted for Leave. If the vote in June 2017 had been a repeat referendum rather than a general election, the result might well have reversed that of June 2016 given that over the previous twelve months, hundreds of thousands of 18-year-olds had been added to the electoral register while a considerable number of over 65s had died. Just four months after 23 June 2016, thirteen post-referendum polls had been conducted, eleven of which indicated that a majority of the British population wanted to stay in the EU (Low 2016). The disparity between these polls and the referendum result can be attributed to the fact that among the 11.9 million people who did not turn out on the day, Remain supporters outnumbered Leavers by a ratio of two-to-one (ibid.). As we have seen, young people in particular did not exercise their democratic right, but in 2017 they turned out in much greater numbers to disconcert Theresa May, partly because university students were better informed, but also because of the Corbyn factor in combating apathy. That cannot change the injustice perpetrated on young people in 2016 since it is difficult to see how redress can be achieved with anything short of a second referendum, and at the time of writing such a proposal would provoke an apoplectic response from Leavers.

That is not to say that the public mood will not shift in the months and years to come; if there is one constant in the British people's attitudes towards Europe it is inconstancy. What is clear is that those Remainers who do not believe that the game is up – the Remoaners according to the right-wing tabloids – have demography on their side: with each month that passes mostly pro-EU 18-year-olds acquire the right to vote and replace the mostly Brexit-supporting elderly people who embark on their final journey. UK politicians will have to respond to that trend.

The referendum result of 2016 was a triumph for *The Sun*, the *Daily Mail* and the *Daily Express*, and the general election result a year later was an unexpected defeat for the same three tabloids. What happened in the interim will be considered below, but first of all it needs to be stated that reports of the demise of Britain's tabloid newspapers have not been exaggerated; they have been plain wrong. The *Daily Mail* still sells 1.5 million copies per day, but that figure is a million down from its peak in 2003. As a news provider, however, *The Mail* today reaches more people than at any time in its history because, far from being driven into irrelevance by the internet, it thrives thanks to the same technology. As Addison (2017: position 6072) notes:

MailOnline is the most visited English-language newspaper website in the world, with around 15 million or so visitors a day. And it is starting to generate cash to cover the decline in profits from the company's newspapers. *Daily Mail* content is now read by more people – more *young* people – than ever before. And it's always hiring: the old newspaper has a shrinking editorial staff of around 330, fewer than half *MailOnline*'s ever-expanding total staff of over 800.

Other newspapers have stayed in business by going digital, and as long as their websites make most content accessible without a paid subscription, they will continue to attract a great many visitors. While the paper editions still have faithful readers who have their favourite newspaper (one that reflects their own values and political views) delivered each day, the online versions do not command the same loyalty and their visitors sometimes disagree strongly enough with an editorial line to contribute feedback attacking not just a specific post, but sometimes the newspaper as an institution. When young people click on the websites of *The Sun* or *The Express* they might decide to share selected content on social media, not necessarily because they agree with it, but often to make its unpleasantness known to others. A decline in sales does not, therefore, mean a decline in readership and influence, which explains why most leading politicians still prefer to be on good terms with Rupert Murdoch and the editor of *The Mail*, Paul Dacre.

As noted in Chapter 12 with reference to an article by Jane Martinson (2016), during the referendum campaign the right-wing tabloids tended to set the agenda, forcing more authoritative and impartial media – notably the BBC – to follow suit. So when Remain wanted to focus on the economic reasons for staying in the EU, the tabloids hammered away at the immigration question and did so with language that stopped just short of being actionable under Britain's race relations legislation. Indeed, Tim Adams (2017) noted that on 'the 23 weekdays before the referendum, the *Mail* led with this immigration narrative on 17 of them'. Of the six days when a different subject dominated the front page, one was 17 June when the murder of Labour MP Jo Cox was reported, and even then *The Mail*'s emphasis was on the killer's mental illness and how the social services had failed him rather than his extreme nationalism. Similarly, the tabloids' employment of metaphors of constraint – *chains*, *shackles* and the like – to attack the allegedly excessive regulation imposed by the EU was ridiculously over the top, but by dint of constant repetition the naturalization process set in to the extent that Remainers tended to concede that something had to be done to slim down Brussels bureaucracy instead of pointing out that much of the so-called red tape protects the environment or consumers.

Andy Beckett (2016) used the headline 'Revenge of the tabloids' to introduce a long article analysing the influence of the popular press over the decades, and specifically the clear evidence in recent years that the power of the tabloids is not diminishing as some commentators have claimed. Their success in the referendum followed the 2015 general election campaign in which *The Sun*, *The Mail* and *The Express* had launched daily attacks on the then Labour leader, Ed Milliband, and played a crucial role in a victory for the Conservatives that the polls, and probably the Tories themselves, had not expected. After the referendum Paul Dacre could also claim credit for Theresa May's becoming prime minister instead of the popular favourite, Boris Johnson; he had for years been an admirer – he was not alone in having been taken in by her new-iron-maiden pretensions – and the Conservative Party has traditionally been willing to listen to a newspaper it considers a loyal and extremely useful ally. Writing in the autumn of 2016, Beckett saw the symbiotic relationship between the right-wing tabloids and the Tory Party as dictating the terms of debate in British politics.

British politics now feels relentlessly tabloid-dominated. From the daily obsession with immigrants to the rubbishing of human rights lawyers, from the march towards a 'hard Brexit' to the smearing of liberal Britons as bad losers and elitists, the tabloids and the Conservative right are collaborating with a closeness and a swagger not seen since at least the early 90s.

From a position of such strength, how did *The Sun*, *The Mail* and *The Express* contrive to get it so wrong just a few months later? Their attacks on Jeremy Corbyn as an unpatriotic communist and a friend of terrorists were brutal yet the Labour Party – which many commentators had believed to be moribund – did so much better than expected that coming a close second felt like a victory, and during the election campaign Corbyn's personal approval ratings soared (albeit from a very low starting point). The headlines and leads to articles by Will Gore (2017) and Suzanne Moore (2017) for *The Independent* and *The Guardian* respectively, both published on 9 June 2017, contradict Beckett by stating boldly that the tabloids no longer exert great power over politics.

The right-wing press no longer wields absolute power in modern Britain. This election proves it

In this era of ever-greater media plurality, voters are better equipped to make political decisions because they can examine a range of views and sources

The *Sun* and *Mail* tried to crush Corbyn. But their power over politics is broken

Voters saw through the tabloids' hysterical attacks on the Labour leader. Now their feared editors just look like strange angry blokes selling hate

Will Gore draws a parallel between a referendum in which Remain overestimated the extent to which voters could be motivated by fear and an election in which the tabloids' similarly monomaniacal insistence on Corbyn's ghastliness overestimated the efficacy of what he overtly calls 'the politics of hate'. His conclusion is that the tabloids have taken a beating, and in stating it he cheekily adopts a little Cockney slang in a way that we are used to reading in a certain newspaper's punning headlines: 'The *Express* is on the ropes. The *Daily Mail* is bruised. The "Currant Bun" is crumbling.'

Suzanne Moore focuses on Labour's ability to connect with the public thanks to their leader's willingness to go out and talk to people, plus the old-fashioned canvassing work done by the party's army of young volunteers. In contrast, the editors of the right-wing tabloids who 'regularly boast about having their fingers on the populist pulse failed dramatically'. Moore's conclusion is as emphatic as Gore's: 'In this one moment they are cut down to size: not fixers of government, not the high priests of the electorate but strange angry blokes selling seven varieties of hate while ranting to themselves.'

The tabloids could not have gone from 'a swagger not seen since at least the early 90s' to being 'on the ropes', 'bruised' and 'crumbling' in just eight months, which suggests that either Beckett or Gore and Moore must be very wrong indeed. I suspect that Beckett is right to see the popular right-wing press as still a force to be reckoned with despite their tactical error in persevering with their character assassination of Jeremy Corbyn when there was growing evidence that it was no longer working. As early as October 2016 Beckett acknowledged that the Labour leader – apparently an absurdly easy target for the tabloids when he took over the party leadership – was proving to be something of an enigma. While one of his predecessors, Tony Blair, emulated the Tories in his determination not to provoke Rupert Murdoch, and others like Neil Kinnock and Gordon Brown clearly harboured a sense of grievance, Corbyn just serenely went on his way as if the tabloids did not exist.

The Labour leader Jeremy Corbyn is 14 months into an experiment in ignoring the tabloids. It may well be doomed; but his leadership has already lasted longer than the tabloids expected, and their ceaseless attacks on him, like their shouting down of anyone who doubts Brexit will be a success, have a small undertone of anxiety about them.

By the final days of the election campaign, that undertone of anxiety had morphed into hysteria, but just as Remainers a year earlier had merely raised the volume of Project Fear instead of trying something different, so *The Sun*, *The Express* and *The Mail* simply intensified their accusations of sympathy for terrorists despite the fact that younger voters had no memory of IRA bombings and possibly did not know what the initials stood for. They are unlikely to make the same mistake again.

At the time of writing the right-wing tabloids are untypically restrained, still licking their wounds after the predicted Tory landslide turned into an embarrassing own goal, and possibly feeling a little foolish about having thrown their weight behind a prime minister who will be burdened with the 'weak and wobbly' moniker for the rest of her career. They will be back, however, baying for blood as never before, because Labour's radical agenda confronts their cherished neoliberal ideology head-on, and the public's positive response to that programme in June 2017 terrifies them. How they choose to attack the opposition after the failure of the 'apologists for terrorism' strategy remains to be seen, but attack they most certainly will. The tactics and the language will change but the objective – the total destruction of Corbyn – will remain the same. As will his determination to ignore whatever they say about him.

As noted in Chapter 14, it was only after their referendum defeat that the pro-EU 48 per cent began to use impassioned language. Young people who turned to social media to express their sense of betrayal in the strongest terms had contributed very little to the debate leading up to 23 June 2016. More mature commentators who had imbued their case for Remain with measured tones, hedging techniques and back-covering modality suddenly sounded strident and devoid of doubt, and the contrast between their pre- and post-referendum language made it easy for Brexiteers to dismiss the latter as the petulant tantrums of a sneering elite unused to not getting their own way. The novelist Julian Barnes (2017) sees the root of the problem as the fact that pro-EU politicians have always stressed the benefits for commerce and business of being part of a European association but have never promoted a vision of European unity as a great ideal and a triumph for civilized values.

> Politicians never tried to sell Europe to the British people as anything other than an advantageous commercial joint venture. Ours has been an entirely pragmatic membership, never an idealistic one. We never bought into Europe as a *grand projet*, or even as an expression of fraternity. All this makes it hard for many here to imagine that idealism about the EU still has breath and life within Europe. After the Brexit vote, many of my European friends expressed disbelief and astonishment. It seemed to them that we had run mad in the noonday sun.

Barnes would doubtless encounter considerably less disbelief and astonishment if he spoke to office cleaners in Wolverhampton or unemployed former miners in Barnsley, but it is difficult to quarrel with his assessment of our entirely pragmatic membership of the EU. Idealism can be expressed in magniloquent language with soaring rhetoric and a poetic flourish; pragmatism is inevitably conveyed in reasonable and measured terms shorn of verbal pyrotechnics. The Brexit debate pitted pro-EU pragmatists against people striving – or claiming to strive – for the high ideals of freedom and democracy, and the language used by the two sides reflected that division.

Whether Britons will one day start to talk of European unity in ardent tones comparable with the Brexiteers' eulogizing of national independence is unlikely but not to be ruled out entirely. In 1979 the Labour prime minister Jim Callaghan, sensing that he was about to suffer a general election defeat by Margaret Thatcher, made an observation that has ensured his inclusion in every collection of political quotations:

> You know there are times, perhaps once every thirty years, when there is a sea change in politics. It then does not matter what you say or what you do. There is a shift in what the public wants and what it approves of. I suspect that there is now such a sea change and it is for Mrs Thatcher.

He was right: the post-war social democratic consensus was about to be challenged by the double whammy of Thatcherism and Reaganomics, and then overwhelmed by the fall-out from the collapse of the Soviet Union. Callaghan uttered those words nearly forty years ago, which means that by his own estimate of the timing of such trends, another sea change is overdue. There are commentators who believe that Bernie Sanders' strong performance in the Democratic primaries, the rise of Podemos in Spain and Labour's revival in the UK are all signs of much more than a rejection of austerity and inequality, but signify the start of a mighty swing against deregulated free-market capitalism. If that is indeed the case – and those hoping for fundamental change have been deceived by enough false dawns not to get too carried away – the EU in its present form could not order back the waves, but would be forced to adapt and reform, perhaps along the lines proposed by Yanis Varoufakis in *And The Weak Suffer What They Must? Europe, Austerity and the Threat to Global Security* (2017). And if that happened, the 18-year-olds replacing elderly Brexiteers on the electoral register could well spearhead a drive to rejoin a Europe united for very different purposes, a European project they could actually talk about with a certain passion.

If no sea change happens, however, the Brexit talks currently in progress will probably not draw a line under the vexed question of Britain's relationship with Europe. The referendum of 1975 was meant to settle the matter once and for all, and the deal, or lack of a deal, that emerges from current negotiations is unlikely to do a better job at achieving that end. Whether you see the whole story as a saga, a drama or a soap opera makes little difference: there will be more twists in the plot in the years ahead.

REFERENCES

Adams, Tim (2017), 'Is the editor of the *Daily Mail* the most dangerous man in Britain?', *The Observer*, 14 May. Available online: https://www.theguardian.com/media/2017/may/14/is-paul-dacre-most-dangerous-man-in-britain-daily-mail (accessed 21 June 2017).

Addison, Adrian (2017), *Mail Men: The Unauthorized Story of the* Daily Mail. London: Atlantic Books (Kindle edition).

Allen, Emily (2017), 'How will the general election result affect Brexit?', *The Telegraph*, 9 June. Available online: http://www.telegraph.co.uk/news/0/will-general-election-result-affect-brexit/ (accessed 16 June 2017).

Ashton, Emily (2014), 'Stick it up your Juncker', *The Sun*, 2 June. Available online: https://www.thesun.co.uk/archives/politics/861295/stick-it-up-your-juncker/ (accessed 7 April 2016).

Austin, John (1962), *How to Do Things with Words*. Oxford: Oxford University Press.

Barford, Vanessa (2017), 'Election results 2017: 20 things you may have missed', *BBC*, 9 June. Available online: http://www.bbc.com/news/election-2017-40211261 (accessed 16 June 2017).

Barnes, Julian (2017), 'Diary', *London Review of Books* 39/8, 20 April, pp. 41–43.

Beale, Claire (2016), 'Agencies' anger at failure of Stronger In campaign', *The Campaign*, 30 June. Available online: http://www.campaignlive.co.uk/article/agencies-anger-failure-stronger-campaign/1400533 (accessed 7 May 2017).

Beaumont, Paul (2016), 'What the Euros 2016 football fan violence tells us about tribalism in Europe – and anger in the Brexit debate', *The Independent*, 15 June. Available online: http://www.independent.co.uk/voices/football-violence-euro-2016-france-marseille-brexit-tribalism-eu-referendum-a7083171.html (accessed 17 June 2016).

Beckett, Andy (2016), 'Revenge of the tabloids', *The Guardian*, 27 October. Available online: https://www.theguardian.com/media/2016/oct/27/revenge-of-the-tabloids-brexit-dacre-murdoch (accessed 22 June 2017).

Beer, Stevie (2016), 'Michael Gove urges voters to "free the country from a sinking ship" ', *The Express*, 21 June. Available online: http://www.express.co.uk/news/uk/681828/Michael-Gove-brands-European-Union-unemployment-creating-tragedy?_ga=1.21796 5846.1284735065.1486896631 (accessed 14 March 2017).

Belam, Martin (2007), 'The "feelthy" French get hold of *The Sun*'s front page', *currybet.net*, 16 December. Available online: http://www.currybet.net/cbet_blog/2007/12/the-feelthy-french-get-hold-of.php (accessed 24 April 2017).

Bloor, Meriel and Thomas Bloor (2013), *The Practice of Critical Discourse Analysis: An Introduction* (2nd edn). Abingdon (UK) and New York: Routledge.

Boult, Adam (2016), 'Millenials' "fury" over baby boomers' vote for Brexit', *The Telegraph*, 24 June. Available online: http://www.telegraph.co.uk/news/2016/06/24/millenials-fury-over-baby-boomers-vote-for-brexit/ (accessed 17 May 2017).

Boyle, Simon (2016), 'Jude Law's minders attacked by Calais Jungle migrants during charity visit', *Sunday People*, 27 February. Available online: http://www.mirror.co.uk/3am/celebrity-news/jude-laws-minders-attacked-calais-7455214 (accessed 7 June 2017).

'Brexit and the newspapers – where was IPSO?', *Hacked Off*, 5 July. Available online: http://hackinginquiry.org/latest-news/brexit-and-the-newspapers-where-was-ipso-2/ (accessed 5 May 2017).

Brown, Penelope and Stephen Levinson (1978), 'Universals in language usage: Politeness phenomena', in E. Goody (ed.), *Questions and Politeness: Strategies in Social Interaction*. Cambridge: Cambridge University Press.

Brown, Sophie (2015), '*Daily Mail* Headline From 1938 Draws Comparisons With Current Reporting Of Calais Migrant Crisis', *Huffington Post UK*, 3 August. Available online: http://www.huffingtonpost.co.uk/2015/07/31/daily-mail-1938-jews_n_7909954.html (accessed 31 March 2017).

Buckley, Jemma, Tamara Cohen and Tim Sculthorpe (2016), 'Luvvie Emma sneers at Britain: I'm European, she claims, in bizarre tirade against us quitting Brussels', *The Mail*, 17 February. Available online: http://www.dailymail.co.uk/news/article-3449390/Emma-Thompson-leads-luvvies-telling-Britain-stay-Europe-not-retreat-cake-filled-misery-laden-grey-old-island.html (accessed 26 May 2017).

Burrows, Thomas (2016), 'June 23 could be UK's Independence Day says Nigel Farage as Boris says an Out vote will be FINAL and urges cabinet colleagues to back quitting the EU', *The Mail*, 27 February. Available online: http://www.dailymail.co.uk/news/article-3466968/EU-vote-offers-Britain-chance-independence-day-says-Ukips-Nigel-Farage.html (accessed 25 May 2017).

Byrne, Ciar (2003), '*Sun*'s French stunt branded "disgusting"', *The Guardian*, 21 February. Available online: https://www.theguardian.com/media/2003/feb/21/pressandpublishing.Iraqandthemedia (accessed 15 April 2017).

Cameron, David (2016), 'PM statement following European Council meeting: 19 February 2016', *UK Government*, 20 February. Available online: https://www.gov.uk/government/speeches/pms-statement-following-european-council-meeting-19-february-2016 (accessed 23 September 2016).

Cameron, David (2016), 'For heaven's sake turn out – or you'll find we're all out', *The Independent*, 20 March, pp. 4–5.

Cameron, David (2016), 'PM's speech on strength and security in the EU: 9 May 2016', *UK Government*, 9 May. Available online: https://www.gov.uk/government/speeches/pm-speech-on-the-uks-strength-and-security-in-the-eu-9-may-2016 (accessed 10 February 2017).

Chilton, Brendan (2016), 'EU does nothing for working people, says Labour Leave's Brendan Chilton', *The Express*, 15 June. Available online: http://www.express.co.uk/comment/expresscomment/679971/eu-referendum-brexit-working-people-labour-leave (accessed 15 June 2016).

Chovanec, Jan (2010), 'Legitimation through differentation: Discursive construction of Jacques *Le Worm* Chirac as an opponent to military action', in Okulska, Urszula and Piotr Cap (eds), *Perspectives in Politics and Discourse*, Amsterdam/Philadelphia: John Benjamins.

Clark, Natasha (2017), BREXIT WOBBLES? David Davis says Brexit talks which are due to start Monday could be delayed – and says he has prepared Britain for no deal', *The Sun*, 12 June. Available online: https://www.thesun.co.uk/news/3778923/david-davis-says-brexit-talks-which-are-due-to-start-monday-could-be-delayed/ (accessed 17 June 2017).

Clark, Ross (2016), 'Even the pro-EU campaign sounds very half-hearted, says Ross Clark', *The Express*, 22 February. Available online: http://www.express.co.uk/comment/expresscomment/646459/Ross-Clark-pro-EU-stay-campaign-half-hearted (accessed 23 September 2016).

Cohen, Nick (2017), 'Posturing behind "the people"', *The Prospect*, March 2017, p. 6.

Congdon, Tim (2016), 'Ignore Project Fear: Brexit Won't Ruin Us', *The Standpoint*, June. Available online: http://www.standpointmag.co.uk/features-june-2016-tim-congdon-ignore-project-fear-brexit-wont-ruin-us?page=0%2C0%2C0%2C0%2C0%2C0%2C0%2C0%2C0%2C0%2C0 (accessed 30 June 2016).

Cooper, Charlie and Oliver Wright (2016), 'EU referendum: David Cameron says Isis and Vladimir Putin "might be happy" with Brexit', *The Independent*, 17 May. Available online: http://www.independent.co.uk/news/uk/politics/eu-referendum-david-cameron-isis-putin-brexit-a7033741.html (accessed 18 April 2017).

Cooper, Charlie (2016), 'Cameron is no Europhile – and that's why his opponents tell a more convincing story', *The Independent*, 6 June. Available online: http://www.independent.co.uk/voices/brexit-eu-referendum-david-cameron-is-no-europhile-tell-a-convincing-story-a7067686.html (accessed 31 May 2017).

Cooper, Yvette (2016), 'Women will get a raw deal if we pull out of the EU', *The Mirror*, 8 March. Available online: http://www.mirror.co.uk/news/uk-news/women-raw-deal-pull-out-7512141 (accessed 22 September 2016).

Cosslett, Rhiannon Lucy (2016), 'If you're young and angry about the EU referendum, you're right to be', *The Guardian*, 24 June. Available online: https://www.theguardian.com/commentisfree/2016/jun/24/young-angry-eu-referendum (accessed 16 May 2017).

Cosslett, Rhiannon Lucy (2016), 'Family rifts over Brexit: "I can barely look at my parents"', *The Guardian*, 27 June. Available online: https://www.theguardian.com/lifeandstyle/2016/jun/27/brexit-family-rifts-parents-referendum-conflict-betrayal (accessed 29 June 2016).

Crystal, David (1994), *An Encyclopedic Dictionary of Language and Languages*. London: Penguin Books.

Dathan, Matt (2015), 'Election results: 10 charts that show how Britain voted', *The Independent*, 8 May. Available online: http://www.independent.co.uk/news/uk/politics/generalelection/election-results-10-charts-that-show-how-britain-voted-10237410.html (accessed 3 April 2017).

Dawkins, Richard (2016), 'Richard Dawkins: ignoramuses should have no say on our EU membership – and that includes me', *Prospect*, 9 June. Available online: https://www.prospectmagazine.co.uk/magazine/eu-referendum-richard-dawkins-brexit-23rd-june-ignoramuses (accessed 10 June 2016).

Dearlove, Richard (2016), 'Brexit would not damage UK security', *The Prospect*, 23 March. Available online: http://www.prospectmagazine.co.uk/opinions/brexit-would-not-damage-uk-security (accessed 26 May 2017).

Dewson, Andrew (2016), 'A Brexit would break up Britain – and dismantle the Commonwealth too', *The Independent*, 30 May. Available online: http://www. independent.co.uk/voices/brexit-boris-johnson-break-up-britain-independent-scotland-nicola-sturgeon-dismantle-commonwealth-a7056181.html (accessed 16 October 2016).

Dixon, Hugo (2016), 'City won't thrive if we quit EU', Mythbust page, *InFacts*, 7 April. Available online: https://infacts.org/mythbusts/city-wont-thrive-quit-eu/ (accessed 5 May 2017).

Dixon, Hugo and Luke Lythgoe (2016), 'EU-bashing stories are misleading voters – here are eight of the most toxic tales', *The Guardian*, 19 May. Available online: https:// www.theguardian.com/commentisfree/2016/may/19/inaccurate-pro-brexit-infacts-investigation-media-reports-eu-referendum (accessed 25 June 2016).

Dixon, Hugo and Luke Lythgoe (2016), 'Six more Brexit myths from the Eurosceptic press', *The Guardian*, 2 June. Available online: https://www.theguardian.com/commentisfree/ 2016/jun/02/six-brexit-myths-eurosceptic-press-vote-23-june (accessed 2 June 2016).

Dodds, Laurence (2017), 'Was this the revenge of the liberal metropolitan elite?', *The Telegraph*, 9 June. Available online: http://www.telegraph.co.uk/news/2017/06/09/ revenge-liberal-metropolitan-elite/ (accessed 14 June 2017).

Dowell, Ben (2012), 'Rupert Murdoch: "*Sun* wot won it" headline was tasteless and wrong', *The Guardian*, 25 April. Available online: https://www.theguardian.com/media/2012/ apr/25/rupert-murdoch-sun-wot-won-it-tasteless (accessed 24 April 2017).

Doyle, Jack (2016), 'Fury at Dave's "Dodgy Dossier": Pro-EU camp accused of new bout of cynical scaremongering', *The Mail*, 1 March. Available online: http://www.dailymail. co.uk/news/article-3470323/Fury-Dave-s-Dodgy-Dossier-Pro-EU-camp-accused-new-bout-cynical-scaremongering.html (accessed 8 April 2017).

Dunn, Megan (2016), 'The Europe debate matters most to millenials – and we want to stay in', *The Guardian*, 15 March. Available online: https://www.theguardian.com/ commentisfree/2016/mar/15/europe-debate-millennials-in-eu-britain-students (accessed 20 March 2016).

Elliott, Francis and Sam Coates (2016), 'Britain votes for Brexit', *The Times*, 24 June. Available online: https://www.thetimes.co.uk/article/closest-call-for-britain-5rcrxnjh0 (accessed 25 June 2016).

Elwes, Jay (2016), 'A result, but no conclusion', *The Prospect*, August 2016, p. 1.

'EU facts behind the claims: Regulation and the single market' (2016), *Full Fact*, 25 April. Available online: https://fullfact.org/europe/eu-facts-behind-claims-regulation-and-single-market/ (accessed 8 March 2017).

'Euromyths', *European Commission in the UK*. Available online: http://blogs.ec.europa.eu/ ECintheUK/category/euromyths/ (accessed 30 March 2016).

'Facts: Jobs' (2016), *Labour in for Britain*. Available online: http://labourinforbritain.org. uk/facts/jobs/ (accessed 15 October 2016).

Fairclough, Norman (2001), *Language and Power* (2nd edn). Harlow (UK): Pearson Education.

Fairclough, Norman (2003), *Analysing Discourse: Textual Analysis for Social Research*. London and New York: Routledge.

Farage, Nigel (2014), 'No one can call Ukip a racist party now', *The Times*, 9 May. Available online: http://www.thetimes.co.uk/article/nobody-can-call-ukip-a-racist-party-now-knzlj52ndn8 (accessed 27 March 2017).

Forsyth, Frederick (2016), 'The EU was never meant to be a democracy, says Frederick Forsyth,' *Sunday Express*, 10 March. Available online: http://www.express.co.uk/comment/columnists/frederick-forsyth/651377/Brexit-referendum-EU-never-meant-to-be-democracy-says-Frederick-Forsyth (accessed 26 February 2017).

'For the many not the few' (2017), *Labour Party*. Available online: http://www.labour.org.uk/page/-/Images/manifesto-2017/Labour%20Manifesto%202017.pdf (accessed 17 June 2017).

Foster, Alice (2016), 'Brexit in the making: Timeline of the road to the EU referendum', *The Express*, 22 June. Available online: http://www.express.co.uk/news/politics/682341/Brexit-in-making-EU-referendum-2016-timeline-road-to-vote-campaign-Britain-leave-EU (accessed 25 May 2017).

Freedman, Des (2015), 'Was it "the *Sun* wot won it"? Lessons from the 1992 and 2015 elections', *openDemocracyUK*, 13 May. Available online: https://www.opendemocracy.net/ourkingdom/des-freedman/was-it-'-sun-wot-won-it'-press-influence-in-1992-and-2015-elections (accessed 29 April 2017).

Gaitskell, Hugh (1962), Speech against British membership of the EEC, *Britain and the Common Market, Texts of speeches made at the 1962 Labour Party conference by the Rt. Hon. Hugh Gaitskell M.P. and the Rt. Hon. George Brown M.P. together with the policy statement accepted by the Conference*, London: Labour Party, pp. 3–23. Available online: http://www.cvce.eu/content/publication/1999/1/1/05f2996b-000b-4576-8b42-8069033a16f9/publishable_en.pdf (accessed 12 February 2017).

Gayle, Damien (2016), 'Wetherspoon chief says staying in EU bad for small businesses', *The Guardian* 26 March. Available online: https://www.theguardian.com/world/2016/mar/26/staying-in-eu-bad-for-small-businesses-says-wetherspoon-chief (accessed 8 March 2017).

Glaze, Ben and Dan Bloom (2016), 'Brexit could trigger World War Three, warns David Cameron', *The Mirror*, 9 May. Available online: http://www.mirror.co.uk/news/uk-news/brexit-could-trigger-world-war-7928607 (accessed 10 May 2016).

Goodhart, David (2017), *The Road to Somewhere: The Populist Revolt and the Future of Politics*. London: C. Hurst.

Gordon, Tom (2014), 'I admit it: The man who coined Project Fear label', *Sunday Herald*, 21 December. Available online: http://www.heraldscotland.com/news/13194407.I_admit_it__the_man_who_coined_Project_Fear_label/ (accessed 5 April 2017).

Gore, Will (2016), 'The right-wing press no longer wields absolute power in modern Britain. This election proves it', *The Independent*, 9 June. Available online: http://www.independent.co.uk/voices/corbyn-success-tories-lose-seats-daily-mail-the-sun-the-express-right-wing-press-no-influence-modern-a7781126.html (accessed 22 June 2017).

Grice, Andrew (2017), 'No matter who forms a government this is the end of hard Brexit', *The Independent*, 9 June. Available online: http://www.independent.co.uk/voices/brexit-general-election-hung-parliament-end-of-hard-a7781006.html (accessed 16 June 2017).

Grice, H. Paul (1975), 'Logic and Conversation', in P. Cole and L. Morgan (eds), *Syntax and Semantics 3: Speech Acts*. New York: Academic Press, 41–58.

Grundy, Peter (2008), *Doing Pragmatics* (3rd edn). Abingdon (UK): Routledge.

Guldberg, Helene (2016), 'What Do Leave Voters Really Think?', *Spiked*, 6 July. Available online: http://www.spiked-online.com/newsite/article/what-do-leave-voters-really-think-brexit/18532#.WQ7lulJabuR (accessed 3 May 2017).

Gutteridge, Nick (2016), 'Europe disintegrates: Now Germany threatens sanctions against EU states over migrant crisis', *The Express*, 22 February. Available online: http://www.express.co.uk/news/world/645778/European-Union-EU-Germany-Angela-Merkel-migrants-Brexit?_ga=1.159862201.502485035.1456252678 (accessed 30 March 2017).

Gutteridge, Nick (2016), 'End of British Army? EU plots "scandalous" military merger if UK votes to stay in', *The Express*, 29 February. Available online: http://www.express.co.uk/news/uk/648052/EU-referendum-Brussels-plot-military-merger-UK-stay-in-British-Army-UKIP (accessed 26 May 2017).

Gutteridge, Nick (2016), '"Your vote means NOTHING" Brussels insists land grab plot WILL go ahead despite Dutch "no"', *Daily Express*, 7 April. Available online: http://www.express.co.uk/news/politics/659147/Dutch-referendum-EU-leaders-Ukraine-deal-Netherlands-no-vote-Juncker-Merkel-Hollande (accessed 24 February 2017).

Gutteridge, Nick (2016), 'Britain has started a revolution against "stupid" Brussels elite and EU is "doomed"', *The Express*, 2 July 2016. Available online: http://www.express.co.uk/news/politics/685286/EU-referendum-Brexit-Black-Swan-Nassim-Taleb-Brussels-elite (accessed 19 May 2017).

Gysin, Patrick (2017), 'A message to Merkel. Little Britain? We've got a simple message for the critics who ridiculed the 17.4 million of you who voted Leave for daring to dump the EU', *The Sun*, 18 January. Available online: https://www.thesun.co.uk/news/2649811/little-britain-weve-got-a-simple-message-for-the-critics-who-ridiculed-the-17-4-million-of-you-who-voted-leave-for-daring-to-dump-the-eu/ (accessed 3 February 2017).

Harris, John (2014), 'Fear and anger in once-wealthy town divided by insecurity and immigration', *The Guardian*, 16 June 2014. Available online: https://www.theguardian.com/society/2014/jun/16/fear-anger-wisbech-cambridgeshire-insecurity-immigration (accessed 1 April 2017).

Hattersley, Roy (1998), *Fifty Years on: A Prejudiced History of Britain since the War*. London: Abacus.

Hawkes, Steve, Craig Woodhouse and Harry Cole (2016), 'Fighting Off The Girls. Boris Johnson fights off extraordinary attacks about Brexit from Tory minister during EU referendum debate', *The Sun*, 10 June. Available online: https://www.thesun.co.uk/news/1259406/boris-johnson-fights-off-extraordinary-attacks-about-brexit-from-tory-minister-during-eu-referendum-debate/ (accessed 14 June 2016).

Hawkes, Steve, Lynn Davidson and Harry Cole (2016), 'Bojo's rallying cry. Boris Johnson urges *Sun* readers "with history in their hands" to back Brexit', *The Sun*, 22 June. Available online: https://www.thesun.co.uk/news/1326774/boris-johnson-urges-sun-readers-with-history-in-their-hands-to-back-brexit/ (accessed 23 June 2016).

Heath, Allister (2016), 'Remainers are moving heaven and earth – but not the polls', *The Telegraph*, 11 May. Available online: http://www.telegraph.co.uk/news/2016/05/11/remainers-are-moving-heaven-and-earth--but-not-the-polls/ (accessed 12 May 2016).

Heath, Allister (2016), 'Brexit will make us richer. That's why Leave could still win', *The Guardian*, 25 May. Available online: http://www.telegraph.co.uk/business/2016/05/25/brexit-will-make-us-richer-thats-why-leave-could-still-win/ (accessed 14 March 2017).

Henley, Jon (2016), 'Why vote Leave's £350m weekly EU cost claim is wrong', *The Guardian*, 10 June. Available online: https://www.theguardian.com/politics/reality-check/2016/may/23/does-the-eu-really-cost-the-uk-350m-a-week (accessed 23 May 2017).

Hix, Simon (2016), 'Is the EU really run by unelected bureaucrats?', *Blog on LSE site*, 21 June. Available on line: http://blogs.lse.ac.uk/europpblog/2016/06/21/is-the-eu-really-run-by-unelected-bureaucrats/ (accessed 27 February 2017).

Hookham, Mark and Dipesh Gadher (2013), 'UKIP candidate barred over his far right links', *The Times*, 28 April. Available online: http://www.thetimes.co.uk/article/ukip-candidate-barred-over-his-far-right-links-m3zc5ldpfn0 (accessed 27 March 2017).

Hope, Christopher (2017), 'Project Fear Brexit predictions were "flawed and partisan", new study says', *The Telegraph*, 5 January. Available online: http://www.telegraph.co.uk/news/2017/01/05/project-fear-brexit-predictions-flawed-partisan-new-study-says/ (accessed 8 April 2017).

'How democratic is the European Union?' (2016), *The Conversation*, 20 May. Available online: https://theconversation.com/how-democratic-is-the-european-union-59419 (accessed 27 February 2017).

'How leaving the EU could set Britain free' (2016), *Daily Mail*, 20 April. Available online: http://www.dailymail.co.uk/debate/article-3548861/DAILY-MAIL-COMMENT-leaving-EU- set-Britain-free.html (accessed 8 March 2017).

Huddlestone, Rodney (1984), *Introduction to the Grammar of English*. Cambridge: Cambridge University Press.

Huddlestone, Rodney (1988), *English Grammar: An Outline*. Cambridge: Cambridge University Press.

Hughes, David and Richard Wheeler (2016), 'David Cameron warns that cheap flights in Europe could be put at risk by Brexit', *The Mirror*, 5 April. Available online: http://www.mirror.co.uk/news/uk-news/david-cameron-warns-cheap-flights-7695974 (accessed 17 October 2016).

'It's Operation Desperation' (2016), *Morning Star*, 8 April. Available online: http://www.morningstaronline.co.uk/a-dca7-Its-operation-desperation#.WLAOKBih03h (accessed 24 February 2017).

'Jean-Claude Juncker's most outrageous political quotations' (2014), *The Telegraph*, 15 July. Available online: http://www.telegraph.co.uk/news/worldnews/europe/eu/10967168/Jean-Claude-Junckers-most-outrageous-political-quotations.html (accessed 24 September 2016).

Jeffries, Lesley (2010), *Critical Stylistics: The Power of English*. Basingstoke: Palgrave Macmillan.

'Jeremy Corbyn on *The Last Leg*' (2016), *vimeo.com*. Available online: https://vimeo.com/170254997 (accessed 16 September 2016).

Johnston, Philip (2016), 'David Cameron, the conquering hero a year ago, is in the fight of his life', *The Telegraph*, 10 May. Available online: http://www.telegraph.co.uk/news/2016/05/10/david-cameron-the-conquering-hero-a-year-ago-is-in-the-fight-of/ (accessed 10 May 2017).

Jolly, Schona (2017), 'The government has no clue how to deliver Brexit', *The Prospect*, 2 June. Available online: https://www.prospectmagazine.co.uk/politics/the-government-has-no-clue-how-to-deliver-brexit#widget_user (accessed 18 June 2017).

Jones, Owen (2016), 'Working-class Britons feel Brexity and betrayed – Labour must win them over', *The Guardian*, 10 June. Available online: https://www.theguardian.com/commentisfree/2016/jun/10/working-class-britain-brexity-betrayed-labour-vote-leave (accessed 1 April 2017).

Kaletsky, Anatole (2016), 'In praise of "Project Fear"', *The Prospect*, 24 March. Available online: https://www.prospectmagazine.co.uk/magazine/in-praise-of-project-fear-european-union-referendum (accessed 8 April 2017).

King, Anthony (1977), *Britain Says Yes: The 1975 Referendum on the Common Market*. Washington: American Enterprise Institute for Public Policy Research.

Kirkbride, Bethany (2016), 'Young people have a right to be angry at Brexit – but not at their parents who voted Leave', *The Telegraph*, 28 June. Available online: http://www.telegraph.co.uk/education/2016/06/28/young-people-have-a-right-to-be-angry-at-brexit--but-not-at-thei/ (accessed 17 May 2017).

Kirkup, James (2014), 'Scottish referendum analysis: How Alex Salmond's core vote sealed his fate', *The Telegraph*, 19 September. Available online: http://www.telegraph.co.uk/news/uknews/scottish-independence/11110450/Scotland-referendum-analysis-how-Alex-Salmonds-core-vote-sealed-his-fate.html (accessed 29 March 2017).

'Labour's apologists for terror: *The Mail* accuses Corbyn troika of befriending Britain's enemies and scorning the institutions that keep us safe' (2017), *The Mail*, 6 June. Available online: http://www.dailymail.co.uk/news/article-4578716/Apologists-terror-Corbyn-McDonnell-Abbott.html#comments (accessed 11 June 2017).

'Leave and Remain EU donations and loans revealed' (2016), *BBC*, 11 May. Available online: http://www.bbc.com/news/uk-politics-eu-referendum-36267668 (accessed 25 May 2017).

Linning, Stefanie (2016), 'Jude Law's security team was attacked and mugged by migrants when the cameras stopped after the Hollywood start left the jungle camp in Calais', *The Mail*, 28 February. Available online: http://www.dailymail.co.uk/news/article-3467795/Jude-Law-s-security-team-attacked-mugged-migrants-cameras-stopped-Hollywood-star-left-jungle-camp-Calais.html (accessed 31 March 2017).

Little, Alison (2013), 'Revealed: How Britain is "£170bn worse off in European Union"', *Sunday Express*, 19 September. Available online: http://www.express.co.uk/news/uk/430571/REVEALED-How-Britain-is-170bn-worse-off-in-European-Union (accessed 12 March 2017).

Littlewood, Mark (2016), 'I used to love the EU. Now I want Britain to leave', *The Telegraph*, 14 March. Available online: http://www.telegraph.co.uk/news/newstopics/eureferendum/12193147/I-used-to-love-the-EU.-Now-I-want-Britain-to-Leave.html (accessed 8 March 2017).

Longworth, John (2017), 'Brits fund EU fat cats. Working people robbed of £35bn to fund EU welfare for the rich, says chairman of Leave Means Leave', *The Sun*, 16 April. Available online: https://www.thesun.co.uk/news/3341650/working-people-robbed-of-35bn-to-fund-eu-welfare-for-the-rich-says-chairman-of-leave-means-leave/ (accessed 19 May 2017).

Lord Green, Daniel Hannan and Patrick Minford (2016), 'BREXIT FACTOR 10 reasons why choosing Brexit on June 23 is a vote for a stronger, better Britain', *The Sun*, 22 June. Available online: https://www.thesun.co.uk/news/1278140/why-voting-to-leave-the-eu-will-save-our-sovereignty-rein-in-migration-and-boost-our-economy/ (accessed 23 May 2017).

Low, Adrian (2016), 'Brexit is not the will of the British people – it never has been', *London School of Economics and Political Science*, 24 October. Available online: http://blogs.lse.ac.uk/brexit/2016/10/24/brexit-is-not-the-will-of-the-british-people-it-never-has-been/ (accessed 20 June 2017).

Machin, David and Andrea Mayr (2012), *How to Do Critical Discourse Analysis*. London and Thousand Oaks (CA, USA): Sage.

Maguire, Patrick (2016), 'Grovelling Merkel and Hollande launch thinly-veiled attack on Brexit', *The Express*, 31 May. Available online: http://www.express.co.uk/news/uk/675015/brexit-merkel-hollande-verdun-france-germany-eu-referendum (accessed 30 March 2017).

'Make the EU Referendum Victory in Europe Day and vote Remain for the sake of the future' (2016), *The Mirror*, 18 June. Available online: http://www.mirror.co.uk/news/uk-news/make-eu-referendum-victory-europe-8227505 (20 June 2016).

Malone, Carole (2016), 'How dare Barack Obama tell the British people we must stay in the EU', *The Mirror*, 23 April. Available online: http://www.mirror.co.uk/news/uk-news/how-dare-barack-obama-tell-7819278 (accessed 25 May 2017).

Marwick, Arthur (1996), *British Society since 1945* (3rd edn). London: Penguin Books.

Martinson, Jane (2016), 'Did the *Mail* and *Sun* swing the UK towards Brexit?', *The Guardian*, 24 June. Available online: https://www.theguardian.com/media/2016/jun/24/mail-sun-uk-brexit-newspapers (accessed 24 June 2016).

Mason, Paul (2016), 'The leftwing case for Brexit (one day)', *The Guardian*, 16 May. Available online: https://www.theguardian.com/commentisfree/2016/may/16/brexit-eu-referendum-boris-johnson-greece-tory (accessed 26 May 2017).

Mason, Rowena (2016), 'Green party "loud and proud" about backing Britain in Europe', *The Guardian*, 14 March. Available online: https://www.theguardian.com/politics/2016/mar/14/green-party-loud-proud-backing-britain-europe-brexit-lucas (accessed 15 March 2017).

Mason, Rowena (2016), 'Leaving EU "could cause catastrophic worker shortages"', *The Guardian*, 27 May. Available online: https://www.theguardian.com/politics/2016/may/27/leaving-eu-could-cause-catastrophic-worker-shortages (accessed 15 October 2016).

Matthews, Alex (2016), '"This vote doesn't represent the younger generation who will have to live with the consequences": Millennials vent fury at baby boomers for voting Britain OUT of the EU', *The Mail*, 24 June. Available online: http://www.dailymail.co.uk/news/ article-3658671/This-vote-doesn-t-represent-younger-generation-live-consequences-Millennials-fury-baby-boomers-voting-Britain-EU.html (accessed 2 June 2017).

Mckenzie, Lisa (2016), 'Brexit is the only way the working class can change anything', *The Guardian*, 15 June. Available online: https://www.theguardian.com/commentisfree/ 2016/jun/15/brexit-working-class-sick-racist-eu-referendum (accessed 1 April 2017).

McRae, Hamish (2017), 'Brexit is now going to be a very different beast – there's no time for a proper deal, so here are our temporary options', *The Independent*, 14 June. Available online: http://www.independent.co.uk/voices/brexit-deal-theresa-may-eu-proper-deal-british-economy-interim-a7790031.html (accessed 15 June 2017).

'Michael Gove' (2017), *Wikipedia*, last edited 24 May. Available online: https:// en.wikipedia.org/wiki/Michael_Gove (accessed 25 May 2017).

Midgley, Neil (2016), 'Word of the Year 2016 is . . .', *Oxford Dictionaries*. Available online: https://en.oxforddictionaries.com/word-of-the-year/word-of-the-year-2016 (accessed 4 May 2017).

Milne, Claire (2016), 'Young voters and the EU referendum', *Full Fact*, 22 July. Available online: https://fullfact.org/europe/young-voters-and-eu-referendum/ (accessed 18 May 2017).

Monbiot, George (2016), 'I'm starting to hate the EU. But I will vote to stay in', *The Guardian*, 10 February. Available online: https://www.theguardian.com/commentisfree/ 2016/feb/10/eu-in-health-wildife-european-union (accessed 22 September 2016).

Monbiot, George (2016), 'The European Union is the worst choice – apart from the alternative', *The Guardian*, 15 June. Available online: https://www.theguardian.com/ commentisfree/2016/jun/15/european-union-eu-britain-sovereignty (accessed 22 September 2016).

Montague, Brendan (2012), '*The Sun* at 40: When Arthur Scargill Was "Mein Fuhrer"', *flashbak.com*, 21 February. Available online: http://flashbak.com/the-sun-at-40-when-arthur-scargill-was-mein-fuhrer-16468/ (accessed 23 April 2017).

Moore, Charles (2016), 'The EU is a huge version of Belgium – and it can't deal with the modern world', *The Telegraph*, 25 March. Available online: http://www.telegraph.co.uk/ opinion/2016/03/25/the-eu-is-a-huge-version-of-belgium--and-it-cant-deal-with-the-m/ (accessed 26 March 2016).

Moore, Peter (2016), 'How Britain Voted', *YouGov UK*, 27 June. Available online: https:// yougov.co.uk/news/2016/06/27/how-britain-voted/ (accessed 28 June 2016).

Moore, Suzanne (2016), 'My instinct is pro-Brexit (and it's nothing to do with Boris)', *The Guardian*, 22 February. Available online: https://www.theguardian.com/ commentisfree/2016/feb/22/my-instinct-brexit-boris-anti-eu-not-anti-europe (accessed 23 May 2017).

Moore, Suzanne (2016), 'Voters will stick two fingers up to those lecturing about Brexit's dangers', *The Guardian*, 8 June. Available online: https://www.theguardian.com/ commentisfree/2016/jun/08/voters-will-stick-two-fingers-lecturing-brexit-dangers (accessed 23 May 2017).

Moore, Suzanne (2016), 'The crumbling of the remain vote shows how hollowed out Labour has become', *The Guardian*, 15 June. Available online: https://www.theguardian.com/commentisfree/2016/jun/15/crumbling-remain-vote-hollowed-out-labour (accessed 1 April 2017).

Moore, Suzanne (2017). 'The *Sun* and *Mail* tried to crush Corbyn. But their power over politics is broken', *The Guardian*, 9 June. Available online: https://www.theguardian.com/commentisfree/2017/jun/09/tabloids-crush-corbyn-power-politics-sun-mail-labour (accessed 22 June 2017).

Morris, Nigel (2014), 'Nigel Farage: Vladimir Putin is the world leader I most admire', *The Independent*, 30 March. Available online: http://www.independent.co.uk/news/uk/politics/nigel-farage-vladimir-putin-is-the-world-leader-i-most-admire-9224781.html (accessed 25 February 2017).

Moses, Toby (2016), 'Leftwing and tempted by Brexit? Remember the Tories are in charge', *The Guardian*, 7 April. Available online https://www.theguardian.com/commentisfree/2016/apr/07/brexit-leftwing-eu-tories-boris-johnson (accessed 27 February 2017).

Mullin, Gemma (2016), 'Nigel Farage as "Hitler" and Boris the basketcase: See Remain posters axed before Brexit', *The Mirror*, 2 July. Available online: http://www.mirror.co.uk/news/uk-news/revealed-eu-remain-posters-were-8335090 (accessed 6 May 2017).

Murphy, Victoria (2016), 'Prince William wades into the EU debate by hinting Brits should vote to stay "In"', *The Mirror*, 16 February. Available online: http://www.mirror.co.uk/news/uk-news/prince-william-wades-eu-debate-7380942 (accessed 19 February 2016).

Nelson, Nigel (2016), 'Open letter from five Labour heavyweights who have changed their minds on Europe', *The Mirror*, 13 February. http://www.mirror.co.uk/news/uk-news/open-letter-five-labour-heavyweights-7366871 (accessed 22 September 2016),

Neslen, Arthur (2016), 'Brexit would free UK from "spirit-crushing" green directives, says minister', *The Guardian*, 10 June. Available online: https://www.theguardian.com/politics/2016/may/30/brexit-spirit-crushing-green-directives-minister-george-eustice (accessed 8 March 2017).

Newman, Cathy (2016), 'A canny Nigel Farage is right to shun Marine Le Pen's advances', *The Telegraph*, 29 May. Available online: http://www.telegraph.co.uk/women/womens-life/10861123/Ukips-Nigel-Farage-is-right-to-shun-Marine-Le-Pens-advances.html (accessed 27 March 2017).

Newton Dunn, Tom (2016), 'Who do EU think you are kidding Mr Cameron?', *The Sun*, 3 February. Available online: https://www.thesun.co.uk/archives/politics/275289/who-do-eu-think-you-are-kidding-mr-cameron/ (accessed 10 February 2016).

Newton Dunn, Tom (2016), 'Revealed: Queen backs Brexit as alleged EU bust-up with ex-Deputy PM emerges', *The Sun*, 28 July. Available online: https://www.thesun.co.uk/news/1078504/revealed-queen-backs-brexit-as-alleged-eu-bust-up-with-ex-deputy-pm-emerges/ (accessed 5 August 2016).

Owen, Glen and Brendan Carlin (2017), 'Wounded May is "on her knees": PM faces civil war in cabinet over hard Brexit plans after MPs plot "no confidence letters" as devastating polls show TWO THIRDS of voters back Hammond's bid for soft exit', *The Mail*, 18 June. Available online: http://www.dailymail.co.uk/news/article-4614492/Wounded-knees-PM-faces-civil-war.html (accessed 18 June 2017).

Parsons, Tony (2015), 'Europe's dream? It crumbled and died', *The Sun*, 1 November. Available online: https://www.thesun.co.uk/archives/politics/116590/europes-dream-it-crumbled-and-died/ (accessed 20 April 2016).

Peck, Tom (2016), 'Nigel Farage's triumphalist Brexit speech crossed the borders of decency', *The Independent*, 24 June. Available online: http://www.independent.co.uk/news/uk/politics/brexit-recession-economy-what-happens-nigel-farage-speech-a7099301.html (accessed 25 May 2017).

Perring, Rebecca and Monika Pallenberg (2016), 'No more shackles: UK could break free of EU laws as early as June 24 if Brexit wins', *Daily Express*, 18 June. Available online http://www.express.co.uk/news/world/680897/Eu-laws-referendum-Germany-Brexit (accessed 6 March 2017).

Petkar, Sofia (2017), 'Is Brexit a giant STITCH-UP? EU talks DELAY as Tories say we SHOULD stay in single market', *The Express*, 13 June. Available online: http://www.express.co.uk/news/uk/815958/brexit-talks-unlikely-next-week-tory-conservative-general-election-disaster-theresa-may (accessed 16 June 2017).

Pickard, Jim, Gonzalo Vina and John Murray Brown (2016), 'Jeremy Corbyn faces no-confidence motion following Brexit vote', *Financial Times*, 24 June. Available online: https://www.ft.com/content/a035f3d2-39c4-11e6-a780-b48ed7b6126f (accessed 11 August 2016).

Pitel, Laura (2015), 'Ukip woman had "a problem with negroes because of their faces"', *The Times*, 8 January. Available online: http://www.thetimes.co.uk/article/ukip-woman-had-a-problem-with-negroes-because-of-their-faces-rxlc5lks8kc (accessed 27 March 2017).

Pollard, Stephen (2016), 'Euro conflict between EU elite and national democracies it is extraordinarily dangerous', *The Express*, 2 March. Available online: http://www.express.co.uk/comment/expresscomment/649020/eurozone-political-economic-failure-Lord-Mandelson-Mervyn-King-Greece-bailout-riots (accessed 23 May 2017).

Pollard, Stephen (2016), 'Scare tactics from Project Fear are ever more absurd, says Stephen Pollard', *The Express*, 15 June. Available online: http://www.express.co.uk/comment/expresscomment/679972/Scare-tactics-from-Project-Fear-ever-more-absurd-Brexit (accessed 15 June 2016).

Prendergast, Lara (2016), 'Brexit was a harsh political awakening for young people', *The Spectator*, 25 June. Available online: https://blogs.spectator.co.uk/2016/06/brexit-political-awakening-young-people/ (accessed 16 May 2017).

Pullen, Emma (2016), 'Leaving the EU will make Britain great once again', *The Express*, 10 March. Available online: http://www.express.co.uk/comment/expresscomment/651645/Leaving-EU-Britain-Brexit (accessed 10 December 2016).

Ramsay, Adam (2016), 'I hate the EU. But I'll vote to stay in it', *openDemocracyUK*, 22 February. Available online: https://www.opendemocracy.net/uk/adam-ramsay/i-hate-eu-but-ill-vote-to-stay-in-it (accessed 22 September 2016).

Rankin, Jennifer (2016), 'Is the EU undemocratic?', *The Guardian*, 13 June. Available online: https://www.theguardian.com/world/2016/jun/13/is-the-eu-undemocratic-referendum-reality-check (accessed 27 February 2016).

Reade, Brian (2016), 'Can you imagine the Tarantino-esque horror of the UK being shaped by the Hateful Eight if we leave Europe?', *The Mirror*, 11 March. Available online: http://www.mirror.co.uk/news/uk-news/can-you-imagine-tarantino-esque-7539521 (accessed 15 January 2017).

Rees, Emma (2017), 'What made the difference for Labour? Ordinary people knocking on doors', *The Guardian*, 12 June. Available online: https://www.theguardian.com/commentisfree/2017/jun/12/labour-knocking-on-doors-jeremy-corbyn-momentum (accessed 14 June 2017).

Rentoul, John (2016), 'Brexit myths: Fact-checking claims by both sides of the EU Campaign', *The Independent*, 13 March. Available online: http://www.independent.co.uk/voices/comment/brexit-myths-fact-checking-claims-by-both-sides-of-the-eu-campaign-a6928831.html (accessed 17 March 2016).

Rentoul, John (2017), 'The election was supposed to clear the way for leaving the EU, but Theresa May's failure has put Brexit in doubt', *The Independent*, 10 June. Available online: http://www.independent.co.uk/voices/theresa-may-s-failure-to-win-a-majority-has-put-brexit-in-doubt-a7783656.html (accessed 16 June 2017).

Rhodes, Anna (2016), 'Young people – if you're so upset by the outcome of the EU referendum, then why didn't you get out and vote?', *The Independent*, 27 June. Available online: http://www.independent.co.uk/voices/eu-referendum-brexit-young-people-upset-by-the-outcome-of-the-eu-referendum-why-didnt-you-vote-a7105396.html (accessed 18 May 2017).

Rodionova, Zlata (2016), 'Pound sterling slump after Brexit boosts tourist spending in UK', *The Independent*, 23 August. Available online: http://www.independent.co.uk/news/business/news/brexit-pound-sterling-economy-eu-referendum-effect-uk-tourism-spending-a7204811.html (accessed 21 October 2016).

Rosenbaum, Martin (2017), 'Local voting figures shed new light on EU referendum', *BBC*, 6 February. Available online: http://www.bbc.com/news/uk-politics-38762034 (accessed 19 May 2017).

Ross, Tim (2016), 'Boris Johnson: The EU wants a superstate, just as Hitler did', *The Telegraph*, 15 May. Available online: http://www.telegraph.co.uk/news/2016/05/14/boris-johnson-the-eu-wants-a-superstate-just-as-hitler-did/ (accessed 16 May 2016).

Runciman, David (2010), *Political hypocrisy: The mask of power, from Hobbes to Orwell and beyond*. Princeton, NJ: Princeton University Press.

Runciman, David (2016), 'Brexit: A win for "proper" people?', *The Prospect*, 30 June. Available online: https://www.prospectmagazine.co.uk/politics/a-win-for-proper-people-brexit-eu-referendum-david-runciman (accessed 2 July 2016).

Sandbrook, Dominic (2007), *White Heat: A History of Britain in the Swinging Sixties*. London: Abacus.

'Scottish independence: Poll reveals who voted, how and why' (2014), *The Guardian*, 20 September. Available online: https://www.theguardian.com/politics/2014/sep/20/scottish-independence-lord-ashcroft-poll (accessed 5 April 2017).

Searle, John (1969), *Speech Acts*. Cambridge: Cambridge University Press.

Shaw, Eric (2014), 'The Scottish Labour Party and the 2014 Independence Referendum',
    in K. Adamson and P. Lynch (eds), *Scottish Political Parties and the 2014 Independence
    Referendum*, 58–79, Cardiff: Welsh Academic Press.

Shipman, Tim (2010), 'By 2066, white Britons "will be outnumbered" if immigration
    continues at current rates', *The Mail*, 18 November. Available online: http://www.dailymail.
    co.uk/news/article-1330734/White-Britons-outnumbered-2066-immigration-continues.
    html (accessed 31 March 2017).

Shipman, Tim and Jack Doyle (2013), '4,000 foreign criminals including muderers and
    rapists we can't throw out . . . and, yes, you can blame human rights again', *The Mail*,
    15 January. Available online: http://www.dailymail.co.uk/news/article-2256285/4-000-
    foreign-criminals-including-murderers-rapists-throw--yes-blame-human-rights-again.
    html (accessed 31 March 2017).

Short, Mick (1996), *Exploring the Language of Poems, Plays and Prose*. Harlow: Longman.

Skwirczynski, Przemek (2016), 'Lisbon Treaty turned the EU into a superstate that could
    become a "prison of nations"', *Sunday Express*, 21 June. Available online: http://
    www.express.co.uk/comment/expresscomment/681928/lisbon-treaty-eu-superstate-
    referendum (accessed 26 February 2017).

Slack, James and Gerri Peev (2016), 'Now Cameron warns that Brexit would lead to
    war and genocide: PM's extraordinary intervention – but Out camp accuses him
    of desperation as Downing St ramps up Project Fear', *The Mail*, 9 May. Available
    online: http://www.dailymail.co.uk/news/article-3580060/Now-Cameron-warns-
    Brexit-lead-war-genocide-PM-s-extraordinary-intervention-leads-campaigners-
    accuse-Downing-Street-desperation.html (accessed 10 May 2016).

Slack, James and Jason Groves (2016), 'Why we must quit the EU, by Cameron's guru: Friend
    and strategist Steve Hilton breaks ranks on Brexit to say Britain will be "literally
    ungovernable" unless we take back power from the self-serving elite', *Mail Online*, 23
    May. Available online: http://www.dailymail.co.uk/news/article-3603793/Why-quit-EU-
    Cameron-s-guru-Friend-trategist-Steve-Hilton-breaks-ranks-Brexit-say-Britain-literally-
    ungovernable-unless-power-self-serving-elite.html (accessed 8 March 2017).

Slack, James (2016), 'May savages the liberal elite: PM will use keynote speech at the Tory
    conference to condemn those who sneer at ordinary Britons' worries and reach out
    to millions of blue-collar workers', *The Mail*, 5 October. Available online: http://www.
    dailymail.co.uk/news/article-3822338/May-savages-liberal-elite-PM-uses-keynote-
    speech-Tory-conference-condemn-sneer-ordinary-Britons-worries-reach-millions-
    blue-collar-workers.html (accessed 5 October 2016).

Stevens, Tom (2017), 'Apologists for Snickers: Twitter users hit back against attack on
    Corbyn', *The Guardian*, 7 June. Available online: https://www.theguardian.com/politics/
    2017/jun/07/jeremy-corbyn-labour-how-social-media-hit-back-against-latest-attacks
    (accessed 12 June 2017).

Stewart, Heather and Rowena Mason (2016), 'Nigel Farage's anti-migrant poster reported
    to police', *The Guardian*, 16 June. Available online: https://www.theguardian.com/
    politics/2016/jun/16/nigel-farage-defends-ukip-breaking-point-poster-queue-of-
    migrants (accessed 29 March 2017).

Stone, Jon (2016), 'Half of Ukip voters say they are prejudiced against people of other races', *The Independent*, 22 February. Available online: http://www.independent. co.uk/news/uk/politics/half-of-ukip-voters-say-they-are-prejudiced-against-people-of-other-races-10062731.html (accessed 27 March 2017).

Stuart, Gisela (2016), Blog: *Gisela Stuart and Team Gisela*. Available online: http://www. twtd.co.uk (accessed 23 May 2017).

Stuart, Gisela (2016), 'Labour's pro-EU stance is "recruitment agent for Ukip"', *The Guardian*, 15 May. Available online: https://www.theguardian.com/politics/2016/may/15/labour-pro-eu-stance-brexit-is-recruitment-agent-for-ukip (accessed 1 April 2017).

'*SUN ON SUNDAY* says vote for Brexit is all it takes to set Britain free' (2016), *Sun*, 19 June. Available online: https://www.thesun.co.uk/news/1306294/a-vote-for-brexit-is-all-it-takes-to-set-britain-free/ (accessed 8 March 2017).

'*SUN SAYS* We urge our readers to beLEAVE in Britain and vote to quit the EU on June 23' (2016), *The Sun*, 13 June. Available online: https://www.thesun.co.uk/news/1277920/we-urge-our-readers-to-believe-in-britain-and-vote-to-leave-the-eu-in-referendum-on-june-23/ (accessed 13 June 2016).

Tapsfield, James (2016), 'Now Brexit could put £3 on the price of 20 cigarettes in the latest dire prediction to emerge about life outside the EU', *The Mail*, 30 May. Available online: http://www.dailymail.co.uk/news/article-3616418/Now-Brexit-3-price-20-cigarettes-latest-dire-prediction-emerge-life-outside-EU.html (accessed 8 April 2017).

Tapsfield, James, Tim Sculthorpe and Allan Hall (2017), 'Scottish Tory leader Ruth Davidson urges May to "reach out" for consensus on Brexit as Cabinet Remainers plot with Labour to "soften" Britain's departure from the EU', *The Mail*, 12 June. Available online: http://www.dailymail.co.uk/news/article-4595498/Juncker-says-dust-settle-Britain-talks.html (accessed 17 June 2017).

'Terror as Gigantic Muslim Spiders Bring Deadly Ebola to UK' (2014), *democraticunderground.com*, 7 October. Available online: http://www.democraticunderground.com/10025633903 (accessed 31 March 2017).

Thatcher, Margaret (1988), 'Speech to the College of Europe ("The Bruges Speech")', *Margaret Thatcher Foundation*, 2017. Available online: http://www.margaretthatcher.org/document/107332 (accessed 25 May 2017).

'The Brexit vote reveals a country split down the middle' (2016), *The Economist*, 24 June. Available online: http://www.economist.com/news/britain/21701257-results-paint-picture-angry-country-divided-class-age-and-region-country-divided (accessed 14 May 2017).

'The new ruling class' (2009), *New Statesman*, 1 October. Available online: http://www.newstatesman.com/uk-politics/2009/10/oxford-universitywealth-school (accessed 25 May 2017).

'The Guardian view on Brexit Britain: A clown not a lion' (2017), *The Guardian*, 16 June. Available online: https://www.theguardian.com/commentisfree/2017/jun/16/the-guardian-view-on-rexit-britain-clown-not-lion (accessed 18 June 2017).

'The Opposite of Democracy' (2016), *Morning Star*, 21 January. Available online: http://www.morningstaronline.co.uk/a-9f4c-The-opposite-of-democracy#.WLRFlBih1cA (accessed 27 February 2017).

'The process for withdrawing from the European Union' (2016), *UK Government*, 29 February. Available online: https://www.gov.uk/government/publications/the-process-for-withdrawing-from-the-european-union (accessed 8 April 2017).

'The right choice is to remain' (2016), *The Independent*, 19 June. Available online: http://www.independent.co.uk/voices/editorials/the-right-choice-is-to-remain-a7090326.html (accessed 22 September 2016).

'THE *SUN* SAYS Don't chuck Britain in the Cor-bin – vote Tory unless you want a friend of terrorists who's ready to open borders and hike up taxes as our next PM' (2017), *The Sun*, 7 June. Available online: https://www.thesun.co.uk/news/3748893/the-sun-says-vote-conservative-dont-chuck-britain-corbyn/ (accessed 11 June 2017).

'Think outside the EU box' (2015), *Stop the EU*, 7 June. Available online: https://twitter.com/stop_the_eu/status/607643541859364864 (accessed 25 May 2017).

'Tied to the EU, growth is 0.3%. Free from the EU it's more', *betteroffout.net*. Available online: http://www.betteroffout.net/tied-to-the-eu-growth-is-0-3-gdp-free-from-the-eu-it-could-be-more/ (accessed 6 March 2017).

Tillmans, Wolfgang (2016), 'Between bridges' posters, *issuu.com*, 25 May. Available online https://issuu.com/bintphotobooks/docs/eu_campaign_wolfgang_tillmans_-_bet (accessed 3 June 2017).

Tonkin, Sam (2015), 'Wish you were here? Refugees are taken on jollies to zoos, theme parks and even to the beach to help them "integrate" into British life . . . and guess who's paying for it all', *The Mail*, 19 December. http://www.dailymail.co.uk/news/article-2256285/4-000-foreign-criminals-including-murderers-rapists-throw--yes-blame-human-rights-again.html (accessed 31 March 2017).

Townsend, Martin (2017), 'A word from the editor: Teremy Corbyn has waged a seamlessly cynical campaign', *The Express*, 4 June. Available online: http://www.express.co.uk/comment/columnists/martin-townsend/812892/jeremy-corbyn-election-seamlessly-cynical-campaign (accessed 11 June 2017).

Travis, Alan (2016), 'Brexit "unlikely to mean deep migration cuts but may lead to 2p tax increase"', *The Guardian*, 10 May. Available online: https://www.theguardian.com/politics/2016/may/10/brexit-unlikely-to-mean-deep-migration-cuts-but-may-lead-to-2p-tax-increase (accessed 15 October 2016).

Trifone, Pietro and Massimo Palermo (2007), *Grammatica Italiana di Base* (2nd edn). Bologna: Zanichelli editore S.p.A.

Vargas-Silva, Carlos and Cinzia Rienzo (2017), 'Migrants in the UK: An Overview', *The Migration Observatory at the University of Oxford*, 21 February. Available online: http://www.migrationobservatory.ox.ac.uk/resources/briefings/migrants-in-the-uk-an-overview/ (accessed 1 April 2017).

Varoufakis, Yanis (2016), 'Brexit is an empire-era trick. Only the radical case for Europe makes sense', *The Guardian*, 28 May. Available online: https://www.theguardian.com/politics/commentisfree/2016/may/28/brexit-empire-era-trick-radical-case-for-europe-lucas-mcdonnell-democracy-eu (accessed 15 March 2017).

Varoufakis, Yanis (2017), *And the Weak Suffer What They Must? Europe, Austerity and the Threat to Global Security*. Vintage: London.

Watt, Nicholas (2016), 'Brexit would be an "abyss of uncertainty and risk", business group warns, *The Guardian*, 24 February. Available online: https://www.theguardian.com/politics/2016/feb/24/brexit-would-be-abyss-uncertainty-risk-warns-eef-business-group (accessed 8 April 2017).

'We must vote Leave to create a Britain fit for the future' (2016), *Sunday Telegraph*, 18 June. Available online: http://www.telegraph.co.uk/opinion/2016/06/18/we-must-vote-leave-to-create-a-britain-fit-for-the-future/ (accessed 15 March 2017).

Weight, Richard (2002), *Patriots: National Identity in Britain 1940–2000*, London: Macmillan.

'What's that party girl Kate Moss has popped out for?' (2008), *The Mail*, 11 December. Available online: http://www.dailymail.co.uk/tvshowbiz/article-1093869/Whats-party-girl-Kate-Moss-popped-for.html (accessed 11 October 2016).

'Who will speak for England?' (2016), *The Mail*, 4 February. Available online: http://www.dailymail.co.uk/debate/article-3430870/DAILY-MAIL-COMMENT-speak- England.html (accessed 5 February 2016).

'Why *The Morning Star* Supports a Leave Vote' (2016), *Morning Star*, 22 June. Available online: http://www.morningstaronline.co.uk/a-1bff-Why-the-Morning-Star-supports-a-Leave-vote#.WSRrvFJabuS (accessed 23 May 2017).

'Why vote Leave' (2016), *Vote Leave Take Control*. Available online: http://www.voteleavetakecontrol.org/why_vote_leave.html (accessed 23 May 2017)

Wilkinson, Matt (2015), 'Softy Calais goes ballistic . . . Frenchies are atrocious', *The Sun*, 29 July. Available online: https://www.thesun.co.uk/archives/news/121049/softy-calais-goes-ballistic-frenchies-are-atrocious/ (accessed 28 April 2017).

Wilkinson, Richard and Kate Pickett (2010), *The Spirit Level: Why Equality Is Better for Everyone*. London: Penguin Books.

Willmott, Nigel (2016), 'Remain and reform is wishful thinking – the left should vote leave', *The Guardian*, 22 June. Available online: https://www.theguardian.com/commentisfree/2016/jun/22/remain-reform-wishful-thinking-left-vote-leave (accessed 15 March 2017).

Wilson, Cherry (2017), 'Election results 2017: The most diverse Parliament yet', *BBC*, 11 June. Available online: http://www.bbc.com/news/election-2017-40232272 (accessed 14 June 2017)

Wooding, David (2014), 'Who do you think you are kidding, Mr Cameron?', *The Sun*, 29 June. Available online: https://www.thesun.co.uk/archives/politics/942654/who-do-you-think-you-are-kidding-mr-cameron/ (accessed 8 June 2017).

Worley, Will (2016), '*Sun* forced to admit that "1 in 5 British Muslims" story was "seriously misleading"', *The Independent*, 26 March. Available online: http://www.independent.co.uk/news/media/ipso-sun-british-muslims-story-headline-significantly-misleading-a6953771.html (accessed 16 April 2017).

Yeung, Peter (2016), 'EU referendum: Turnout among young voters "almost double" initial reports', *The Independent*, 10 July. Available online: http://www.independent.co.uk/news/uk/politics/eu-referendum-brexit-turnout-young-voters-youth-vote-double-a7129181.html (accessed 23 May 2017).

INDEX

Abbott, Diane 182–5
Adams, Gerry 184–5, 188
Another Europe is Possible 93–4
approximators 21
Article 50 of Treaty of Lisbon 181, 191, 196
Attlee, Clement 124

Banks, Aaron 54
Barnes, Julian 208–9
Batten, Gerrard 89
Beckett, Margaret 13
Benn, Hilary 7, 13
Benn, Tony 133
Berlusconi, Silvio 156
Blair, Tony 143–5, 154, 207
Bloom, Godfrey 65
Blunkett, David 13
British National Party (BNP) 95–6
Brown, Gordon 207
Bush, George W. 143

Calais Jungle 102, 105, 145–6
Callaghan, Jim 209
Cameron, David 14, 28, 31, 69, 78, 117,
    122–3, 147–8, 153, 15
  danger of low voter turnout 115
  individual voter registration 77
  reasons for allowing referendum 57
  risk of war in Europe 113
Carswell, Douglas 95
Castle, Barbara 134
Chilton, Brendan 124–5
Chirac Jacques 143–4
Clegg, Nick 161
cohortative mood 46
  exhortative subjunctives 47

Common Agricultural Policy 130, 132
Common Market *see* European Economic
    Community
Cooper Yvette 12
Co-operative Principle 22
  Maxims of Manner, Quality, Quantity
    and Relation 22, 194
coordination **10–17**
  syntactic parallelism 10
Congdon, Tim 89–90
Corbyn, Jeremy 7–8, 203
  alleged unelectability 182, 189, 199
  attacks by tabloid press 182–90, 206–8
  For the many not the few 191–2
  parodies of tabloid attacks 187
  unconvincing Remain campaign 7–8
Council of Europe 133
Cox, Jo 126, 205
Cresson, Édith 76
Cummings, Dominic 3
Curtice, John 191

Dacre, Paul 101, 204–5
Dad's Army 122–3
Davidson, Ruth 193–4
Davis, David 195, 197–9
Dawkins, Richard 133
De Gaulle, Charles 131–2
Delors, Jacques 136–7, 141–3, 147–8
Democratic Unionist Party (DUP) 193,
    195, 198
Die Welt 149
Dijsselbloem, Jeroen 72
Dorfman, Lloyd 53
Draghi, Mario 72
Duncan Smith, Iain 4, 157

Eagle, Angela 161
English Defence League (EDL) 96
Euromyths 148
European Commission 29, 75–6, 135–6, 148
European Council 14, 75–6
European Court of Justice 76
European Currency Unit (ECU) 141–2
European Economic Community (EEC) 13,
    91, 124, 129–37
European Parliament 75–6
Eustice, George 80–1
Exchange Rate Mechanism (ERM) 136

factive verbs 17, 87
Fallon, Michael 15
Farage, Nigel **54**, 57, 123, 154, 157
    countering accusations of racism 96–7
    distancing UKIP from Front National 95
    Independence Day 57–8
    victory declaration 54
Foot, Michael 133
Francken, Theo 156

Gaitskell, Hugh 130–1
Galloway, George 157
Good Friday Agreement 185, 198
Gorbachev, Mikhael 73
Gove, Michael 4, **55**, 63, 81, 116, 125, 157, 195
Grayling, Chris 157

Hacked Off 154–5
Hague, William 121
Hammond, Philip 121, 198–9
Hannan, Daniel 61
Harding, David 53
Hargreaves, Peter 54
Harmsworth, Harold *see* Lord Rothermere
Hattersley, Roy 131, 136
Heath, Edward 130, 133, 187
hedging **19–44**, 197, 208
Hodge, Margaret 7
Hollande, François 99, 145
hypotaxis *see* subordination

imperatives **45–52**
implicature 14, 50, 156, 184, 194
inclusive and exclusive *we* 46, 48, **56**
Independent Press Standards Organisation
    (IPSO) 100, 147, 154–5, 161

Jenkins, Roy 135
Johnson, Boris 4, **54–55**, 63, 80, 97, 121,
    126, 152–3, 157, 205
    personal attacks 160–1
    praise for Sun readers 125
Jones, Toby 102
Juncker, Jean-Claude 9, 72, 114, 123,
    147–8, 155
jussives **48–52**

Khorsandi, Shappi 102
Kinnock, Neil 13, 145, 149, 207

Lagarde, Christine 156
Law, Jude 102
Le Pen, Marine 95
lexical verbs 21
lexit 3, 12, 38–44, 62, 73, 83, 91, 93, 105, 124
Lisbon Treaty 73
Lord Rothermere 101, 120
Lucas, Caroline 92–3

Macmillan, Harold 130
Macron, Emmanuel 194
Major, John 137, 140, 148, 187
Mandelson, (Lord) Peter 7, 154
Martin, Tim 156
May, Theresa 121, 146, 149, 175–6, 199, 202,
    205, 208
    'no deal is better than a bad deal' 192
    post-election pressure for soft
        Brexit 192–8
    reasons for calling general election
        181–2, 190
    'strong and stable leadership' 189
McDonnell, John 93, 182–5
Merkel, Angela 98–9, 147, 149, 156–7

Messina, Jim 57
metalingual glosses 22
modality **19–44**, 208
    boulomaic modality 23
    deontic modality 22–3
    dynamic modality 34
    epistemic modality 22–3, 197
    expressive modality 23
    relational modality 23
Momentum 190
Monnet, Jean 73
Movimento Cinque Stelle 95
Murdoch, Rupert 140, 144–5, 204, 207

naturalization 86, 205
News Corporation 140
nominalization 85–94
non-factive verbs 21
Norway relationship 196, 198

Obama, Barack 58
Odell, Tom 102
Osborne, George 78, 81, 189

parataxis *see* coordination
Patel, Priti **55**, 125, 157
Pompidou, Georges 132
post-truth 116, 151
Powell, Enoch 133
presupposition 17, 86
    change-of-state verbs 87
    logical presuppositions 87
Project Fear **109–17**, 154–5, 160

Rees-Mogg, Jacob **55**, 157
Rudd, Amber 161

Sainsbury, (Lord) David 53
Santer, Jacques 76
Scargill, Arthur 140
Schäuble, Walter 194
Schulz, Martin 72
Speech Act Theory 48
staycation 30
Straw, Jack 13
Straw, Will 3
Stuart, Gisella 38, 106
Sturgeon, Nicola 29, 161, 168
subjunctive mood 48
subordination 10–12
    syntactic hierarchy 10

Thatcher, Margaret 56, 62, 187, 209
    Bruges speech 56
    clash with Jacques Delors 136–7,
        141–3, 147
    relations with *The Sun* 140–1
The Hateful Eight 157
The Sun **139–50**
    hostility towards France and EU 140–50
    puns 140–2, 145–7, 207
Thompson, Emma 64
Tillmans, Wolfgang 15–16
Treaty of Rome 16, 130
Tusk, Donald 72, 114

Ukraine 70–2
    free trade deal with European
        Union 70–2

Varoufakis, Yanis 93–4, 210

Wilson, Harold 14, 124, 131–5